About the a

Salena Godden is a writer, poet and broadcaster who has been described as 'the doyenne of the spoken word scene' (Ian McMillan, BBC Radio 3's *The Verb*); 'the Mae West madam of the salon' (*The Sunday Times*) and as 'everything the *Daily Mail* is terrified of' (*Kerrang!*). Her most recent book of poems, *Under the Pier*, was published by Nasty Little Press in 2011. To mark twenty years of poetry and performance, a new collection *Fishing In The Aftermath / Poems 1994–2014* will be published with Burning Eye Books in the summer of 2014.

Salena Godden tops the bill at literary events and festivals nationally and internationally. She can be heard on the BBC as a guest on *Woman's Hour*, *Click*, *From Fact To Fiction*, *The Verb* and was a resident poet on BBC Radio 4's *Saturday Live*. She currently works alongside award-winning radio producer Rebecca Maxted. *Try A Little Tenderness: The Lost Legacy of Little Miss Cornshucks* was broadcast on BBC Radio in May 2014. This follows the success of their last collaboration *Stir it Up! – 50 Years of Writing Jamaica* also for BBC Radio 4. *Stir It Up* included excerpts from the literary memoir *Springfield Road* and was broadcast in 2012.

Springfield Road

Springfield Road

Salena Godden

unbound

mum and dad, springfield road, hastings

This edition first published in 2014

Unbound
4–7 Manchester Street, Marylebone, London, W1U 2AE
www.unbound.co.uk

Where correspondence has been reproduced, errors and omissions have been retained. Some names have been changed to protect the innocent and to amuse the dead.

Typeset by Bubblegum
Cover design by Mecob

A CIP record for this book is available from the British Library

ISBN 978-1-78352-054-1 (limited edn)
ISBN 978-1-78352-055-8 (trade edn)
ISBN 978-1-78352-056-5 (ebook)

Printed and bound in India by Replika Press Pvt. Ltd.

For my mother

The continuity of this love remains,
And shall remain unbroken.
There is nothing encountered big enough
To fracture or reduce, what's bigger than time
And shall outlive time's use.

Do not be afraid then, worry nor even
Miss me overmuch. Between us, over us
Longer than us both, this love.
Circumstance, separating miles
Or chance, but aspects of the one
Insoluble thing, this love.

Paul Godden
excerpt taken from *Birthday Ode A Month Late*
A poem written by my father, Paul Godden, to his mother,
22nd October 1964.

Contents

PART THREE – WINTER

PART FOUR – SPRING

footnote: this book has been separated into four pieces and named after the four seasons rather than the years. More for the emotional images that come with each season than the actual date or time. Whilst writing this I found there was a time of innocence and with it came sunshine and there was a time of grief and with it came the darkness. For me, whatever year it was, it was always spring-like and summery at Springfield Road and when I was there it always seemed to be alight and hopeful. Autumn and winter in my recollection were times of cold hardship and difficulties and so these sections reflect this. You will notice the summer section is longest, because of course the summers were longer in the seventies

PART ONE – SUMMER

my brother gus and me, danesholme, corby, 1975

1 / introduction
– Andalucia / Spain 2010

La Casa De Las Almendras
Andalucia, Spain
August 2010

My Dear,

These are the memories of my life as a child. This is the story of the world before I was here, the universe I was born into, that I came to love before I had to grow up, find rent and suffer hangovers. This is the story of how I became this overgrown adult with crooked teeth and scars.

I am alone in the mountains behind Malaga, at the highest point of Andalucia. The truth is, I feel as though I am peeling myself off the ceiling, coming down from the gigs and festivals, and I'm swapping the microphone for a pen.

I came here with the sole intention of writing some new work. But something happened here yesterday, and I'm now compelled to open the pages of this memoir and share this story with you – and this new version I write for you – especially for you, who have waited so patiently to read it.

This is the memoir of our old house, our family home in Hastings. How I remember those first mornings of the school holidays, stretching under musty blankets and cotton candy-striped sheets, in that house, in that bedroom, on Springfield Road. Awaking to the sounds of Grandpa's mantelpiece clock chiming downstairs, the distant church bells and seagulls.

This is the story of that home and those who lived here, namely my absent father – Paul Godden – who left such a trail of debris in his wake that as I read and write this memoir I feel like his personal road sweeper, picking through the litter and leaves, letters and photos, for nuggets of truth and revelation.

It's important you should know this is not written from the perspective of a time travelling superhero – quite the opposite – this is just how I can best remember my child self, how we have all changed, and yet not at all.

Now all I require you to do is read this and click your fingers and say *Hey! I remember, we did that too!* I want you to say you remember not how things could have been, but how they really were. You might say, I remember being closer to the ground, to the cracks in the pavement; I remember liking being upside down; I remember being afraid of the dark; I remember being lost in daydreams; I remember discovering life is unfair; I remember riding my bike with my feet off the pedals and I remember freewheeling down hills with the wind in my hair; I remember losing my front teeth; I remember being forced to eat my greens; I remember summers were longer and how oranges were bigger; I remember struggling to comprehend sex and death, heaven and hell, war and God and perhaps, you'll say, I remember I missed my dad too.

In my life as a writer, I have found it much easier over the past twenty years to get up on stage in front of people and talk openly, humorously, about cervical smears and one night stands, rather than reveal the story of my interior world, my childhood and especially my father. But someone once told me, you cannot climb a well from the middle, you must fall right to the bottom. Once you are there, in the cold, alone and ankle deep in slime, you'll look up and you'll get a real sense of the dark and the work involved to climb towards the light, the truth.

If this book were an animal, it would be a stray tomcat that has been passed around between us, fed and stroked. This story has grown into a strong and handsome alley cat, but an animal that will most likely bite and scratch you.

I have often wondered if this book is cursed, sometimes I have believed it is haunted, for it has surely haunted me. This writing is my *Red Shoes* and when I hear its tune I dance, even though I know I am dangerously close to leaping off the edge. And as I fall, time and time again, I catch myself re-thinking and re-writing this book. We see what we want to see, and sometimes we are shown the threads that connect us all. I believe that if you are focused on a certain person or a particular time and place, if you listen keenly, the world will reveal clues, like bridges and doorways, that guide you onto the right trail and encourage you to keep going against all odds. No matter what I do, all roads lead me back to *Springfield Road*.

It's August 2010, I left London and came to Spain for a month, alone and quite impulsively. The solitude and silence were startling at first. As I write this, I am overlooking almond and olive trees under big starry skies. The moon is full, white and hot. I've been working on new poetry, reading a stack of books and talking to myself out loud. On the drive from the airport and up the mountain I saw a sign with the word *Cardobe*. I couldn't figure out what memory it was tickling, then yesterday serendipity came knocking as I drank coffee and smoked – *Cardobe* – I threw the word into my computer's search engine and it led to the folder of the first ever draft of this book from 2006. My gaze fell upon a discarded letter from my dad to his mother, Edith, a letter we found in the basement of Springfield Road, that had been edited out of the manuscript, considered inconsequential, back story, because it was written before my father met my mother. But I now notice the postmark of this letter: my dad posted it from here, this very spot, in the mountains behind Malaga, Andalucia, 1965.

Did we forget that my father, as a young jazz poet and bachelor, ran away to Europe in 1965? Is this fate? Is this significant or even relevant? Am I being led by nostalgia? Am I grabbing at straws?

I phone home and speak to my mother. She believes that yet again my dad is watching over me, guiding me back on his trail, this trail.

'*I have taken to myself a Spanish "Cardobe" hat. It is a wide brimmed black hat they use to dance flamenco in…*' he writes, and yet again my present is illuminated by a light from the past, just like a lighthouse. In 1965 he is describing *the silent white houses, the twisting streets and the glittering sea*, it is the very view I can see now, as I write this in 2010. So what choice do I have, but to continue pushing on with this story and for it to be told my way for you. Here I am quite literally walking in his footsteps, down narrow Andalucian streets. I sit at bars he must have drunk in more than forty years ago, for through the rise and fall of Franco, nothing much has changed in the heart of these tiny villages.

Like many of his letters it is written in a steady hand, in green ink, looped and slanted words like music notation on light thin paper. The envelope is marked with the red and blue striped edges of airmail. I am guessing 'Easter 1962' is the title of a poem but so far there are no clues who 'K' might be.

Casa Del Poeta
Pedragelejo, Malaga
Somewhere around 8th Dec.

Dearest Mum,

Thank you for your regular, encouraging and ultimately lovely letters. K– hasn't written still. Don't understand but maybe I am a little slow. Listen I shall telephone you Christmas Day at 4pm afternoon if you can pay for the call. It costs 10/- a minute. Is that OK? I shall probably just cry for three minutes but there you are. I feel so terribly lonely at the moment, I'm vastly terrified to come straight home. What would that prove? That I was just as weak as everybody else, wanting security and peace. I want peace but of a different kind. You understand, so why do I talk so much.

The Rector wrote and said he sent 'Easter 1962' to a publisher, just for an opinion. Might be very interesting. We must wait and see. There is a full moon tonight and it glitters silver on the sea and lights the white and silent houses and the twisting streets. On Saturday we went up into the mountains behind Malaga. Was very exciting, you looked down on the whole coast or so it seemed.

The trumpet is <unreadable> very well. All afternoon I have been practising carols. Incongruous in that I was sitting on the porch in a bathing costume at 65 in the shade, sweltering from the hot sun playing 'In the bleak mid winter'! Its early days though. We are thinking of going into Malaga at Christmas to perform and see if we can get any money.

You know my usual outfit, jeans, Pa's jacket, jumper, it has taken an addition. I have taken to myself a Spanish 'Cardobe' hat. It is a wide brimmed black hat they use to dance flamenco in. Anyway exhibitionist as oft— I am well known throughout the (dives) town as 'Cardobe Poeta'. Cardoba is the place where they dance most flamenco. Flamenco is just the <unreadable> dance. In the little bar in Pedragalejo on Sunday nights they have a sort of beano. The bar is no bigger than my bedroom at home. Last Sunday night two little girls aged 10 or 11 were dancing. It was quite

Springfield Road

beautiful but awfully disturbing for both before the age of puberty had all the bumps and grinds necessary. I have become vaguely acquainted with a Spanish girl but all that happens is an exchange of language lessons. I wonder why K hasn't written. Anyway I am writing quite a lot, some not too bad. I miss you, shall hope 4pm Christmas day. OK? Lots of love. F in F. G.B.W.Y, Love Paul

***

I now have no choice but to open the kitchen door to this gnarly tomcat of a book. I will give it some food, some light, water and warmth knowing this is bound to hurt a bit. There are going to be things we all thought we had forgotten and also things we wish to forget. Things that will remind you of yourself. I came here to begin a new story, but maybe all my stories begin with this one story – this love story, this ghost story – and as I type that the tinny radio fizzes with Bob Marley singing 'Buffalo Soldier', his lyrics ask that if I know my history, then I will know where I am coming from, then they wouldn't have to ask me, who the heck do I think I am.

I was born in 1972. This means that I have been nurturing these stories for you for thirty-eight years. I never married and I do not have any children – yet. Home is a run-down fishing town by the sea called Hastings, East Sussex. And home is London. I didn't go to a posh school or even university. With my thesaurus and my first love Piers Thompson, I left Sussex and travelled to London at the age of nineteen. I began my big city life by working two jobs – backstage at the Drury Lane Theatre at night and as an A&R assistant at Acid Jazz Records by day. As a young poet in the 1990s I lived predominantly on Marmite on toast and instant noodles. I was constantly hungry, I feasted on books, nourishing my writing in the warmth of Swiss Cottage and St Pancras libraries on masculine literature – namely Hemingway, Bukowski, Orwell, Fitzgerald, Brautigan, Maupassant and Fante – at night I read my early poetry in the backrooms of pubs and bars for free wine and laughs; or I spat lyrics over beats in clubs and raves hiding under the punk-poet moniker, Salena Saliva. I always called myself Jamish: Jamaican, Irish, English. I have very few regrets, I have nothing to lose and I have no savings. They say that it is always poets that die in wars, and I never got over a sense of being in the trenches. I rarely quit anything or anyone and I am too forgiving. I have a bizarre and outdated sense of fair play and team spirit. I am my own worst enemy. My heart is wide open. I have fallen in love too quickly, too often and too easily. I believe we are running out of time, I don't believe we have any time to waste. For this I give myself a hard time and people tell me I am impatient. I am impulsive. I throw in all I have in a game of poker, but I reckon that is the only way to truly win. And these are some of the phrases I use to define who the heck I think I am.

I spent the latter half of the last decade dwelling in the flesh and blood of this story, our history. It ought to make a person a special kind of weird to live in the past for so long. I feel a special kind of strange every time I sit here reading through these pages. But the past is here in the present and on the tip of my tongue. I now know I was always heading to this very ledge here today, on a mountain top. I contemplate the space I inhabit between the past and the future, between the deep night sky and the rocky drop below. And as I do so, I remember home and Springfield Road.

How I would peer from that attic window and imagine my father looking out of that very same window when he was a boy. Outside, Hastings would be easterly, fresh with spring, the buds and pale blossoms hanging on the apple and pear trees. That attic room was my father's bedroom when he was a boy and I suppose I was always looking for him, the materials of his existence. I remember the lavender mothballed paper-lined drawers of the furniture in that particular room. I remember once finding a king-size marble, how I held it up to the light, squinting with one eye into the swirling blue and green glass. It was well scuffed and a sure winner. I told myself it was once my father's marble, I gave it a squeeze as I tucked it safely into the pocket of my pink pedal pusher jeans, convinced it would be lucky some day. In the distance I could make out the steel-blue line of sea on the horizon and overhead I heard the constant cry of seagulls on the slanted slate roof. I imagined what it might be like to call the house on Springfield Road my home and what it would be like to live in the holiday forever.

Salena Godden / Spain, 2010

2 / *when we were three*

The day we left my father I remember orange lights. I was wrapped in the familiarity of my soft blanket, and the lights, the luminous orange streetlights, were wrapped in their own black blanket of night. Lying on the back seat, I watched them pass the car window like the blips of a life support machine. They sped towards me and then slowed down. We were on a long journey. We were in motion, moving forwards, fast, and we would never go back.

Stars dangled, I saw the lights dancing on see-through strings. I called out for my mother. She turned to pat me and made a *shush* noise, *there, there,* she said, *shush.* Her face, though smiling, was strange, contorted with shadows and ghosts of amber lights. I struggled to sit up to see the world the right way round, to see where we were, and she said,

Lie still, be a good girl, we are nearly there now love.

My eyes fixed on a yellowish light moving towards me from the other side of the road, it was a lighter orange than the others. It stuttered like a falling star, disappearing into the distance. I tried to stay awake to watch this particular light as long as I could. My eyelids grew heavier until it was pin-sized and lost, the hypnotic lights blurred and the monotony of the car engine lulled me back to sleep.

***

I remember I was in a jungle one hot afternoon. At least, I believed I was in a jungle, and there in the tall grass nothing kept still for a minute. It was crawling in there, fizzing with life. Millions of tiny bugs buzzed and jumped, flew and hopped about me. I could not see over the top of the long grass, with its spikes and thorns. My nose tingled with the smell of earth and grass. There were fluffy spores in the air, dandelion clocks. A white butterfly settled on a cowslip and as I moved to touch it, I can recall my chubby hand reaching out as it flew away, up into the endless blue above me. Down in the grass it was cool, shadowy. I looked up into the cloudless sky and listened. There were no human voices, nothing familiar, just the rustling of insect monsters and a humming of six-legged traffic. Suddenly for me it was all over, it was the end of the world, I was lost and I was crying. I dropped my empty jam jar and sobbed. It was hay-yellow in every direction and my ears burned with the itch of grass life as something jumped on my arm. I cried out, then stopped to listen, then cried out louder. Suddenly he appeared like a giant saviour, the sun his halo,

Ah, come, Salena, don't cry, look.

My big brother Gus, my hero,

Don't cry, look, I caught two grasshoppers!

His jam jar was filled with grass and spindly legs. He was proud but I didn't know what a grasshopper was. He started singing the song from *Pinocchio*.

My name is Jiminy Cricket! Jiminy Jiminy Cricket! Come on…

He lay down and rolled off down the hill. My big brother Gus, four years older than me, and hurtling ahead. Outstretched pointed fingers, we rolled fast down the slope, tumbled down the bank laughing. Until the grass was suddenly soft, short and green and I now knew where we were, we were at the front door of our new home.

***

Then this is one beginning. I was coming up to my third birthday in the early spring of 1975 and this was our fresh start. We were three, my brother, my mother and me. Our dad went away to play in the resident jazz band on a ship called the *QE2*. My mother had moved us to a house on an ugly concrete council estate called Danesholme, near Corby, Northamptonshire. Northamptonshire is in the midlands, the green and flat middle of England's waist.

In this new house, we lived around the corner from my mother's parents, Nanny and Grandad, and my Uncle Gerry. My brother had gone ahead of us and was waiting for us when we arrived. He was so relieved to see us again that he cried at first. He missed us horribly – I could tell by the way he clung to Mum – he hadn't done that so much before. The houses in Danesholme were grey boxes, built in squares facing each other, with a hump of grass and bush in the middle of each, identical to the last. It was a Legoland of concrete play bricks. It was very different from the pastel fishermen's cottages of Ramsgate and the seaside where we had lived in a marshmallow-pink house with my father before.

I remember we didn't have much furniture, and certainly not enough to fill an entire house. When I ran across the uneven wooden floorboards the rooms echoed, resounded hollow. I can picture my mother with her headscarf on, smiling, the portable radio playing. She was always busy, my mum. She'd smoke her ciggy and she'd whistle and sing along to the radio. She'd wink down at me, then take a swig of tea from a pint glass and gasp, *Ah that's better.*

She threw the doors and windows open while she painted the house. I remember the kitchen was bright green and she painted a hippy daisy chain along the wall. This is a borrowed memory, I don't remember the daisy chain – she does. I do however remember this industrious DIY period. Most of all I remember she painted my bedroom in tones of violet and lavender. My mother taught me the words for colours, the names of rare and subtle hues. I loved these pretty words my mother used. The words for my new bedroom were indigo, lilac and purple, and when she put me to bed for my afternoon nap those particular colours were lit in shafts of sunshine, ultraviolet swam behind the backs of my eyes and etched into my memory forever.

***

I had a friend, her name was Mary and she lived across the square from me. She was Irish, with black hair and I never forgot her vivid violet-blue eyes. I recall we played together every day, pushing our prams, wearing our mother's beads and high heels. We collected and squashed berries with sticks. Whilst we played, we listened out for the ice cream van, the tinny trickle of the 'Teddy Bears' Picnic'. Although we were not to talk to strangers, the ice cream man was a pink and jolly man, I remember he took us by the wrists and ankles and gave us swings and aeroplanes. He gave us penny sweets and drumstick lollies for nothing.

One day Mary and I wandered further away from our square than we had before, we were hiding and spying on my brother and his friends. We followed them through the tunnel that led under the motorway and towards the woods on the edge of the estate. We weren't allowed to go there. It was dark and cool beneath the underpass, with the steady roar of traffic above us, we made a racket, roaring and shouting as we ran through the dark and the urine stench towards the sunlight.

We believed that there were real grizzly bears in Danesholme woods, so we didn't follow my brother any further at first. We stayed safe in the sunshine, peering at the edge where the trees started, before the long forest shadows began. We ran back excited and scared, we jumped and squealed at the sound of anything rustling in the bushes. *It's the bears*, we repeated to each other, clutching each other's hot hands, dipping into the cool gloom of forest and then dashing back into the sunshine.

Our bare arms goosepimpled as we eventually dared to step through puddles of shadows, dapples of sunlight trickling through the canopy of forest above us. Gus and some boys were looking up into a tree.

Shushh! I've found some chicks… be very quiet or you'll scare them, my brother Gus said, as he very carefully gathered the tiny creatures in his jumper. He set off and we followed him, the chicks cheeping as we were chirping and begging to hold one.

Once at home, we looked at the three chicks on the kitchen table, fragile, purple and papery, their eyes were hardly open. Their beaks were wide, letting out tiny croaks and cries. I asked,

Where's their mummy gone Gus?

Don't know, they've been abandoned…

Why?

Don't know, maybe the mother was scared off or something…

Our mother said softly, *Poor things!*

The mother bird would smell us humans on them now, wouldn't she, if she came back, wouldn't she, Mum? Mum?

Mum didn't say anything as Gus continued urgently,

Mum, we can't take them back to the woods, they'll perish out there in the wild.

Springfield Road

Mummy, would the mummy-bird smell human bean on them now?
Human bean? It's human being!
Yes, I am afraid she would and then she'd abandon them…
Yeah, so we best keep them, hey? Mum, can we, hey?

Gus butted in and then we pleaded at a high pitch until Mum smiled and said we could keep them if we looked after them properly. Gus said,

They'll be eaten by cats or foxes if we don't take them in, hey Mum…
And the bears will eat them all up, won't they, Gus?
Yes, Salena, if you say so.

We made the chicks a cosy nest in the airing cupboard where Mum said it was warmest. Mum remembers we let them free and they cheeped and hopped along the top landing of the house. We gave them tiny pieces of bread dipped in warm milk and broken-up cereals.

Then, one chilly morning before Gus left for school, we went to feed them their breakfast but found the corridor silent. When we opened the airing cupboard door they were all dead, probably scared to death in the dark airing cupboard. My brother and I had shaken hands, choosing which chick was to be whose. We had imagined a future with our bird-chicks for pets. One day, they were to be our own tame birds. We could have trained them to follow us to school, to sit on the school fence and then follow us home again. Now, wiping our eyes, absorbed in our young grief, my brother and I made the necessary arrangements. We filled a shoebox with toilet paper and tissue, and an old cotton handkerchief to cover the chicks up and keep them snug. We dug a hole with spoons and buried them in the public front garden, right by our front door. Mum led with a sombre funeral speech, then helped us say our prayers, and said,

Ashes to ashes and dust to dust.

Mum told us the chicks went to God in bird heaven. I squinted up into the cold morning sky to see bird heaven. I imagined it was behind the clouds and just before the stars. We made a lollipop stick cross to mark the final resting place, but a few days later they were dug up by cats.

3 / the right excellent nanny of the maroons

Every morning in Danesholme, my mother dropped me off at my grandmother's on her way to her new job working in the local Co-op supermarket. She sat me quietly in my grandmother's living room and told me to be good and put the radio on very low for me. I knew that I had to be very quiet, Nanny worked nights as a nurse in a hospital and I had to wait for her to wake up to see to me. I'd play alone, taking in the spicy smells, the tall leaves of the rubber plants and the exotic red ginger flowers. I remember the collection of wooden ducks on the stairway, the maps of Jamaica on bamboo trays, and a blue and yellow budgie in a cage. I'd lift the night-cover on the cage to see if the budgie was sleeping. I chattered to the little bird, hearing the rustle of its feathers, I'd poke my fingers into the cage to feed him seeds as he nipped me with his beak. Whenever his cage door was opened, he'd fly aimlessly around the living room and perch on the curtain rail.

Waiting for Nanny to get up, I'd listen to the radio whilst spinning around in a circle for hours. This was my favourite game – to try to stand for as long as I could no matter how dizzy I became. I loved the melodies of 'Lazing on a Sunny Afternoon' and 'Raindrops Keep Falling on my Head'. I sang, spinning on the spot, until the fuzzy shagpile carpet came up to meet me, orange waves of brown circles and red patterns rising. I stood there fixed, trying not to fall over, with the room spinning about. Once I had fallen and the room stopped racing before my eyes, I struggled up to do it again and again. I never grew tired of the rush of blood to my head and making myself dizzy, either by spinning or hanging upside down off the back of the sofa and being drawn to these sensations, enjoying being dizzy and upside down has followed me into adulthood.

Eventually I'd hear my grandmother in the bathroom upstairs. I'd creep up to the L-shaped landing halfway up the stairs to watch her. I crouched and spied on her, ducking down out of sight when she looked over, though I think she must have known I was there, it was all part of the game. Watching my grandmother dressing fascinated me; the preparation and piecing together of this magnificent tiger-eyed woman. Just out of the bath, she was engulfed in clouds of powder, a sweet dusting of sweet scents of lavender, lily of the valley or roses. Chalky white talc against her soft brown skin.

I studied my grandmother and her underwear. My nanny's bra was just like my mother's, but so much bigger and stiffer to hold her wondrous bosoms in pointed peaks. Each breast was protected, separated and mountainous. Even though I had seen this a hundred times, I was mystified by my nanny's pillowy bosoms. She'd put on another contraption, a girdle, with a million hooks and buttons, until it seemed she was bound in with bone and lace. The process was unfathomable to me; the undergarments were masterpieces of engineering. I felt it was important for me to watch, because one day, I hoped I might develop such a chest and I'd need to know how to ease myself into such interesting articles.

I moved up a step and held my breath, watching as Nanny sat and gathered the nylon material of her stockings expertly in her hands. I liked the way she pointed her toe into the silken material. Then she stood and pulled her full petticoat over her head. She called my name and I went and sat on her bed as she put on her beige skirt and buttoned her blouse and cardigan. Finally, she sat at her dressing table and brushed her hair through, the brush making a rasping noise through her tight knotted curls. With her lips clenched around pins, I watched as she gripped her wig into place. She wore a reddish-auburn wig, with shiny fat curls.

***

Nanny, my maternal grandmother, was the fifth of ten children born to Rudolph Robinson and his wife Theresa in the hills of Clarendon – there were thirteen babies in the Robinson brood, but only ten survived to adulthood. Clarendon is high up on Colonels Ridge on Bull Head Mountain, a couple of hours' drive from Kingston, high up into rainforest-lined, winding roads bordered by sugar cane plantations,

3 / the right excellent nanny of the maroons

in deepest Jamaica. My grandmother was the daughter of a tailor and farmer. My great-grandfather, Papa, was also a lay preacher and elder at the Mount Carmel Church, which Nanny told me meant among other tasks, he had to give the sermon if the priest was away. *But everyone did a little bit of everything,* Nanny always said, *everybody helped each other as best they could, not like now, there was no, not my job, not your job, we all just got stuck in as best we could.*

Nanny told me that although it was beautiful on Colonels Ridge, life was very hard. Every morning before they walked the many miles, in the heat down the potholed track to school, Nanny and her many siblings bathed in the river and did their chores, milking goats and fetching the water from the river on a donkey. The Robinson children loved school though and were very eager to go, school and church were social events too.

She had the most beautiful gold eyes, like a tiger's eye. As a child I was convinced my great-great-grandmother Marma was somehow magic – to the English ear it sounds like Mar-ma although I never saw it written. There were always black and white photographs of my elders on both my mother's and Nanny's bedside tables. The picture of Marma is the most striking and unforgettable, she looks happy in her rocking chair, she wears a bandana, long lace petticoats and she smokes a pipe. I believed as a child, that my nanny's eyes had turned that pale amber and saffron-gold from one of Marma's spells to cure her from going blind from staring at the sun too long, and as is often the case, these stories had some vein of truth in them.

Nanny's grandfathers were Scottish and Irish farmers. Both of her grandmothers were Maroons, the great rebel Jamaicans who today are recognised as an indigenous people by the United Nations. As far as I know she was no relative but 'Nanny of the Windwards' was a courageous warrior in the First Maroon War from 1720 to 1739 against the British invasion. By using military tactics, she became so powerful she was rumoured to be a high priestess and a witch. The Maroons would camouflage themselves with leaves and ambush their enemies at night. They were said to be able to slit a man's throat before he'd seen or even heard them coming. They were fierce and proud and rumoured to be unafraid of death, I read that the Maroon mantra was this: *to never bow head or knee, to hear only their own voice, to stand in the shadow of none and to be masters of their own destiny.*

Springfield Road

The British called them the 'relentless rebels' as they made cross-country travel treacherous in Jamaica. Many plantations simply surrendered or were abandoned. An initial offer of land and freedom was shunned by the Maroons, resulting in irregular warfare. Eventually, peace treaties were signed in 1739 and bribes accepted in return for land, freedom and independence.

Some of my elders were Maroon, like my grandmother's grandmother, Marma. I've been told she was also what we might today call a herbalist or a healer. Nanny said that even though Marma couldn't read or write, she instinctively learned the properties of all the herbs and plants through a lifetime of watching. She had an intuitive natural talent for what we might call alternative medicine. Now all grandparents have stories they tell the grandchildren over and over and my grandmother always told me stories about her grandmother, Marma:

Back home if anyone went into labour Marma was there, when people were sick she'd be there for them too. Then when I got malaria I got so sick… I went blind and I couldn't go to school, I'd just sit on the porch all day and hear the other kids come and go and playing. I felt very lonely and left out. Marma, she go fill a metal bathtub with water, roots and herbs. Then she leave them in the water to soak and let them get sun-drenched. She boil up herbs and make me drink it down, boy oh boy it was bitter. I would have to sit in that tub as Marma pressed the sun-drenched leaves on me, applying pressure, over and over again. I got better, eventually, but my eyes were like this, light, from that day on. You know, when Marma died she told me, I'm going to follow you, uh huh, that's what she said. I am going to follow you. And she did, oh yes, she keeps an eye on me.

As Nanny told me these things, with her face so deadly serious, I would look past her shoulder and above her head for the ghost of Marma. Nanny taught me to believe there are greater forces in the world than us and I trusted her every word. I always take it for granted that my dead are watching me – not just God, or the tooth fairy and Father Christmas, but my elders too. This was a confusing contradiction for how could people be both in heaven and also down here watching us? Bedtime was quite crowded, what with all the dead people, ghosts and spirits, standing at the end of the bed and watching over me. I feared the dark.

Nanny had a quiet influence and she captivated me as a small child. She was kind but firm. She could be quite strict, and so I was sure to be particularly well-behaved for her, I would do anything she said whenever she finished the command with *for Nanny*. And she used it to full effect: clean your teeth for Nanny, tidy your toys for Nanny, finish your greens for Nanny.

Nanny made steamed greens and she got her fish fresh from the fish-van man who drove around the Danesholme estate and rang a bell so you'd know he was there. I'd pull a kitchen chair to the sink and stand on the seat to watch her gutting the bloody veins, all that filmy, grey mucus and muck out from inside the fishes. I'd watch with great morbid fascination as she dismembered a mackerel with practise and precision, opening the gills with her thumbs under the running tap and scraping off any scales. The skin seemed slippery but she held it sure and fast in her firm grip. There was tissue to cut through and fibre as she cut the heads off with a sawing motion.

I hated fish, loathed it. I disliked the taste but was mostly afraid the bones would get trapped in my throat and choke me. I always complained, but Nanny was convinced the properties of fish made children brainier somehow. She made me stay at the table until I finished my lunch. Sometimes I was there almost all afternoon, staring at my plate of cold fish and soggy cabbage, my legs swinging, agitated, my bottom getting numb. Screwing up my nose, I would chew it with my very front teeth to keep the bones away from my throat as Nanny said,

Don't play with your food.

I pretended to eat, chewing fresh air and swallowing imaginary bites whilst I watched Nanny have her lunch, the way she ate all of it, she sucked the skin and the bones. I studied her as she spat bone into her hand delicately and left it carefully by the side of the plate. She was like an owl, regurgitating pellets. I would look up in astonishment at the way my grandmother ate, the way she consumed apples whole, even the core. My nanny, she sucked the marrow out of chicken bones.

At school I used to boast that my nanny had a choice between either Grandad or Harry Belafonte. The truth was that Harry was a school friend of hers. She told me nobody then had any idea what he would go on to achieve. Harry was to be one of the first great Jamaican singers to cross over into mainstream America and Europe.

Springfield Road

At the age of ten, Nanny left Colonels Ridge and went to live in Port Antonio with her eldest sister Viola, to study millinery and dressmaking. While she was there she liked to ride bicycles, go to church and the choir and the cinema to see films with Tyrone Power and Errol Flynn. Errol Flynn lived in Port Antonio at the time; Nanny and her friends would often talk to him and ask him when another film was coming out.

He was very friendly, like one of the locals, Errol Flynn was a very nice man.

Nanny's house smelled spicier than ours; a combination of Grandad's home brewing projects in various stages of fermentation and Nanny's cooking of rice and peas, oxtail or chicken. It was noisy too, with the barking of my grandfather and his gravelled laughter.

My Uncle Gerry was usually hovering in the background or upstairs in his bedroom playing the albums of Bob Dylan or The Beatles, still in his late teens and yet to leave home. My mother's brother, Gerry, was always very much in his own world, keeping himself to himself, appearing only for tea. He was skinny and tall, religiously he wore skintight black t-shirts and drainpipe jeans, he looked like a rock star. He'd snigger to himself and leave the room as soon as he could, head upstairs and close his bedroom door. To me he seemed to spend hours lying on his bed, staring past the garish floral yellow wallpaper, lost in space, deep in poetic dreams. Or playing his unplugged electric guitar, his plectrum strumming the chords of his muted rock solo.

Downstairs, my grandfather was a noisy man; you felt his presence before you heard him, whistling and singing. His voice was a booming tenor and he had a dirty rum-toasted laugh. When my grandfather was home from work, I recall a chaotic household, a jostling place, with the news on the radio and the television, blaring, my grandfather shouting at the screen that the politicians were all crooks and sucking his teeth. It seemed this was a place where kids were to be seen and not heard, where children were not to get underfoot. I remember peering through the baby-gate fixed across the kitchen door to keep us out of the way. My grandfather drank brown coloured liquor, whisky or rum, the ice jangled in his tumbler. I remember bottles of camp coffee, chicory and his beer brewing in the pantry. How he rattled his pocket change and chewed on his tongue as though he were Humphrey Bogart. You did well to be quick off the mark, you made sure to keep out if his way and to stay on the good side of him.

My grandfather was an only child, born in the early twenties; he was brought up by his grandmother from the age of four. I have always been lead to believe that he had a particularly hard childhood – but he never spoke about his boyhood in any detail. I know he originally studied agriculture and during the Second World War, he signed up to the RAF. Occasionally Grandad would take the bamboo tray with the map of Jamaica on it off the wall, and point out the geography, the names of the places where the family were born and where they all grew up. He came from the Buff Bay area. Nanny and Grandad met when she was seventeen and he was nineteen on holiday in Balaclava. Then Grandad went to live in the States for a year studying agriculture. By the time he came back they were recruiting volunteers for the war. *It seemed to be the thing to do, everybody was signing up and getting paired off,* Nanny said. *There was this big rush to get married and well, we loved each other, so we went to Kingston and got married on the third of May 1944.*

During these rare and softer moments with my grandfather, I thought of Jamaica as a faraway place on a shiny, varnished bamboo tray with the different parishes of Jamaica, depicted by images of hummingbirds, flowery birds of paradise, palm trees and coconuts.

In 1951 Nanny followed him to England with my seven-year-old mother. Grandad was stationed in Dover. Soon after she arrived in the UK, Nanny came down with malaria again. And here is Nanny's other story, the other one to tell the grandkids – one night her fever was so bad they got their heavy great coats and laid them on her to try to make her sweat it out; Grandad's coat and four others, were piled high. And that night Marma appeared to Grandad and told him to give Nanny nothing but pure Jamaican coffee and pure rum she had just brought from home.

… Pure coffee… the real stuff and the 100% proof pure white rum we used to have back home, uh hum… and it was so strong, it knocked me out and I was sweating under those heavy great coats. Your grandfather, he says, 'you are not to be sick, you keep it in', and I did but I was so out of it. I never touch that rum again without it making me want to be sick.

Springfield Road

The next morning Nanny was up and out of bed, getting my mother ready for school. When the doctor came to check in on her and told her she should be back in bed she said,

Oh, I am all right now, thank you.

And she was.

***

Every day Nanny and I would take a walk and go to the shopping precinct to get the day's newspapers where my mother worked in the Co-op supermarket. There she would be in her turquoise-green gingham supermarket uniform with her pricing gun. The cool refrigerators made the hair on my arms stand on end.

How much am I today Mum?

Clin-ker-ching went the gun,

38p! I am 38p!

I wore the 38p price tag with pride. The other ladies who worked there fussed, telling me I was going to be a right heartbreaker when I grew up. It didn't sound very nice, the breaking of hearts, but they cooed at me and made a fuss about my curly hair and the colour of my eyes.

Green? Or are they blue? Ohhhh! She's going to be a heartbreaker that one all right, aren't you, eh? Little heartbreaker!

They are blue, green and grey, it changes with her mood, my mother told them proudly and squeezed me around the back of the neck. My mum always told people that. She said that my eyes changed with my mood. She said that if I had been crying they appeared more green, when I was happy my eyes were blue and when I was angry they turned a stormy grey. I grew up believing my eyes were as easy to read as the weather, as the sky and the sea.

Little heartbreaker.

The ladies grinned down at me making me squirm. I looked over at the yogurts. If it was a good day Mum would let me choose one to take home; if it was a supreme day I could pick a miniature pot of my favourite blackcurrant cheesecake.

With our dad away, my brother at school and my mother working in the supermarket, I treated those plump and idle days with my nanny

3 / the right excellent nanny of the maroons

as my God-given right. I watched *Sesame Street*, *The Monkees* and movies with the young, handsome Elvis in Hawaii. I lay on the carpet, glued to the television screen when Elvis movies were on. I sprawled on cushions on my belly and watched Elvis kiss the ladies. My very first crush was Elvis in Hawaii.

In those pre-school days I remember making mud pies, carpet tea parties and picnics for my dolls. I buried the cutlery in the garden as though it was treasure and I had my mother in fits trying to find it again at dinner time. I recall I had a play nurse's uniform to dress up in to mimic my grandmother. While my brother played on his bike and seemed to get away scot-free with such dull domestic tasks, Nanny ensured I was programmed to be self-sufficient and capable. This is the Jamaican way – girls in the kitchens and boys free to play. My grandmother taught me to sew on buttons; she showed me how to iron and steam Grandad's handkerchiefs and the pillowcases; she told me to be helpful around the house. I learned how to peel potatoes and to make my own tea and toast for breakfast; to wash the dishes and to vacuum. I was a very independent child. I was three years old, I asked *why* to everything and my repetitive mantra was *I can do it* and that has not changed.

4 / the man of the house

When Gus began to go to primary school every day I remember how I would try to follow him to his bus stop. I remember he kissed me goodbye by the underpass, before the bears' woods and he'd say, *Be a good girl, you look after Mummy, now go back home, I'll be back later, OK?* Gus was the man of the house now. Mother and Nanny often told him so, and he took this title very seriously. Gus could run fast and jump off high walls. He could ride his bike, gather speed and then skid, to do wheelies like Evel Knievel. He was rarely ever out of his Spider-Man pyjamas.

While Gus was at school, I played in the dirt with my dolls and waited for his school bus to bring him home at teatime. With that earthy iron taste of mud in my mouth, I was content but I soon started to go to a preschool nursery every morning. It was in a pointed building, shaped like a witch's hat, situated opposite my mum's supermarket. I liked it there; they gave us biscuits and orange squash. We painted and sang and they read us stories. There were lots of other children to play with and so I was very happy to go.

My brother was always a lovely looking boy. With shiny black curls and striking eyes, dark as coffee beans, and very long curly eyelashes. He has a Y-shaped scar between his eyebrows because he once ran into a metal pole in the launderette before I was born. The scar accentuates the crease when he frowns and knots his brow. He was always browner and redder in skin tone than me. As an infant I was blondish, pale yellow and chubby, where Gus was dark and lean with a slighter bone structure. Often to our absolute horror, people would think he was the tall and slender girl and I was his robust and rotund, pot-bellied little brother.

I remember when we took our baths together he'd squeeze in the sailor-shaped bottle of Matey bubble bath and scoop white handfuls of bubbles onto our faces to make Santa Claus beards and say *Ho Ho Ho.*

And when we cleaned our teeth side by side we used to aim to spit at each other's hands accidentally on purpose.

I copied everything my brother did, and being a curious little girl, I tried to straddle the toilet seat to wee standing up like my big brother. This was something I attempted more than once and every time I made a mess everywhere. Once, I remember Gus busting into the downstairs toilet and catching me mid-experiment, I was facing the cistern and toilet bowl and trying to take aim as he burst in and into laughter, yelling,

Mum! Come and look what she's doing this time! Quick, Mum…

It seems my brother was always laughing at me. And it's worth mentioning that his laugh is an unusual, fast machine-gun laugh that rat-a-tat-tatted from the back of his throat and resonated in his chest and belly: ha-ha-ha-ha. There are two things that always follow this laugh; his tutting *what's she doing this time?* or if it looked as though I'd hurt myself, *you all right, sis?* To this very day these are still the two phrases I most often hear Gus say to me.

***

I have pale memories of two visitors during those early times in Danesholme and the beginning of life without our father. Grandpa George came on the train all the way from Hastings. He had known us when we were babies, Gus being older remembered him more than I did. Grandpa George smelled like sandalwood, mothballs and dusty books. I sat on his knee at the kitchen table and I could tell that although he was very kind he was not used to affection or children climbing on him. He sat stiffly and gave me funny little pats on the head. His white hair was combed to the side, and he wore a three-piece suit and a tilted green beret. He sat with my mother at the kitchen table and they had cakes and tea from the teapot. He spoke courteously and drank his tea from a proper china cup and saucer. My mum told us to go out to play and they talked in shushed adult tones.

We were also visited by an Uncle Peter from Germany, who was brought up with my father on Springfield Road. Not a real uncle and not my dad's real brother – but kind of. He spoiled us with sweets and gifts.

Springfield Road

He gave me a Slinky, a wire spring that climbed down stairs.

What I recall most though, is that during these two particular visits, Gus and I knew the adults were talking about our dad. I remember we asked after him intentionally, because there were strange pauses when we came back into the room, and my mother shot us looks and gave contradictory replies in front of the guests. Gus and I picked up on the awkwardness that came with the answers, *he's away at sea* or *he'll soon come.* Mum always said that Dad was coming back one day to see us, the standard reply to our questions was always – *wait and see.*

During those early days, I'd catch my mum sighing into the washing-up, looking out of the window into the distance, lost in worries. I saw her weepy after phone calls and muttering over the post. She dreaded letters. She'd say *what is it this time?* then she'd take a deep breath and roll her eyes heavenwards as she opened the mail.

I know now that my mother must have found it difficult to ask her parents for help. I also now know that it was a struggle being a single parent in the early seventies and working at the supermarket to keep us together. I have a distinct memory of her cleaning up a spillage on the kitchen floor – she has stopped wiping, she sits on the floor with her hands covering her face. I bend down to look at her, I am trying to peel her fingers away. She shakes and makes no real noise, I begin to cry, hating seeing my mum weep like that and she says, *Stop now, don't you start crying, love, you don't understand, you're too young.*

I understood enough to know my mother's heart was broken; to know there were bigger things than puddles of spilt juice on her mind. Wishing I were bigger, I remember trying to wrap my arm around her neck. She blew her nose, avoided eye contact; she stared at the floor and at the mess. Then, looking up, she got a tissue to wipe under her eyes and smiled, the corners of her mouth forced upwards, her dark eyes still sad with black streams of mascara running down her cheeks.

My mother's moods were always hard to predict. I remember after our baths how we would happily scamper about naked, and how Mum laughed and chased us to bed, threatening,

Bite your bum, bite your bum, here I come to bite your bum.

But at other bath times she'd cry out,

How am I supposed to cope without your dad if you kids are going to play up? I thought I told you to get into your pyjamas, you'll catch your death running around barefoot!

And with that she'd burst into furious tears.

I soon understood there was a pressure and a strain, I knew she was often tired but I also couldn't tell whether she was play-acting or serious. She could play-act that she was angry to tease me and I could be overly sensitive and believe her. But I knew there was a boiling point, that there were times when it wasn't an act but something deeper and darker. It wasn't that she was quick to anger or bad-tempered, I believe that she got exhausted wearing that optimistic sunshine mask. My mother was a fine actress, mostly she appeared either in serene mode or sunny-positive. She always put her chin up and her best foot forward. But it did depend on the colour of the day, how much energy there was, how tight money was. The messy toys or muddy shoes were never the real issue.

Once the drama was over there was a long and awful silence. The only sound was the crash of crockery as she washed up or the scratch of the brush as she attacked the stain with vigour, on her hands and knees, working up a sweat. It wasn't until I was much older I found out that this was perfectly normal, that universally when mothers are angry they do fierce housework. My mother vacuumed up a storm and slammed the kitchen cupboard doors. She swore under her breath, as she crossed the street in her slippers and hurled the rubbish into the back of the dustbin man's truck *her bloody self*. She wouldn't speak to us for what seemed hours, as she cleaned and battled and cursed inanimate domestic objects like the jammed ironing board. We knew she meant business when she had her apron and pink rubber gloves on.

We'd beg her to speak to us; we'd write notes or draw pictures and promise to be ever so good, to never ever be naughty again, beside ourselves for want of her affection and forgiveness. She would finally call us to come to her. Gus and I would be quiet as she spoke to us firmly and asked us if we had learnt our lesson. These speeches were delivered in a slow, stern voice used specifically to make us listen. Often she said something wrong or backwards and we would all crack up laughing, because Mum was funny that way. She got muddled and used the wrong words; she would *put her foot down with a firm hand*.

Springfield Road

Then we'd say sorry, my eyes welling up with relief that she was speaking to us again, and we'd all be laughing and crying at the same time. At times like these her frown dissolved and the sunshine mask returned, her forgiving smile was like sunlight through a cloud as she hugged us and told us she loved us very much. Then we'd put the dishes away together, the three of us, industriously, picking up what was broken, clearing away what was spilt and putting the kettle on. She'd promise something nice for tea, like our favourite chewing-gum cake – malt loaf – a doughy fruitcake which was delicious toasted and heavenly with melted butter.

As I grew older I learned to read the changes of tone signalling one of my mother's thunders. When I was much older I even became an accomplice in them. We mirrored each other and eventually we learned to laugh at our reflections. I came to understand that as much as there are sunny yellow days there are blue days, grey days and black days, days when it's all too much, depressive days when the wintry rain is as sad as tears. There were also days to see red, days when Mum smashed empty milk bottles against the wall at the side of the house on purpose, her eyes glittering with satisfaction. (Many years later, after a pubescent teenage disagreement, I remember my mother saying *don't take it out on me* and taking me around the side of the house on Springfield Road to smash empty milk bottles against the wall. She was right – the explosion of glass was hugely gratifying and momentarily relieved my teenage angst and frustrations.)

During my childhood, on more than one occasion, I caught my mother alone in her bedroom crying. She'd ask me if I thought she was a bad mother. I never had any idea what prompted her to ask me that. I'd throw my arms around her and kiss her wet cheek and tell her over and over again, *you are the best Mum in the world and I love you forever and ever.*

This was the time when my universe was my mother and my infant images of her and of those days are a sum of this: I remember her now – a grey day with a constant mizzle. She sits curled on the sofa, eating something salty and tangy like tinned sardines on toast, utterly absorbed in a Dick Francis novel. She has washed all the bedclothes and hung the damp sheets on the radiators to dry. The house is hot; it smells of clean laundry, humid and soapy, and the windows are steamed up with condensation. Later that day, she sits at the kitchen table holding a pen, smoking, pensive and staring into space. The cigarette smoke rises and curls, and she is silhouetted by dusky light at the window. There are opened envelopes in separate piles in front of her, official-looking letters from the bank and her solicitor, leaflets about single-parent child support. She's trying to make sense of them all. She is dyslexic and she bites her lip and writes very carefully, arduously, with loopy handwriting on a lilac writing pad. She always uses the lined guide so her writing will cross the page in a straight line. Remembering her like this, I sense my mother's solitude. This was our early life living without our dad, there was a big hole and we were standing on the edge, waiting. We could not turn around or go back, we were in transition and biding time.

5 / my mother's words
excerpts from my mother's diary written in 1974

I am seven years old. I come from a warm place, a settled home on the plantation in Jamaica, to a cold and indifferent father. The war is over but I do not know of any lack of chocolate, fruit, sugar or know the terror of bombs. I am full of trust, a free child, natures child. I could have died twice though, at birth and at the age of four when I had pneumonia. I believe everything happens for a reason, I am full of love and trust.

I arrive in Dover 1951, winter. Who is King George, Mummy? I ask, and why is the flag at half mast? Quiet child, can't you see I am talking to your mother? That is the first thing he said to me. I drop back one pace and follow behind and see my mother change. I sense I am alone from now on and looking back I never knew how right I was.

It's England and it's so cold and I have only a cotton dress and jumper, white socks and red shoes, I hate to wear shoes. The tall block of flats we live in are cold. It's not a friendly place. Crying is out of the question, I unpack. Oh, to be in my feather bed where the hot rain beats on the tin roof and lulls you to a sweet slumber.

My mother falls very sick and I am not allowed to go to her. He says go downstairs with the nice lady, go do as you are told. Yes sir, I say and turn on my heels. I want my mother so much, I fell silent and I didn't speak until I saw my mother again.

I have nightmares. The bedroom is cold and still unfamiliar. My mother comes to comfort me and my father storms in and says what the hell's going on in here? There's somebody at the window! I say and so my father switches off the bedroom light and we wait until we see it was my malt bottles making shadows on the walls. I have to drink malt to build me up because I am too skinny, my father says. I ask if I can sleep in the bed with my parents and my father tells me, no, you are a big girl now and your mother is too soft with you. I find solace in remembering Jamaica, the noonday sun and walking with my grandfather. I remember how I went to stay at my loving aunties sometimes and swim in a sea the colour of malachite with white, white sand. I remember the sugar mill, the smell of the bubbling golden sugar, Mangoes fresh off the tree, swimming and splashing in the cool river and walking through the coffee groves. In the evenings there is storytelling and my great-grandmama, Marma, feeds us fruit and smokes a clay pipe and wears a red bandana. One morning I slept in past the cock crow and they found me asleep in Marma's bed. When she died, my afternoon naps were taken on her grave of white marble under the mango tree. Sleep was always a great healer.

My father taught me to polish his RAF buttons and badges and his boots and shoes and if they were not to his satisfaction or liking I was beaten and if mum got in the way she got it too. I remember him waking me from bed to beat me because I had forgotten to brush my teeth.

We moved to London, where I join the International Ballet School, but then we moved on to Hong Kong. We sailed on the Georgie, a lovely ship. In Hong Kong, Mum and Dad are out most nights and I go to ballet classes. My school is twenty miles away. To get there I travel first by RAF lorry with a crowd of others to the Hong Kong Ferry then across the harbour and by bus to Lion Hill. We are in Hong Kong for three and a half years. I learnt from the Chinese and I enjoyed their way of life. I absorb it all, go everywhere, see everything, nothing is hidden and nothing my father could do can harm me. I learn tolerance.

By the age of thirteen I break the school sports records and jump my own height, 5'1. I saw Richard Third and I dance in nightclubs and start to learn to play the drums and to sing to please people. I had spoken to Robert Wagner and Kitch Kendal whilst still going to school.

Then, one day my teacher notices blood on the back of my shirt and how I flinch if anyone tries to put an arm around me or touch my back. For the first time I am encouraged to talk and my dad has to see the headmaster. I see school as an escape and I perk up and take more interest in my studies and my father lays off for a while.

Leaving Hong Kong was like a bit of me dying. I loved that place and still do. My babysitter Lee with her one gold tooth and chopsticks. The rooftops with everybody doing tai chi every morning. I learnt something about inner calm there, inner strength.

I am fourteen when we go to live in Deal, where my father has been posted, mum having not found much work as a nurse in London. We live in a grand house with Susan's aunt and uncle. Susan and I hang out in our Smoky Joe's, sloppy jumpers with a belt, we have frothy coffee and walk down the road with our thumbs in our jeans, singing, and go for fish and chips. That was our big splash, walking home eating fish and chips; jumping out of the dark to frighten each other.

We move to Bournemouth. They stop calling out my name every Monday in assembly for my weekend achievements wherever I had been running and winning, in

Springfield Road

Southampton, Portsmouth and everywhere else. Dave, John and the gang all called me their shapely javelin or iron drawers.

Dave is the first to kiss me. I am fifteen and he is seventeen. He has a motorbike and is off to college at the end of that term. He comes to meet me from school one day and all the other girls run into the school cloak room at Boscombe, all talking at the same time and saying there is a fabulous boy on a motor bike asking for me. I take my own sweet time and when I see him I wave nonchalantly. All the other girls are two paces behind me talking in loud voices but I stay cool and quiet. He takes my books and puts them in his side-saddles of the bike and we ride off, waving.

We go down the beach and walk and then he takes me in his arms and for the first time in my life I am really kissed. My knees give way and we flop on to the sand dunes. I wish he'd stop and talk about the track and the following weekend inter-school sport of England meet in Southampton, but he has other things on his mind. He is kissing my ear and I start laughing and say, it tickles. We laugh and roll about in the sand, chasing and dodging, and he rugby tackles me and my school shirt comes untucked from my school skirt and he kisses my belly and for a brief moment he puts his hand on my thigh and then I sit upright and we sit side by side. I don't want to spoil the moment but I say, we had better be going home. My voice is no more than a whisper as I brush the sand off his cheek. He takes my hand and kisses my palm, he gets up and helps me to my feet. He jokes about the sand getting everywhere then we ride home. He parks and takes both my hands in his and says, you are still a virgin aren't you? I won't bite you. I stand there smiling and say, I am, does it matter? I take my books and my hands are trembling. No, he smiles, and he kisses me on the cheek, starts his bike and rides off.

Then when we got to Southampton I didn't notice Dave until the event had started. I could see love in his eyes and it is enough for me to drive me to come second in the All England Championship.

One day I come home tired from my usual daily five-mile run and notice my mother has been crying. She says goodnight and goes to work her night shift at the Boscombe hospital. My father has been drinking. I smell whiskey on him.

I run into the bathroom and lock it and then he comes looking for me and he bangs on the toilet door it seems for hours. He keeps saying, you are no good at anything, you will never be any good at anything. I drink port, thinking it would keep me awake all night until mum got home…

6 / love drunk

It was summer and suddenly my mother became a sing-song of girliness and she seemed to laugh more. She played Gilbert O'Sullivan records and sang along triumphantly to the songs 'Matrimony' and 'Nothing Rhymed'. She took my hands in hers and danced with me. I followed her and got under her feet, as she got ready to go out. I watched as she ironed her hair in the kitchen. The flat irons heating and glowing blue and searing orange on the gas cooker rings. There was a tub of turquoise straightening lotion and a mirror propped against a pot and that smell, the sizzle of steamed hair,

Promise me you will never straighten your hair…

I promise.

It makes the hair break and weakens it… You promise! I wish I hadn't started…

I watched her as she morphed from this soft curly mother to a beautiful and elegant lady, with hair all sleek and glossy.

Does it hurt?

No Darling…

She grinned down at me from her reflection in the mirror patting at her fine silken hair.

My mother sprayed my wrists with Chanel No.5. I watched her putting the finishing touches to her make-up, gazing at the way she used those delicate brush strokes applying mascara with her mouth half open and her eyes wide. Her pretty perfume hung in the air. Being only so tall, I admired the shine of her stockinged legs and turn of her tiny ankles in strappy high heels, the shimmer of her silvery evening dress. Then she tucked me up in bed, she leant over me, engulfing me in her loveliness and told me to be good. *Sleep tight and don't let the bed bugs bite* she always said as she kissed me on the lips, then when she was most mesmerising, and so intoxicating, she kissed me so I can have some of her lipstick staining my own lips. I'd feel the lipstick on my mouth and rub my lips together, and as I fell asleep I sniffed my wrists.

Springfield Road

The next thing I remember was my mother's bedroom becoming out of bounds. I recall my bare feet padding across the floorboards to find myself at her now closed bedroom door, hearing voices and hesitating to go in. My early morning time snuggling in her bed seemed interrupted. I was nosy and curious hearing someone else in there but when she heard me she called out,

Go put your slippers on, there's a good girl or you'll catch cold, we'll be down in a minute.

We'll be down. There was now a *we*, not just Mum.

In the stillness of the sleeping house, I can easily picture my child-self in the dark kitchen making tea, climbing on a chair to reach the cupboard with the intention of getting two cups down, instead of just Mum's. I can see my pleasure in making a tray of breakfast, clumsy toast and jam, proud as a house cat with a dead bird. I had been taught to knock, so with my hands full I said *knock knock* out loud, balancing my offering, my bid to be allowed to join the laughing people behind the closed bedroom door.

That whole first year with Mum's new boyfriend Paddy was a rush of impressions, a speeded up montage of falling in love. For me, it was a roller coaster of sensations signalling the arrival of an easy-to-assemble new daddy. Paddy took us out in his car for trips to the countryside, to see castles and stately homes. At one, perhaps it was Hampton Court, I remember a beautiful rose garden with water fountains and a maze of tall, trimmed hedges where we lost them both, Paddy and my mother, in a game of hide and seek. I remember the anxiety of being lost in a maze. That my mother had got herself lost with her new friend, but worse than the initial sense of abandonment was the nagging feeling that although it was a game, she did so intentionally.

With Paddy we had water fights, pillow fights, snowball fights. He gave us aeroplanes, swinging us by our arms and legs, spinning us through the air. He gave us killer dead legs and Chinese burns and pinned us in wrestling holds. He had one trick where he bent my finger in on itself, towards my palm, pushing the fingernail up into itself. It hurt. He squeezed my knee hard just above the kneecap and he wouldn't let go until I repeated *surrender, surrender.*

6 / love drunk

One lazy summery day we went on a family picnic. There were millions of fluffy dandelion seeds in the air and we took a rowing boat down a slow river, water splashed the seat. I leaned over the edge of the boat, staring into the algae-green water looking for fish. It was a dreamy summer's day and I was witness to a blossoming love affair going on above my head in the realm of the adults. I recall my mother smiling and laughing, looking so gorgeous in a pretty pink gingham sundress, a stalk of straw between her teeth as we walked through fields, we climbed into a tractor and sat on hay bales.

Have you ever had a close friend besotted with a new lover and do you remember how annoying it can be? Although we want to be happy for the friend and we are excited to meet the new addition, sometimes we all secretly wish things hadn't changed. You suffer tiny stabbing pains of possessiveness and jealousy. You feel you must try extra hard with him, because you need to be liked by the new boyfriend so he won't freeze you out or turn her against you. More to the point there is a love-drunk glaze that comes over your friend as she falls under the spell of the new man – and so it all seemed with my mother. Often with new couples there is a noticeable power shift where one partner is more controlling. There is a power struggle, a balance to find. Someone is the lover and someone is the loved, someone does the running and someone does the chasing, someone is the giver and someone is the taker. And so before we knew it Paddy was at our house all the time and swiftly things changed. Now when we asked for anything Mum began to reply *ask Paddy*.

Paddy became the law, policing the washing of hands and the tidying of toys. Soon he installed more regimented routines, bedtimes and teatimes. Paddy already had two children from a previous marriage, who lived with his ex-wife. Paddy knew how to bring up children. He was about ten years older than my mother and she thought he knew best.

But the truth is you cannot make a first impression twice:

I was three years old, overexcited and overtired or maybe I was having a tantrum but when Paddy looked down at me and said,

Do you want a real spanking? You carry on like that I'll give you a spanking...

I laughed nervously and answered yes, believing he wouldn't really do it, thinking this was a new game. But Paddy lifted me up in a flash by my arms, he swung me around, put me over his knee, pulled down my knickers and slapped my bare bottom hard with the flat of his hand. With the shock of this I urinated all over him and his lap and he quickly threw me off. Towering above me, Gus, Mum and Paddy looked down, the expressions on their faces a mixture of anger and amusement. Gus sniggered and Paddy made a huge fuss about the wet on his jeans. Blood rushed, flushed under his skin and his top lip curled as pointed to the wet stain on his trousers. I never forgot the look of disgust on his pink face or the precision with which he grabbed me and pulled my pants down. I never forgot that when he swung me by the arms and slapped me, it wasn't a game, he meant it.

***

Shortly after this my mother disappeared and we had to stay with Nanny and Grandad for what felt like ages. Nanny ran a tight ship and Grandad frightened me. Gus was always in Gerry's room playing records and locking me out, keeping boy secrets and teasing me. We all had to be on our best behaviour and I remember just crying a lot and missing my mum.

When everyone was still asleep in the early morning, I climbed out of my cot and crawled to the corner of the room to a box where Mum put some of her precious belongings for safekeeping, including a blue jewellery case. I especially liked to play with my mother's seahorse necklace. It was a seahorse skeleton with silver eye sockets set in a diamond shape of clear Perspex, surrounded by tiny rainbow-coloured air bubbles. It hung down to my feet from a black velvet ribbon when I put it around my neck. Just as the seahorse was frozen and suspended, I was waiting for my mother to come back to me.

When my mother did return she was glowing and grinning and she was married to Paddy. She must have asked our permission to marry Paddy; perhaps Paddy even asked us himself. I don't remember, but I know I would have gone along with it. Whatever Mum wanted I wanted too, and I simply liked things to be organised. In my childish mind it would be two grown-ups and two children, we were a four, two girls and two boys, and now we'd all live together happily in our house in Danesholme.

However, I now realise that my big brother Gus was no longer *the man of the house*. More to the point, Gus knew that this meant our real father was not coming back. My brother was loyal to our real dad. Remembering our father more clearly, he also understood that from now on if our dad ever returned it would be only as a visitor. During this period my brother started getting into trouble, aged seven or so, he was expelled from his first school for breaking a boy's nose with a dustbin lid. In his defence Gus told us the boy was a bully that had been picking on the smaller children. For the rest of our lives as children together, this became a pattern with my brother, always getting into scrapes for standing up for the underdog, being singled out and scapegoated. I remember my mother taking us with her to talk to his headmaster about Gus's behaviour. His school was an austere red brick building that smelled like hospitals, bleach and rubber-soled plimsolls, the empty corridors echoed with the determined click of my mother's heels as she frogmarched the doomed Gus out of the school with an angry *Wait until I get you home!*

***

It was to be our first Christmas together as a family unit and we went out shopping. Fizzy with excitement I skipped ahead down Kettering High Street. I looked back to see Mum and Paddy arm in arm and I cried out,
        Come on Mummy! Come on Daddy!
    We were outside Woolworth's, with the flashing fairy lights, the glaring Christmas carols and garish tinsel, when I was told quite clearly,
        Don't ever say dad or daddy. This isn't your daddy. This is Paddy. You are to call him Paddy.
    I recall that moment as clearly as if it happened this very morning, as succinctly and sharp as that first spank, I suddenly saw the trick and realised this man was to be my stepfather and that he would never replace my real dad.

7 / *paint it black*

During the early honeymoon days of their marriage, on Saturday mornings, Paddy and Mum dropped us off at a local community centre to attend a Saturday school, with creative activities and sports. I remember there was a balloon game at the end of each session, and at home time, all of us joined in, scrabbling to bop the balloons up into the air so they never touched the floor.

I remember my favourite song was 'Paint it Black' by the Rolling Stones. I thought the lyrics were *I see a window and I want to paint it black*. I first heard that record when my Uncle Gerry played it to us and I imagined painting window panes so no-one could see in or out. I found that idea and the song itself exciting, it made me feel rebellious as I sang: *I see a window and I want to paint it black*. I sang it at the top of my lungs. I'd gallop, punching the air, leaping higher on the chorus of *black, black, black*, to the recollection of the rhythm of the drums, which sounded to me like racing horses' hooves.

At the Saturday school they separated us by age groups. My brother was at the other end of the hall with the big boys. I was alone with my painting, wearing an old man's shirt with the long sleeves rolled up to protect my clothes underneath. I was humming to myself, *I see a window and I want to paint it black,* painting with a rainbow of colours, a picture of a pink house, red apples growing on green trees and the yellow sun in a blue sky.

Blackie! spat the mouth of a plump seven-year-old child with a red face and crooked plaits. The child with her chubby fingers, stood close enough for me to smell the cheese and onion crisps on her breath. *Blackie!* she said again. She frothed the word up, over and over, in a singsong of spit, *Blackie, Blackie, Blackie!*

I looked over her shoulder across the hall for my brother but I couldn't see him. My heart pounded and my eyes misted over so I couldn't see to pick the colours. I knew this was a bad word. I took my brush and slathered the end of it in gloops of black paint. Concentrating on the paper in front of me, keeping my chin tucked in and my head down, I drew the brush across the painting. I looked through hot watery eyes at my house now swimming in ugly mud, the butterflies I had been trying to conjure were now a swirl of brown mess.

Blackie…

I smelled again the acridity of cheese and onion.

Blackie, Blackie, Blackie…

It was over as soon as it started. I stood with all the fury of a nearly four-year-old who believed she was in the right and I threw myself at the girl, who was twice my size. It was so fast and so sudden, it was easy. She fell to the ground, and I sat on her chest, pinning her down with my knees, while I painted her scrunched-up face black. Paint splashed and flicked off my brush, a half-chewed mush of crisps between her teeth mingling with black globs of paint.

I was picked up by my arms and ripped off her and my paintbrush was snatched away. I looked up at the adults who had suddenly appeared as they fussed over the seven-year-old, as she howled, *it went in my mouth!*

They washed her face and mouth out while she bawled. I was scolded and told to fold the soggy paper that had once been my glorious, colourful painting and throw it in the bin. That was the part that made me cry.

Gus thought it was hilarious. He shook his head and put his hand and over his mouth to hide his laughter, saying *ha ha that's my sister, look what she's doing now*. Then he helped me get cleaned up and as usual he told me to say *sticks and stones may break my bones but names will never hurt me*. No matter how many times he said that it was not true, those names did hurt and they made me feel dirty. Kids in the streets often yelled 'golliwog' or 'blackie' at us when we were out playing. *Golliwog get back on your marmalade jar* was the comment we heard most of all, and I never learned to ignore it completely.

And then as suddenly as it flared up it was all forgotten. It was nearly home time and then we all played the balloon game, keep the balloons up, keep the balloon in the air, whatever you do don't let the balloon touch the ground. Gus and I never went there again, to that strange Saturday school, and shortly after that we moved to our new bungalow in Desborough.

8 / paint it white

Our new house was a two-bedroom, semi-detached bungalow in a village called Desborough also in Northamptonshire, in the green belly of England. My newly wed mother had to give up her job in the supermarket and this meant she stayed at home to look after me. I recall enjoying having my mother to myself for this brief time before I started full-time education. I also remember the new house was white, spotless and modern.

In the two-bedroomed white bungalow I now had to share a room with my brother. We slept in bunk beds in new sleeping bags, we thought it was what camping must be like, and being the smallest and lightest I got to sleep in the top bunk. The decoration of this new house was minimalist, painted slate grey and glaring white. Even the television was a white space-age cube.

There was an oval framed picture of Mum and Paddy's wedding day above the mantelpiece. I wished we'd been invited to the wedding, it seemed that my mum had looked so pretty, her dress was all lace about her throat. In that photo Gus and I always sniggered that our stepfather looked like the Hulk with an afro.

In the new house there were many precious things we weren't allowed to touch, tennis trophies and crystal glasses to be kept for best. Looking back I think it was bizarre, this man had married my mother with her two rough and tumble children and then proceeded to carpet the whole place in a scream of tell-tale white. And that white carpet was our worst enemy: it not only betrayed tiny drips but also showed up indented footprints; giving away any scuffle or play. And we soon discovered that Paddy was fastidious enough to know if we had been in the living room by whether the nap on the carpet was brushed wrong or lay differently. Before long, we were forbidden from being in the living room at all – except for special occasions or when we had visitors.

My stepfather installed cowboy saloon doors in the archway to the dining room. When Paddy was out the swinging saloon doors were excellent for games of Cowboys and Indians; we'd fall through them pretending to shoot each other. There were rush wicker baskets for our laundry, which were nearly as tall as me and big enough to climb in and hide. I played my recorder and writhed, slithering up through the lid like a hypnotised snake. I recall my early childhood in that white bungalow was ruled in this way and by two sets of rules – the way we were when Paddy was in or when Paddy was out.

My stepfather was a curly-haired Irishman. He was very vain about his hair; he fluffed it up in the mornings with an afro comb so it doubled in volume. He had sharp features and pale skin that burned lobster red in the sun. He smelled of Germolene all the time, a pink antiseptic cream. He had pale ice-blue eyes. He looked a little like Paul Michael Glaser, the curly-haired one in the hit TV show *Starsky and Hutch*. With Paddy at the head of the house, there were now petty laws and strict new regimes. Gus and I were not permitted to watch television. We were not permitted in the house alone. If they went out, we had to go out too and we could come back inside only when they returned. We would roam the streets waiting for them to return. We were taught to feel that we are in the way, noisy and messy. If my mother was too soft towards us, she was told not to spoil us. I assume looking back this was where I first learned to go without, to take the back foot and to fake an apology to keep the peace, even if I don't mean it.

Before long, Paddy decided that my brother and I were to eat in the kitchen, standing up at the counter. He said we were messy and we ate like pigs. He said he was sick of the mess we made in the dining room after meal times. At tea time they closed the partition of frosted glass, slid the door shut between the dining room and the kitchen, between them and us. It was not so bad eating standing up. My brother and I still fought for the one cherry in the tin of fruit cocktail and swapped food we liked and disliked. We learned to wolf our food down fast to get meal times over and done with so we could go back out on our bikes or skates, to find our friends to play in the street. So perhaps it's because of this I still eat fast sometimes.

My stepfather liked processed, English, bland food – shepherd's pie, sausage and mash, bacon sandwiches, roast dinners. Nothing too fussy or foreign. This didn't stop Mum constantly trying to add exotic flavours and Jamaican spices to her cooking. She made curries and took pride in using the herbs, fruit and vegetables she had grown herself in the back garden. But I recall food being a huge issue. Amongst other things, my stepfather was bizarrely territorial about cheese. He ate cheddar cheese and pickle sandwiches on Saturdays watching sport on television whilst smoking Rothmans cigarettes. He'd often take the cheese out of the fridge and scrutinise it, weigh it with the palm of his hand and say accusingly,

Who's been at my cheese? You been eating my cheese? That's my cheese that is…

It was difficult to look innocent when you really were – the idea of being wrongly accused and found guilty was so terrible. Believe me, I never ever ate my stepfather's cheese. It was always me that stole the cream off the top of the milk without shaking the bottle, but I promise I never touched the cheese.

***

Soon after moving to Desborough those brief days of being at home with my mother ended. On my first full day at infant school I remember being alarmed by the number of children who were crying and afraid to go inside the school. Some mothers had to come into the building and struggle to pull coats off rigid, stubborn arms. Children clung to their mothers' legs like koala bears, hiding their faces in their mothers' laps.

But not me. I waved goodbye from the playground, leaving my mother at the gate with other parents, teary and choked up. A tiny Asian girl bawled with tears and was given a lolly. I wanted one too; it didn't seem at all fair that the cry-babies got rewarded with sweets. All around me there seemed to be blubbering hysteria, a snuffling of sucked thumbs, snot bubbles wiped across cheeks. The teacher seemed kind and soft-spoken and I could see there was plenty to do: there were coloured bricks, pictures on the walls of numbers and letters and a wooden playhouse. During that first day one child worked himself up into such a fit he had a nosebleed and had to be taken to a special quiet room. There was a smell of disinfectant in the corridor.

Mum always said I tried to run before I could walk, and those first days at school I was eager and impatient. I had watched *Sesame Street* daily, and my mother and grandmother had read and sang to me and fed me books. Like a parrot, I repeated my numbers and letters, so as a result, I could write my own name and count, and knew my alphabet before I started school. I confidently shouted out answers in class and when the teacher sang us a song, I was the only child who could click my fingers as required. I picked up the sing-along fast and sat in class bolt upright, able to click the fingers on both hands, a feat that even the teacher couldn't manage. After a day or two of this overzealous, admittedly annoying behaviour, the teachers took me into a special quiet room and gave me a little test with picture cards. I was hoping for a lolly. The next day I was put up a class and placed in the year above in the second years. The children were so much bigger than me, I stopped shouting out the answers and I listened and took my first brave steps on that brilliant journey of learning to read and write all on my own.

9 / tales from my mother's kitchen

On Sunday afternoons my mother and I would cook the roast together, and we often made apple crumble. For the crumble part, I was the boss, I rubbed the butter and sugar and flour together between my thumbs and fingers and ate sweet, buttery nuggets. The greasy, crunchy, crystals dissolved on my tongue. At times like these, the kitchen was a cacophony of bubbling pots infused with the sweet smell of apples stewing with cloves, nutmeg and cinnamon.

My mother checked the apples by poking them with a knife, leaning over the pots steamed up the lenses of her round owlish spectacles.

She nodded and then said,

Oh that's strange look at that! Look at my arms…

What?

I looked up from my crumbly, sugared world as she held out her arm for me to examine

Goosebumps! she answered. *Look.*

Her arms were goosepimpled, but I didn't understand what this signified.

I could swear I just felt a cat wrap around my ankles, it tickled, how funny, just then… Oh there it is again.

We looked at her feet but there was no cat there. I looked up at her face and then back at her feet, I looked at her face and feet in turn again. Her face was lively with mischief and her dark eyes glittered.

I think it's the ghost of our old cat Pres! I just felt its tail wrap around my legs. Come on boy, come on Pres, outside…

I watched as my mum opened the kitchen door and motioned as if to a cat. She waited with the door wide open, smiling at the cold air as she ushered clean nothingness out with her hand and softly whispered,

Outside now, there's a good boy, there you go.

I shivered and watched my mother as she shooed air, saying *Outside, Pres, there you are good boy…*

Then, as if that was the most normal behaviour in the world, she closed the door and returned to the cooker, lifted the lid and stirred the apples. There was a very long pause, while she knew I was looking up at her, waiting for her to laugh and tell me she was joking. Her eyes shone as though lost in memory, and then finally she smiled and said,

You see, your dad and me, we used to have this cat called Pres. We named him after Elvis Presley. Pres was a lovely tortoiseshell tomcat who followed me everywhere around the house. He'd even be there at the bottom of the street waiting for us when we got in late from a gig…

She paused and lightly bit her bottom lip. Even though she had told me these stories time and time before, I always couldn't help smiling. I liked to hear them as much as she liked to re-live the time when we were babies and when my real father and my mother were young and hopeful. I loved to hear tales about my father being a good dad and a loving husband, and to imagine the two of them happy together.

The thing is… she continued *I didn't know I was pregnant with you at first. I was still dancing, go-go dancing until four, sometimes five in the morning, and there would be Pres, sitting on the steps of our pink cottage. It was in Shaftsbury Road in Ramsgate, where all the fishermen's cottages are, all painted different pretty colours, ours was the pink one. We'd take your brother with us… he would have been only two or three then. He'd sleep backstage in the dressing room… he'd be fine, such a good little boy.*

My mother sighed remembering happier times. She always sighed like that when she brought my father up. They were married for seven years before they split. Mum told me that they thought it was for the best. They were skint, totally broke, when he was offered the job on the *QE2*. It was steady work and well paid, and she encouraged him to take it. When he left she hoped for a new life, something more stable, away from the touring, the rock-and-roll and the financial uncertainty. We never heard from our father, and Mum would say it was because he was still away at sea and that it would upset us too much to see him – Gus and I however always suspected it was because Paddy wouldn't like to meet the real love of my mother's life.

Springfield Road

Piece by piece, I created a mental scrapbook story of who the other half of me was. By borrowing memories from these stories I imagined our life before he left. I vaguely remember the house in Ramsgate and shadows of railings against sunny pink walls. As I rubbed buttery sugar to make the crumble fine, with that sweet smell of stewing apples, I wanted to remember it all, remember my father's presence, remember the cat called Pres, the ghost that curled around my mother's feet that afternoon.

I have seen a photograph of Pres, lying on his back in a pool of sunshine with his paws in the air, wanting his belly scratched. In the family album it sits beside one of the only photographs of my father and me together. It is a black and white photo but I have coloured it in. We are sitting in the sun on the doorstep, I am in between the legs of my father, there are shadows of the railings against the pink sunny walls behind us. Half of my dad's head is cut out of the picture because the photographer, probably Mum, hasn't stepped far back enough, but my father is smiling. He has long hair to his shoulders. He has Jesus sandals on his feet, his ankles are skinny, and he wears a long-sleeved t-shirt covered in a pattern of bath time rubber ducks – he looks like a hippy. A cigarette dangles from his lips and he grins down the lens never knowing the top of his head and his eyes are out of the frame. There he is then, one bright morning, he sits on the doorstep in the sunshine with me sitting the next step down and I am his toothless daughter, grinning, sitting between his feet and holding onto his legs.

***

My father flirted with my mother when they were driving from Margate to London for a gig, performing with The Skatalites. My mother was riding in the Bedford van with the equipment in the back and Dad was shotgun in the other car, a dark green Humber, with the trumpet player and the other dancer. He dared her and my mum passed the bottle of wine across the busy motorway to my father, the trombone player wearing the cravat and the shades. And that night my mother was the leggy dancer in sparkling tights whilst my father looked up admiring her from below playing in the band. That's my dad, there, down in the pits looking up at the legs. In her words, he threw her a rose and she caught it and has kept it forever.

9 / tales from my mother's kitchen

As happy newly-weds in the late sixties, my mother and my father lived in Leeds but often stayed in the house on Springfield Road, my father's family home, with his parents, George and Edith. Mum fell pregnant and had my brother almost immediately. Gus was a beautiful eight pound ten baby with a full head of jet-black hair. At the indignation of being slapped on the bottom Gus screamed relentlessly until he was locked onto my mother's breast. He was a very loving and easy-going baby and, being the first born, he was pampered and spoilt rotten by everyone, namely Grandma Edith and her home cooking. The house on Springfield Road in Hastings was always a pit stop between gigs and a place for my parents to gather themselves on rainy days.

***

With the late afternoon sun streaming through the small square of gold, with the windowsills cluttered with plants and the leaves casting shadows on the kitchen's turquoise wallpaper, my mother regaled me with these tales of the past.

I remember that kitchen wallpaper so well; it had a pattern of sea blue and green heart-shaped flowers with violet centres. I remember the wallpaper so vividly partly because of the hours I spent watching my mother cook, and also because we covered all my school books in it to keep them nice. Sitting up on the side with my legs swinging against the cupboard below, I felt I could ask my mother almost any question. As she peeled, chopped or stirred, I coloured in the outlines she drew of our life before.

I was conceived during the lazy dog days of the summer of 1971, at a holiday camp on the Isle of Man. Dad was playing in the jazz band and Mum was go-go dancing. They lived in a caravan with three-year-old Gus.

It was the end of the summer season and we were at the Douglas holiday camp, your dad was playing with Ray Ellington…

I interrupt, *There was a magic bridge right?*

Mum rolls her eyes, then nods, indulging me.

Yes, there was a fairy bridge. When you cross it to go from Douglas into Castletown, you have to say 'hello fairies' three times and make a wish or you would be cursed by the witches who were burnt at the stake at an old mill nearby.

Springfield Road

As a child, I loved this story and I imagined this place of wizardry and fairy magic during that warm Indian summer, nine months before my birth. I imagined a ducking stool by a humpback bridge over a fast green river, the spirits of Sirius whispering through its rickety wooden frame, surrounded on each side by wild flowers that littered the grass and nearby woodland. I could see the river, winding towards a crooked windmill on the distant horizon, where ghosts of drowned witches haunted the cold shadows of the rocky river bed. I imagined the mischievous laughter of fairies skipping across the glimmering, sunlit surface of the shallows. Then I pictured my mother laughing, being chased by my father across the bridge, hiding beneath it as he caught up and kissed her. He might have said something daft and sloppy like, *if we weren't already married I'd ask you to marry me*. That was when I was a twinkle in my dad's eye and that was when my parents were in love, kissing under the dog star.

Really? I was made under that magic bridge?

Well, no! Not exactly there, under the actual bridge, but later on, when we knew I was pregnant, we did always wish for a little girl there.

***

As a child, I stared at the sun. I tried to capture a memory of what it was like to be inside my mother's womb, to then be born, the first sensations of first light. I believed that if you look through your eyelids directly at the sunlight, maybe that is something of what you saw, you saw the veined inside of red skin.

When I was a very little girl, I dreamt I was inside my mother's belly. For many years, I was convinced it was my first and earliest memory, as it was as vivid and real as a memory:

I was inside my mother, I could think and feel, but I was wordless. I was inside a dark place with a glimmer of red, a dim glow in the dark like a ruby in the bottom of a pint of Guinness. I called that warm glowing colour a made-up word – *rubiessence*. I could hear music, the way you hear sound from below the surface of the bath water. There was a muffled rhythm, something like a drum, my mother's heart beating, blood in my ears, pulsing. Most prevalent and unforgettable though was the sense of total peace I felt, and an acceptance that this was all there was, all there ever could be and whenever I remembered this, be it a dream or a memory of a dream, I could conjure how I had once felt there, safety, peace, comfort and a pure contentment.

Tipping my face towards the sun, and through my closed eyelids, I compared this memory-dream of my birth to scenes in films of people drowning, the serenity on the face of the drowning person once he or she stopped fighting for air. It seemed peaceful, beautiful, the most graceful of deaths, to sink down below the surface forever, like floating off into space. I imagined that being born was like drowning but backwards, as violent as not being able to breathe any more. From the essence of ruby, the dark red cave and heat of the womb to the bright, white glare of a hospital. Noise and first light would feel like a sharp, cold slap and I believed that was why babies screamed so when they were new born.

Maybe this is what all mothers tell their daughters, but my mother always told me that they wanted a little girl and that I was made on purpose. She told me I was a love child. I was born in June, midsummer, and I arrived early, impatient as ever. When my mother went into labour, my father was performing in Canterbury in a jazz concert. In one version of the story she told me, when my father heard my mother was in labour, he literally leapt, grabbing onto the velvet curtains and joyously swung across the stage. Either way she told it – and the story does alter – my father was wild and excited at the news. A band-mate drove him to the hospital to be at my mother's side and, as my mother put it, we both popped our heads out at the same time. He appeared as I arrived. I weighed eight pounds six, but when I was born I was silent and refused to scream or cry. Apparently, I started breathing on my own and then immediately put my own thumb in my mouth. Mum always says, *it was as if you had been here before, you just stared at us and sucked your thumb as though you knew us.* The doctor told my mother *you've got an independent one there,* whilst my father kept telling Mum how clever she was. Dad was pickled, merrily singing in the hospital corridors to anyone who'd listen *come and look, I've got a beautiful baby girl!*

Mum insists that I was also a mother's dream, an easy-going baby. She says we were a happy young family, and my parents believed that somehow things would work themselves out. However, a dancer and a session musician do not make much money, particularly off-season and between gigs. So my mother picked potatoes at a local farm for fifty pence a day. In those days, we lived hand to mouth and she could make a chicken last seven days: a roast chicken on Sunday would be a stew come Tuesday, then by adding some spice and love it became a chicken curry and after boiling the bones for broth, it was reduced to a soup by the end of the week.

I have pale but warm, talc-powder memories of our pink fisherman's cottage in Ramsgate. For as long as it lasted, with a smoky jazz soundtrack in the background of Dicky Wells, Gene Krupa, Coleman Hawkins and Lester Young, this era was a rose-tinted time. My brother Gus remembers it more keenly. He remembers our dad taking him behind the bar in a pub and teaching him to pour a pint, and he remembers going go-kart racing. My brother remembered my father more clearly and during our shared childhood his absence was suffered most acutely, and also privately, by Gus.

PAUL GODDEN (trombone)

Paul is our trombonist, although he is another newcomer to the show this is no new venture for Paul as he started playing trombone at the age of 12. After University he played a night club in Vienna. Has played with the well-known "Sounds Incorporated" and in 1967 recorded on the Sergeant Pepper L.P. Summer seasons in Blackpool and engagements on the Q.E.2 go to make up Paul's wide experience. He is married and has one child. He met his wife in the business, she is a dancer and they live in Hastings.

programme from granville theatre, ramsgate, 1970

10 / our real dad

When you travel to a new city, you can imagine what it must be like, even if you have never been there. You can conjure up London, New York or Paris by their names alone, picturing your destination whilst on your way there. This journey is in reverse, my father is the stop I missed, he is the station I dreamt of when I was sleeping.

We all have a store of scenarios of how it might have been. I have imagined him being a loving father. I have pictured him throwing me into the air and catching me, then sniffing me the way I have seen all parents do, putting their faces close into the centre of a bare-bellied baby and blowing raspberries. I am sure my father did this to me: threw me high in the air, made me fly and blew onto my belly. When he changed my nappy, I imagine I caught my own foot and sucked my toes. My skin was once as soft as all babies', and just like all our fathers must have – your father, our father, my father – he held me and I was safe in his arms. With his mouth pressed against the crown of my head he inhaled as he soothed and patted my back. He saw himself in me, I'm sure, in my features. I was his echo and he must have said what all fathers have always said, that looking into my face was like looking in the mirror.

I can picture the familiar shape of my father in the early morning. Then I can imagine my chubby infant self, dribbling, standing up in a cot in a messy bedroom. There's a gas fire, the bars are glowing orange, and I smell toast. I have torn off my nappy from the night before and thrown it out of the cot. I am naked and laughing, funny Daddy, I clap, although when I clap I let go of the side of the cot and fall. I am only just learning to stand, so I must be seven or eight months old. I haul myself back up by the cot bars and he says something like *that's my girl*. He would, wouldn't he? I think he'd say something like *that's my good girl*.

It is dawn, early in the morning and he is melancholy, probably hung-over. It's the grey morning after a gig and he didn't get paid or he subbed all the fee already. The money is always spent before he sees it. He has post-gig blues, unshaven, and his mouth tastes of stale fags and beer. He looks down at me and wonders how on earth he is going to cope. He licks the cigarette paper and puts the rolled up fag in his mouth, sighs, shakes his head. He lights a match and inhales smoke.

I can now recognise sounds and shapes, objects and people. Shoe. Dog. Milk. Mummy. Daddy. I must know that word and try to use it. This is one time when I get to say 'Daddy' to my real dad. If I am eight months old then it is winter. Cancel the summer sunshine I had previously imagined, making an arc of light across the smoky, shabby room. If I am eight months old, let's say, then it is cold and about to snow outside on the cobbled street in Ramsgate, on the pink house, on the row of pretty fishermen's cottages in February 1973.

Or maybe we are visiting Springfield Road, maybe we are not in Ramsgate but we are in Hastings. Now I do know what the view looks like from that window, I have touched the old wallpaper in the room we would have slept in. I know the red brick and slate rooftops of the houses opposite and the grey sea on the distant horizon. Snow is falling diagonally and disappearing as it touches the wet ground.

That moment then, he loves me, doesn't he? Dare I write that? Yes, I dare and I know it. If there is one thing I know, it is that in this snapshot, this imagined scene, he loves me. He scoops me into his arms and takes me to the window to show me the snow. Let's say he did, for now it makes no difference. I am in his arms and I can see the snow outside, feathers falling from above. I can also see our reflection in the glass, my dad is holding me in his arms, us together, father and daughter. The hairs on his arms and the warmth of his chest against my soft, naked baby form. I nuzzle into his neck, his unshaven bristles and sideburns. We are framed by the windowpane and faintly etched into the glass. The snowflakes are tapping the windows, erratic as shoals of fast white fish in light and water, changing directions in swirling gusts of salty wind.

Dad. Your cheek is pressed against me, you sniff my hair and kiss my head. 'Daddy' you say slowly. You put my hand on your mouth and I feel the sound, the resonance of the word vibrating through my fingers. 'Dad.' You are holding me and moving from foot to foot, slowly rocking us as we look out at the grey-mauve of first light, the sky is the colour of pale wisteria, swollen, mottled and trembling as the young seagulls' crying throat.

This is what we all owe ourselves: the shape of a memory of a moment of love and intimacy. A flash of how it might have been, how they told you it was. Once upon a time, when you were too small to remember, there was tenderness and you were cherished. Imagine your own father. Your real dad brushed your hair away from your forehead with gentle fingertips, he gave you the sweetest light kisses and watched over you when you were in your cot. That is all always yours, forever. This life, it is a long journey and this is the station you passed when you were sleeping but will always dream about

***

My father was born in Kent on April 24th 1941. According to my mother, he was a clever and gifted boy with a propensity towards chubbiness. Mum said he was nicknamed Porky at school and this made him self-conscious about his pot belly. He was very smart, and he shot through school and was awarded a scholarship to grammar school. He lived on Springfield Road from the age of about ten.

As a young man my father went travelling around Europe. He visited Spain and Italy, he studied music in Vienna and then came back to England to study at the new music college in Leeds. During this time he met my mother Lorna. He played sessions for the BBC then he graduated to playing session work for The London Philharmonic. He also played sessions for Miles Davis and played on The Beatles' *Sergeant Pepper's Lonely Hearts Club* album.

The summer when I was born, my father was playing with the great jazz singer Salena Jones – my namesake. My parents toured with the likes of television game show host Larry Grayson and The Skatalites, until my father took that job playing in the jazz band on the *QE2*. By the late seventies, he was resident at the London Palladium and then…

I combined my mother's accounts of my father with the odd snippets I gleaned from Grandpa George and the anecdotes that came out during rare visits from his old jazz pals in my teens.

I heard that my father was a brilliant musician, that he could play almost anything you put in front of him – the piano, the trumpet, the clarinet, the trombone. He was a drinker and a great laugh down the pub. My mothers tells me that as a young man the local police in Hastings knew him by sight and often found him after closing time, singing in the street and along Hastings seafront, and would bring him home to Springfield Road. He hated to wear a suit; when he did it looked like it had been thrown at him and just missed. He was a writer of poetry, a lover of jazz, a wearer of cravats and neckerchiefs. He was a bohemian and a libertine. The life and soul of the party, he had time for a drink with everyone and Mum told me this was his downfall. He gave it all away, he left nothing for himself. He gave himself such a hard time that the people who loved him had to work hard too. He never went straight home, he never did anything the straight or easy way. Yes, he gave himself a hard time and he'd drink until drunk after every single gig.

As I grew up, when I played the fool or read my stories or poetry aloud, my mother's face would light up and she'd tell me I was being like my father. That was how I was rewarded and how I grew up to know this much and this little. My mother tells me that we would have had great debates, we'd have had each other running in circles of word play. I revelled in the notion that my father was a showman; that he was infectiously funny, mischievous and above all that we would have made each other laugh. I reckon that I could have drank him under the table and beat him at pontoon too. But all I could ever do was digest these statements and deduce truths from the materials of my own DNA. Nature or nurture – could I really be a copy of a man I never truly knew?

Often I didn't want to believe my mother's portraits of my father, based as they were on her memories of being in love with the smell of the man and his laughter, and the details always changed with her mood and the weather of her own remembering. Her ex-husband Paul Godden was not the dad-man-hero I invented. The father I knew was in my bones and blood, I felt I knew him in the reflection behind my eyes in the mirror. My creation of him was all my own.

When your father is absent you collect all they have said and all they have told you, you look at photographs and letters and stir these ingredients together and bake your own dad. It doesn't matter now if he had faults and flaws. When you haven't known your father, he can be anyone you like and anything you choose to believe. So I made my father out of jigsaw pieces of other extraordinary men. I believed he was gentle and quirky like the American author and poet Richard Brautigan. I imagined he could be a merry rogue like Oliver Reed in *The Three Musketeers*. He had the flair, I thought, of a young and distinctly English Dirk Bogarde. Something of the poetic heart and wanderlust of author Laurie Lee. He was rock and roll with the hedonistic jazz persona of a haplessly destructive and depressive Chet Baker. My version of my father was anything but ordinary.

When I was at Springfield Road I was closest to his life there as a boy and young man. The fact that he had lived there, in that very house, was all I had. I knew he was confirmed and that he sang in the choir at Christchurch, and I knew that he read and wrote music and poetry. I imagined he probably composed those songs and poems whilst walking on Hastings' pebbled beaches and later as a teenager I often tried to re-create or emulate this.

It is necessary to mention that my father was adopted and that he searched all his life for his true birth parents. So more than anything, my father and I shared a perpetual sensation of seeking, the unbearable state of looking. His children inherited that longing, the space of waiting to be found, to be rescued.

It's not that we are not loving, living in the present with our loved ones, but when you have an absent parent or parents, there is an itch and yearning to have more. It's as though we are looking over your shoulder when we say hello. We are gazing across the water at the receding horizon, with a glimmering hope to find lost blood, to catch a familiar eye across a strange and crowded world.

11 / a letter from paul to edith

Hello My Dear Old Mum

How are you this bright windy day? Thanks very much for the bread my mum and for Cressendo which has just arrived. I am glad to hear you had a nice birthday, I thought of you all day. I have written a begging letter to Nell, I asked for 30 quid to pay the rent. That way she might send ten but if she comes around moaning don't blame me it was your idea. Tonights the night I find out about the job. So by the time you get this... we'll know. The food parcels haven't arrived yet but I expect they'll take a little while. Thanks for them in advance. Dyson my trombone teacher is a gas. He's teaching me things I never knew on the horn and he's got such a beaut tone. He's a gentleman like Mr Chapman. Truly family man with nice hands and a little moustache. He thinks I should grow one (a tache not a family) to strengthen my lip, so don't be surprised if? What do you think of the enclosed, my first (BBC) contract. One whole guinea, hang on to it we'll frame it one day. Well I must go and do some more practice. Lorna says she'll marry me which would be nice but I will say it for you "What on?" Its nice to know she goes along with the idea. Sorry this letter is late I have been so busy. Take care of yourself, love your unworthy son, Paul x

12 / tea and crumpets

It was a long drive from Desborough to Hastings to visit Grandpa George for the holidays. It took all day, the entire family rising as the sky was just light and lavender. We were like an army about to go on manoeuvres. We crawled along motorways behind queues of cars pulling caravans heading for holidays on the coast. The radio announced that it was *going to be a scorcher*, making us fast-forward to images of Hastings Piers, the promenade, Knickerbocker Glories and splashing in the green and salty sea. My brother and I were squashed among luggage and the picnic bag. There was a stink from the grey hard-boiled eggs in our packed lunches. Gus had a growth spurt and was suddenly very tall and spindly. He sat with his legs wide apart and constantly complained of cramps, *I need more leg room!* I wore shorts, the leatherette seating always stuck to the back of my bare legs, leaving a red mark of the linear grooved pattern on the backs of my thighs.

On long car journeys I remember I had an annoying preoccupation with needing the bathroom or with car sickness, and thinking of either made it worse. Trying to concentrate on not thinking of it made long car journeys unbearable for me. Being told that it was impossible to stop and warned *go now because we are not stopping*, instilled a terrific dread and panic that stopping, that pulling over, was a very bad thing. Now as an adult I must admit I get a little overexcited at petrol stations and truck stops, on road trips with friends, I look forward to the pit stops most of all and wonder if this is the root cause.

For the first half hour or so, my brother and I read out the road signs and bet on who would be first to see the sea, which was still a good seven hours' drive away. We played games; I-Spy, Battleships and Top Trumps. He cheated, I cheated, we bickered. The air outside was hot through the open windows but it was suffocating, stifling with them closed. There was no such thing as air conditioning – not in Paddy's queasy margarine-yellow Mazda, a clapped-out rust-bucket that rattled down the motorway.

Springfield Road

Heat oozed off the tarmac, shimmering like water in the distance, and I'd say to myself *it looks like an oasis*. With the windows wide open, the car filled with country smells; the ripe stench of cow dung, the nose tickled with petrol one time when the car was filled in the garage.

Gus drew an invisible line with his finger down the centre of the back seat, marking his territory. We squabbled about which was my side and which his, hoarding prisoners of war, claiming toys and comics. We passed fleas, playing IT, which escalated to dead legs and silent, swift, thigh-stinging punches. Gus gave me a Chinese burn and I tried to bite his hand as he twisted my wrist. He said *she started it*, I said *he started it*, and then we were told to *Give it a bloody rest for Christ's sake or you can both bloody get out and bloody walk!*

The car was quiet after that. I escaped into my top three favourite indulgent daydreams of discovering I was adopted or being an Olympic gymnast or a pop star whilst staring at the countryside and listening to the radio DJ say, *it's gonna be a scorcher and, you know folks, you could fry an egg on your car bonnet, today we are reaching highs of ninety-two in the south... and now I'd say it's about time for some summer loving, here's John Travolta and Olivia Newton-John...*

When we were all in the car Paddy would make his little joke.

Look Lorna, isn't that your cousin?

I think that joke started when Mum told him how big our Jamaican family is or how small Jamaica is, how you'd be surprised who may be related to whom some way or another. His joke invariably came up when we were all in the car and we saw a Jamaican or African in the car in front or crossing the road. *Isn't that your cousin?* It made Paddy really laugh, but we saw it upset Mum. I am ashamed to admit it but we'd giggle nervously too. *Hey Mum isn't that one of your cousins?* This made Paddy roar with laughter, we liked to be in with Paddy and his jokes. It was better than being at the other end of them. Eventually Mum would snap sharply and we would all go very, very quiet and feel ashamed.

It would be the late afternoon when we finally left the thick traffic of the motorway. Then we glided through Kentish countryside, up and down the swooping hills, passing villages with strange names, farms selling fresh eggs and potatoes, *pick your own strawberries*, and winding roads with humpback bridges that made my stomach leap. Mum gasped at dream cottages covered in wisteria and tea roses. *We'll have a cottage like that, one day, when we win the pools,* she sighed. Trees canopied above us, the sky was duck-egg blue between the lush branches, as we drove past the glorious rolling green of Kent and the Sussex hills and valleys. As soon as the word Hastings appeared on the road signs, we sniffed for the piquant smell of it, the first taste of salted air, eagerly searching for the line of aquamarine shimmering on the horizon.

I spy with my little eye something beginning with… sea!

Sea! Sea begins with S!

I know! See the sea, there look!

I saw it first!

We leaned out of the car windows, the wind making our eyes water and our hair blowing wild, opening our mouths, tasting the salt.

The house on Springfield Road was olive-yellow. There was a pretty front garden with antique rose bushes growing in it. When the door opened the same distinct smell always hit you first and foremost, a musty combination of Lifebuoy soap, Earl Grey tea, mothballs and a whiff of kippers. It also reminded me of the pages of dusty leather-bound books. The house on Springfield Road was a shrine to the dust of old things. There was an old cuckoo clock in the hallway and worn linoleum on the floor. On the first floor landing, the window was stained glass, red and blue shafts of light hit the walls. The house on Springfield Road was enormous compared to the bungalow we lived in, with unused bedrooms, a dusty attic and the murky basement.

Grandpa George showed us to our rooms on the first floor. Lovely, stuffy, homely rooms. There were fireplaces, but the chimney was blocked, so instead an electric three-bar fire filled the grate. The old springy beds in each room squeaked when you sank into them. A crucifix hung on the wall above each and every bed and there was often an old china potty beneath. Along the mantelpieces were figurines from Lourdes and statues of saints. There was a clutter of yellowing black and white photographs of old monks, priests and nurses in frames. Also photos of my brother and me as babies there in that very house, in the same armchairs but being held by people we didn't recognise or remember. And there were pictures of our real dad as a schoolboy grinning at us cheekily.

Springfield Road

Looking back, it occurs to me that all these photos might have made my stepfather uncomfortable. Grandpa George was always very fond of my mother. He came out on Mum's side when my parents separated, harbouring, but never voicing, the opinion that Paul was irresponsible by shirking his duties to his children and breaking his wedding vows. He rather thought it was '*a great shame they didn't work it out*' somehow. I remember throughout childhood Grandpa George maintained a closeness with my mother, a steady stream of phone calls and letters. He never forgot a birthday and sent food-parcels monthly, with teabags, bars of soap and packets of soup, I recall how he always included sticks of pink Hastings rock too.

We arrived in time for tea, and it was always time for tea, which was served in the ground floor front room with great yet sloppy ritual. Thick slices of brown bread were carved, cut into triangles and spread with soft yellow butter and church fete jam. Tea was stewed in a chipped brown teapot and kept warm under a burnt tea cosy and served in porcelain china cup and saucers with red roses on them. There were cakes from the bakery at the bottom of the road. That tiny bakery was crammed with a magical selection of cakes; ice cream cones filled with marshmallow, deliciously moist bread puddings and gingerbread men. We had tea, listening to the ticking of the dark, wooden, mantelpiece clock, its loud chime interrupting us at fifteen minute intervals. The four o'clock sun streamed through the yellowy net curtains, toasting the bread on the table, the first slice was always a little stale from being left out and the milk was always a little too warm. When we visited for Easter there were hot cross buns, and always there were crumpets and these were speared with a metal prong and toasted on the bars of the gas fire, as one might before a real open fire.

Grandpa George had an unusual way of eating. He exhaled noisily from his nostrils and his jaw sometimes clicked. He nearly always had cream or gravy down his tie or food trapped in the corners of his mouth. He had a very sweet tooth, like me, and loved marzipan and liquorice and fudge. I would look up at him in wonder at the way he ate sweets like me, with me, and with so much delight, not in tiny bites with the usual care of adults, but hungrily, making that noise through his nose. To me

Grandpa George was a testament that being grown up meant that you could have sweets, you could have your pudding for dinner and always a second helping of cake too.

As the kettle was boiled for yet another pot of tea, I was finally allowed to leave the table to go exploring. The basement and attic were my favourite places to snoop through old, out of date things, things that were maybe here when my father was a boy. In the attic was the room that my mother said had been Dad's, and the back bedroom that was once Uncle Peter's. I'd stand in the silence of it and imagine my father's boyhood. I looked out the window and tried to imagine being him, seeing things as he might have. In the basement I found books of sheet music that my mother said were his. I once found a tiny notation pencil in a silver tube with a lid that she told me he wrote his music with. In earnest I wrote sheets of nonsense treble clefs and semi-tones with it to try to conjure something of him.

The basement was dark and damp smelling. Mum said there was a ghost on the narrow back stairs, and I always got a cold chill, goosebumps walking down the creaking and dimly lit stairwell. Through the basement back door there was an outside loo that hadn't been used for decades. I'd dare myself to look into it, opening the door to see the toilet bowl was full of moss and spiders. Once I was in the back garden there was an apple tree that I climbed, and sitting in its branches, I said to myself *I bet my dad sat up here*. He probably didn't – the tree would have been much smaller back in the fifties – but I'd sit there and pretend anyway. Though there was the grave of his pet dog named Francis right beside the apple tree, I knew that he loved that dog, I knew that much was true.

13 / grandpa george

Excerpt transcribed from a recording of Grandpa George talking, made in Hastings in 1988:

I think there should be more periods of calm and quiet. I think there should be belief and dependence on God. I get involved with questions about God and spiritual matters and of course I don't know and cannot answer… but somehow with God there are lots of things I don't understand but I just find I accept it … We must try to have quiet times to reflect. I do think that prayers help an enormous lot. I don't know how, but they do. If you ask for things that you want, sensible things, not selfish things, the answer comes somehow, in my experience. Also we should try very hard to think the best of all people. All sorts of people try to irritate and annoy, but we should try to think the best and think good of them. I think one of the terrible things that I have always hated is class distinction. It is one of the things I had to put up with when I was a youth. I found the army a good experience in that direction. You were thrown together in a barrack room with all sorts of different types that, as a youth, you would not be allowed to mix with. I found that they were not so bad and they probably found that I wasn't so stuck up as they thought. I am not saying this in a communist sense, but I think there is good in all people.

***

Grandpa George had bright white hair, cropped high above the collar and parted slickly to the side. Even in my mother and father's wedding photographs from the sixties, he looked like an older gentleman. He seemed to have a lifetime supply of grey-brown chequered gentleman's three-piece suits, which he wore fully with braces, pocket watch and waistcoat. On his head he wore a cap or bottle-green soldierly beret. When he shaved he often missed a bit on his neck, I would spot some soap there and a few grey hairs, usually on his Adam's apple or by his ear.

When I was a very little girl we would sit and chat on the third step from the bottom of the stairs and wait for the cuckoo to poke its head out when the clock chimed the hour. Grandpa George had soft pink scrubbed hands and I tried to teach him hand-clapping games.

Who stole the pies from the baker's van? Number one stole the pies from the baker's van, one two, three, four, that means you!

I'd sing and Grandpa George could never keep up, no matter how many times I explained the rules or tried to show him how it was done.

Aren't you funny, he always said that to me, *Aren't you a funny little girl? Come on try again, it's easy just copy me.*

You are a funny little girl now aren't you?

I tried to teach Grandpa to rub his belly and pat his head at the same time. He could never get that right either no matter how much I insisted it was easy.

***

Grandpa George was born in August in 1916 in Peterborough. His parents met in the department store, Boots, on Robertson Street in Hastings. In those days, Boots had an art department and his mother worked in the silverware department. His father was an art dealer and picture framer. After being made redundant, they eventually moved south and settled in Hastings and ran a small art shop on Norman Road, a ten-minute walk from Springfield Road. The shop hardly made any money and so they also sold cigarettes, tobacco and stationery. They found they still couldn't make ends meet and so they took in lodgers and summer visitors. Grandpa George remembers losing his bed to guests sometimes and his mother staying up half the night cleaning. It is quite likely his father, George senior, may have tried to flog his own paintings too, vast landscape work, often depicting churches. There was always one of George senior's big oil paintings hanging above the dining table in the front room in Springfield Road. I recall an impressive landscape of rolling yellow hay fields and golden hedgerows with a steeple in the distance.

When Grandpa George left school, although he was mostly fond of aeroplanes, he got turned down by the Air Force. He did a few menial jobs in garages, until eventually he was called up in 1940:

… and the next thing I knew I was on a boat to Egypt. We weren't supposed to know we were going to Egypt of course. The boat was called Sobiski *– It was a*

Springfield Road

British-built motor-liner but it was Polish owned…It got very hot, terrible conditions, and they put us on guard, guarding stategic points on the ship, I don't really think it was necessary, just something to keep us busy. They were always trying to catch you out and give you jankers if they could. Major Gibson, he was on our side all right… but the ship is run by the commanding officer, so what he says goes… and anyway, they had class distinction with a capital C. You had to stand around and you had the most primitive, rough food… and the officers were up on the upper deck… you had to stand a few yards away from the officers who were la-di-da-ing it around, eating ice cream and jelly… whilst some poor blokes standing guard there, not even speaking to him… of course officers don't talk to common people.

Anyway then we went through one of the worst storms they'd ever had. The propeller came right out of the water. You'd see great mountains coming right up above the ship and then the next minute you'd be looking down into a valley .When you went across the deck you'd hang on to a rope, you wouldn't dare to let go or you'd be a goner. Anyway we were put in at Durban… we missed Cape Town… The ship was damaged and so it had to be repaired…

Anyway we had our pep talk from one of the officers before going ashore, that we weren't to go back-slapping and familiarising with the natives and so on. If they weren't kept in their place someday they'd only… Talking about natives, well, the general view among ordinary troops like myself was that if a chap was good enough to stop a bullet for you, he was good enough to be treated decently, well, I still have that view, don't you? We went to a soldiers canteen, one of the ladies said to me it was winter weather, how could we want ice cream in this weather? And well, that is what we wanted all right and ice cream was nice for us…

During the Second World War, Grandpa George was a wireless operator on a tank in the Middle East. However to read the stack of letters he wrote his mother from the front line you would be hard pushed to believe they are from a grown man at war in a tank with guns. George writes about the heat and thanks his mother for the Palm Sunday cross and the socks. He tells her about *a little doggy* that comes into their camp, that he has made friends with. There are details of a Palestinian orchestra he listened to, the overtures and religious services he managed to tune into on the wireless, and places of historical and biblical interest that he visited. But, this was Grandpa George, where other soldiers might have worshipped pin-ups and had pictures of wives and girlfriends under their pillows, I imagine Grandpa George had a picture of his favourite cathedral pinned on the wall next to his bunk. It's a certainty he had a crucifix. He returned to civilian life with medals that he never ever mentioned. If he ever spoke of the war it was only to illustrate the importance of discipline but more so the importance of manners and kindness.

When Grandpa George returned to civilian life he was the verger at Christchurch and it was during this period he met and married my grandmother, Edith Godden, who I will introduce you to in the next chapter. It was Edith's idea that George become a male nurse, and he worked at various hospitals until he retired in 1981.

Grandpa George used tools as they were properly intended, shoehorns and letter openers. He spoke with the gentility of another time. His pockets were always weighed down with handkerchiefs, coupons and string. He loved animals and he gave filled envelopes to all animal charities when they knocked at the door. As he grew more elderly, his love of animals led him to products that didn't use animal testing. He loathed any form of animal cruelty and anti-animal testing posters were put up in his lounge windows. Natural lavender soaps, local honey shampoo and rose geranium bubble baths begin to appear in our Christmas and birthday parcels.

But he kept to the rules of his childhood: fish, often kippers, on Fridays, which made the house stink something awful because he had a tendency to forget about them and burnt them. He was to be found at Christchurch throughout the week and twice on Sundays. He never missed the Proms – that was when classical music would boom even louder than usual through the house. His great splash out was that he always had a season ticket for concerts by the Philharmonic society. He referred to steam engines as *proper trains*. His work in the church was a job and something he loved. He also loved the royal family and his queen and country. And anything modern was described as *new fangled claptrap*.

***

Christchurch is a beautiful sandstone church in the centre of St Leonard's. On school holidays I'd often accompany Grandpa to church to help him change the hymn boards and replace the altar candles. We'd talk in whispers whilst doing these tasks and I was curious about being permitted up the narrow steps into the bell tower and backstage into the priests' musky dressing rooms, where the cassocks and robes hung like stage costumes.

I remember being inspired by Grandpa George. How one morning, when the sky was moonstone, milky as opals, I lay awake and counted the chimes of a distant clock. It was six in the morning and the house was still and quiet as I crept downstairs to the front living room. Looking through a crack in the curtains, I saw the sun was doing the God-thing, when one ray of sun beamed through a silver-lined cloud. It was as if it was God's own finger was that single shaft hitting the horizon.

With a framed reproduction of Holman Hunt's allegorical painting *The Light of The World* above me and the monotonous ticking of the mantelpiece clock in the background, I opened the enormous leather bound family bible. I had set myself the project of copying the entire bible out word for word. That particular school holiday my fevered obsession with religion had no limits. At night I dreamt of kissing Jesus – how I loved Robert Powell with the bright blue eyes. And how I roared my eyes out every single Easter when they showed that epic drama. With a mouthful of chocolate egg I'd sit and weep, particularly in the scene when they whipped Jesus and made him carry his own cross and daubed his wounds with vinegar.

I attacked this bible-writing work with great vigour, making my first letter bold and ornate, trying to trace over the swirl of calligraphy loops. I believed everyone – principally Grandpa George – would be very pleased that I had taken the trouble to write my own handwritten bible. I wrote until my hands ached, until I had a red raw bump on my finger. I remember wishing the bible would hurry up and get to the good bits about Adam and Eve but there seemed to be loads of waffle I didn't understand, before the creation of any animals or man. This was to continue every morning. I swore I would rise each day at dawn to complete this work. However, it was Grandpa George who took me aside and told me it took monks many centuries to write the bible out by hand. Then he patted me on my head and said *aren't you funny?*

***

We rarely had photographs taken and that summer was no exception. Perhaps that holiday there would have been pictures of Mum and Paddy playing tennis, or Gus and I playing on the beaches of St Leonard's, making new friends with other holiday children, all of us splashing each other and jumping waves. I distinctly remember when we took the cliff-lift up onto the top of the East Hill, how it creaked precariously. It was a short ride, but from the top I could see the stretch of pebbled beaches, the curve of the coast and the horizon. Hastings Pier was in the distance and the amusements and arcades were below.

It was nearly the end of August, the end of the summer holiday and I remember how we sat up on the East Hill together in a patch of daisies, eating ice creams looking out across the cliffs towards Fairlight. Above us was a haze of cream and blue and the breeze off the sea was clean and fresh. We walked along narrow footpaths of cowslips and yellow gorse, heading towards the sweeping Firehills and Fairlight. Mum named flowers and insects in a dreamy voice while butterflies, red admirals, cabbage whites and tiny pale holly blues fluttered around us.

14 / the heart of springfield road

If the heart of the home is the kitchen, then it is the soul that rules that kitchen that makes that heart beat. At Springfield Road, this was Edith Godden, my paternal grandmother and Grandpa George's wife. The stone-floored kitchen occupied the basement of Springfield Road. Even as a child, I could imagine this kitchen in its heyday, I could almost smell it, picture a hive of activity, billows of flour, the steady kneading of dough and the rolling out of pastry on the table in the centre of the room. I could imagine farm sausages on the griddle, the Sunday joint in the double oven, dripping and gravy in blue and white striped china jugs; a picture book home-made pie cooling on the windowsill looking out into the yard at the apple, cherry and pear trees beyond.

Down in the kitchen there was a larder, with a light that came on when you opened the door, like a modern fridge. It was a triangular shaped pantry with shelves filled with out-of-date tinned food. I walked inside the larder to see if the light stayed on when the door was closed. This provided a ripe opportunity for Gus to lock me in there from the outside. I soon discovered that it was indeed dark when the door was closed. Fearing the dark, the spiders and the mice, I'd plead with him to let me out from among the dusty tins of powered Colman's mustard, Bird's custard and Heinz baked beans. The Atora suet dated back from before we were born, because Grandpa George never threw away anything after Edith.

Edith Godden. In every one of the old black and white photographs you could see the good inside her. She loved children; in all photos she was most often holding a child. She had ruddy cheeks, her white hair a wild mess of pins. She always wore her apron. She was all bosom, with baggy stockings and had red soapy-looking hands. I always pictured her with arms full of clean linen, folded to put away upstairs in one of the rosewood, mothballed drawers in the upstairs bedrooms. Clothes pegs still attached, clipped to the front of her pinny pocket.

Hastings is forever the archetypal British seaside holiday resort that needs a holiday, all faded grandeur and peeling façade. So too was the house on Springfield Road, with the walls still echoing a time when the rooms were full of life, laughter and love. When fires burned in all the rooms, when each mantelpiece was crammed with religious effigies and fading photos. There was a time once when the bricks of the house vibrated with the laughter and tears of dozens of children who were taken in or fostered here over the years, like my real dad and Uncle Peter and other people that were homeless; refugees or immigrants seeking some shelter. This was a house for the lost and found. Everyone who came here, it seemed, came looking for something; everyone who came here had lost pieces of the jigsaw. I imagine Edith being run off her feet but loving every minute, bossing people about, ordering and organising chaotic bath times according to limits of hot water. Most of all, I liked to imagine lovely cramped tea-times with too many at the table. A slather of jam and toasted crumpets. Edith probably never sat down but hovered with a crumpled tea towel in her hand.

***

Edith Josephine Godden was born in September in 1906 at home on Beaconsfield Road in Dover, the daughter of a submarine diver. She was a district nurse in the war. In 1930 she completed her nurse's training at Connaught Hospital for Walthamstow, Wanstead and Leyton, then went on to work in a convalescent home in Bearstead, Kent. Whatever else went on there, it was a place where they sent girls who had got themselves in 'trouble', a place designed to relieve them of their burdens, war-babies, accidents. These illegitimate bundles were then put up for adoption and sent to orphanages until, it was hoped, they found good homes.

On April 24th 1941, a baby boy was born to a teenage Irish girl named Joyce Winifred Tremlett. This newborn was my father Paul, then named Anthony Paul Tremlett. We will never know what it was Edith Godden saw in this baby; for all the children she helped to bring into the world as a district maternity nurse, she didn't legally adopt any others. Perhaps a ray of sunshine lit the room as he entered the world and something inside Edith moved. Perhaps she saw him in a dream the night before, or in the tea leaves in her cup. Most likely I imagine she shared a particular bond with the teen mother, Joyce, who was as young as only fifteen and may have been alone here in England. I imagined that her Irish family didn't know about her predicament. Or that they found out and disowned her with a Catholic washing of hands. Either way, to me, it is not that difficult to picture Edith, then aged thirty-five, unwed and without a child of her own, seeing before her a young frightened Irish girl with a baby and nowhere bright for either mother or child to go.

I have indulged in a scene of the two of them together, Edith and Joyce:

It is spring, a crisp late April morning. The daffodils and crocuses have burst through the grass outside the windows of a white, sanitised room. I see a trembling Joyce, my real grandmother, as a teenager. I see her big round eyes, the same eyes as my father and I, an absinthe greenish blue, all welling with tears. I see the two women holding hands. Tears trickle down Joyce's face and I see Edith reaching out and holding her hand as Joyce asks in her Irish accent, *You'll take good care of him, won't you?*

In reality, I expect Joyce probably had little control over her destiny and that of her illegitimate son. It is a fact that the case went to juvenile court though. Filling in the gaps in what I have been told or overheard, the real story goes a little more like this: it is 1940. We have a teenage Joyce over from Ireland, working as a scullery or kitchen maid for a rich Kent family. She is seduced by her boss, an anonymous older gentleman. She falls pregnant and is sent to a home in Bearstead, Kent to have the baby, and this is where Edith Godden steps in and saves the day.

It's highly likely my unnamed father's father, my true paternal grandfather, was a rogue and a coward. Needless to say, he was an older, probably married man, affluent, with a large house. He had a property big enough to still warrant staff during the Second World War, when rations were scarce and for most people luxuries such as servants had been forsworn. He kept his identity secret and his hands nice and clean. After the birth and adoption of my father, Joyce disappears from the record books without trace. Did she go home to Ireland? Did she run away in pursuit of a new identity? Somewhere far away like America? Was she committed to an asylum or hospital? Did she live or did she die? Nobody seems to know. My father looked for her sporadically throughout his life and always came up empty handed, but for the titbits I offer here. My mother has told me that my father was convinced Joyce had committed suicide and that the not knowing, the searching and the coming up empty handed at every turn pained him deeply. It is unfinished business and gaping holes in the material of who on this earth you are really made of. Who made you? Wherever Joyce went, the truth of my father's birth went with her. But another truth remains, the adoption papers plainly state that as of 22 August 1941 Edith Godden was the sole parent to my five-month-old father and from then on he was known simply as Paul Anthony Godden.

Single mother Edith and her new son moved to Hastings and started a new life. I cannot imagine how difficult it must have been to bring up a child in the forties. In a way she may have fitted in with other single women, war widows struggling as single mothers also. As a regular churchgoer and Sunday school teacher, Edith attended Christchurch, that sandstone church in the centre of St Leonard's, and this was where she met and befriended the indefatigably shy, church verger Grandpa George. They grew closer and closer, until in 1952, both Edith and George were marrying for the first time and quite late in life. I really couldn't tell you how they went about courting each other. I imagine they most likely shared a love of dogs and music, evening walks or concerts. During these early years Edith ran a nursing home with her sister Helen and brother-in-law. When they wed my young father would have been a boy of around ten or eleven years old. In the wedding photos my father is in a blazer and cap and looks very much the cheeky schoolboy. After the modest wedding at Christchurch and a honeymoon in Buckfastleigh, George took his new wife and new son Paul and they made a home in the house on Springfield Road in the year, 1952. And so here is the beginning of the story – another beginning anyway – though Grandpa George never legally adopted Paul and my father's name remained Godden. And later still, in the late sixties, Christchurch is where my mother and father were married too.

Edith had a great love for children and was a member of The Mothers' Union. As a member she was persuaded to take on various children. Soon the house on Springfield Road was filled with temporary foster children, some from London, others local, all allocated to Edith through the church and the union. These included Uncle Peter, a mixed-race boy who was a few years younger than my father. I imagine there must have been a cacophony of teasing, tears and laughter, of instruments being played, homework being slaved over, the chaos of meal and bath times and in every room there was another story. I am idealising it, of course I am, but it seems that house was run by kind and generous souls who took strangers in. Grandpa George said it wasn't always a happy ending: for example, there was a child called Donald who was always in trouble for stealing. Edith was convinced Donald had some good in him because the dog always went mad with delight whenever he saw him. One of Edith's litmus test was how kind people were to animals and how animals were to individuals. Donald wound up in borstal in the end, but maybe he wasn't a bad person, just good with animals and at getting caught.

I have a brown leather case that belonged to Grandpa George; it is battered and barely closes. Inside it there are birth and marriage certificates, ration books, food tokens and a day-pass giving leave from army barracks. There are picture postcards of the old Hastings clock tower and the Hastings tram running alongside it. The messages on the back of these postcards start *Dear Mother* and then talk about the weather and end with *lots of love and God bless George*. They are dated 1955 and 1956 and sent from London, where George was completing his nurses' training, and they are written to Edith. It seems even Grandpa George called her mother. Grandpa told me:

I was working at the hospital. It was December 20th 1972. I can remember that date all right. It was in the evening I was doing a late turn. I was working on the male block of the hospital. It was the twentieth, so just before Christmas, there was a lady who asked me if I would have a drink with her and I was having a drink and chatting to her... then a staff nurse from the other block came over to see me and said 'There's a policeman downstairs, he wants to see you about your wife,' and she said 'terrible,' so I went downstairs to the office. The policeman was there. The staff nurse said 'here he is' and then she said 'shall we tell him or shall he just sit down?' So he said 'Make him sit down.' She said 'shall we give him something?' and got some brandy out of the drug cupboard and said 'shall we give him this?' and the copper said 'yes' or something like that and then he told me and I couldn't make head or tail of it. I knew she was dead. The police took me down to the police car and drove me to Royal East Sussex Hospital where I had to identify her. I will say this about the police, they were extremely kind. I said to one policeman 'I have said things about the police but I take back what I have said.' I stopped at home the next day. The man who ran over Edith was very young... it happened on The Green, just at the top of the road... The week before, I had been to a medical lecture in that same room they held the inquest in, it all made me feel very peculiar. I don't know how I felt – it took me several years to adjust to it, I am still not quite adjusted.

It was Christmas 1972, when Edith Godden was killed in a road accident at the top of Springfield Road. In George's old brown leather case there are dozens of letters and flowery cards kept safe and bundled up with ribbon from people who were touched by her: nurses, patients, churchgoers and friends. It seems Edith touched people, they all echo the sentiment that *Edith was so good, it was like it shone out of her.*

In the basement kitchen the heart of Springfield Road stopped beating once Edith was gone. Grandpa George never moved or changed anything, nothing at all, after the day she died, and for more than thirty years – my whole lifetime – the basement became a damp, cobwebbed shrine, stocked with pre-1972 tinned goods. Dust covered the boxes of buttons, her handwritten recipes, her meticulous housekeeping accounts; sewing silks, thimbles and packets of dress patterns. Her fine china crockery faded, silver cutlery grew bent and tarnished. I would find newsletters about forthcoming fundraisers, jumble sales and coffee mornings scheduled for 1973 and stacks of old *Reader's Digest*s with recipes marked for later. Huge cooking pots rusted in the sink. But the light still blinked on when the pantry door was opened, as though Edith had just popped to the shop at the top of Springfield Road for a pint of milk and she would be back in a bit.

At the time of her death I would have been only six months in my cot. Now as I write this, it dawns on me that this was my brother's first loss. Grandma Edith doted on him, she enjoyed spoiling him. I imagine him knowing something was missing, that Edith was gone. Perhaps Mum and Dad explained it to him quietly together when they saw Gus running around the house calling her name. Perhaps my brother thought she was hiding and looked for her in the kitchen, in the back garden, before it was explained to him that she wasn't there anymore. Gus was a sensitive and bright little boy, he must have understood something of what had been lost and mirrored our parents' and Grandpa George's grief.

At Springfield Road, I always listened for the heartbeat whilst I played with lost things. The pieces of a life, evidence of love, left by Edith and my real father and all the people that had once been here; pencils, thimbles and coins. I'd pick at a crumbling bit of wall with my thumbnail and imagine Edith's ghost passing me on the stairs. Her chubby arms full of clean laundry and linen, her cottony white hair, her pinny all clothes pegs. Edith's ghost was a steaming apple pie cooling on a windowsill, just a feeling, an image in my mind that wasn't ever really there, but I could still taste it.

15 / the wendy house

During the late seventies, money became really tight and since I was settled into school, my mother had to start looking for a new job. These strains echoed in the outside world; on the news I remember men in donkey jackets shouting, miners in a furore over cuts and union strikes, there were angry picket lines and race riots. Closer to home, the closure of the nearby Corby steel works put hundreds of people out of work and this included my stepfather who was made redundant, losing his job there as a statistician. Even as children we were aware of a hate campaign against Margaret Thatcher and in the school playground we sang with vitriol *Thatcher Thatcher... the milk snatcher!*

I was at Loatlands primary school full-time and old enough to go to and from school alone when my mother took a job at the Desborough shoe factory. This was toxic labour and her hands became hard and scarred from the stress, the chemicals and the leather glue. Meanwhile, my stepfather went into a re-training programme to become an accountant. In the beginning I had an after-school babysitter called Mrs Bright. She was the lady with so many children she didn't know what to do. She lived just down the hill and I'd go to her house after school and play until Mum came home from work at teatime. I remember that garden was a chaos of toys and children from the neighbourhood. Until one day one of Mrs Bright's little girls, Charlotte, got her finger trapped in the back door. Mrs Bright fainted at the sight of all the blood. I was the eldest, the little kids were crying at the sight of Mrs Bright collapsing and I dialled 999, it was something they had taught us in Brownies. However, after that, none of us had Mrs Bright to babysit us after school anymore.

Following that, after school every day, I'd go home to find the plastic bottle of orange squash and malted biscuits my mother hid in my Wendy house. The Wendy house had been given to me one Christmas by Grandpa George. It was permanently erected under the mossy corrugated plastic porch down the side of our house. It was yellow plastic, with a red sliding door and aluminium poles to hold it up; a blue plastic roof, a green rug on the floor and two see-through plastic windows. It was, essentially, a small house-shaped tent but I even made curtains for it. Inside there were two cardboard boxes: one was a washing machine and the other a cooker. I had drawn on buttons, dials and gas rings and cut holes in the front, a circle for the washing machine and a square for the oven. In the summer sometimes, I was allowed to have a school friend sleep over in the Wendy house, but when it was cold and wet the wintry wind and rain licked up the sides, making it flap open. I tucked the walls under the base poles and wished my mother would hurry home.

***

Occasionally after school, if I timed it right, I'd walk down across town to wait for Mum outside the red-brick leather factory. To me the old factory smelled good, leather and glue, and I liked the noises that came from inside, I imagined engines whirring, gigantic sewing machines, roaring furnaces. The windows were prison-like, small and sooty, barred and high. I'd sit on the railings, hook my legs over the bars and hang upside down. The lower steps became my beam and I rolled over the poles into somersaults. When I grew bored, I'd go to the corner of the car park where the wall had collapsed. Beyond the bricks, the junk, the shopping trolleys and industrial bins there were bramble patches and twisted gnarled trees in a wasteland, I'd go scrumping for crab apples, sour plums or blackberries.

Then when the bell finally rang shrill and when the doors opened, there was a waft of warm air, hot leather and new shoes. I'd sniff and look for my mum among a clatter of gossip, headscarves and a blur of blue matching overalls.

What are you doing here monkey face?

Waiting for you monkey face!

The factory ladies smiled down at me and I'd find myself staring at the corner of my plimsoll, and the kerb. My mother would look worn out, exhausted, but happy. After a very long goodbye gossip over a fag, we walked home together and I'd tell her about my day at school. There was an ulterior motive for meeting my mother from work of course – for if it was a good day we'd stop to go shopping and I could help choose the groceries, keeping a steady eye on the cheesecakes of course, but if it was a really magic day I could cajole her into stopping at the newsagents to buy me the latest *Tammy* or *Twinkle* comic. Whilst she paid for it I'd sneak a flick through the slightly older *Judy* or *Jackie*, which had love stories with real kissing at the end.

16 / kiss chase

There was always something magical and beautiful about those first shiny days of spring when the world was snowy with blossom. When new buds were sticky and strawberries appeared, tight and pale green, waiting to be painted red and softened with warm sunshine. Asparagus was purple in the fields, and in the far off distance, there was a sudden shock of oilseed rape, glaring neon yellow on the horizon.

When the scent of freshly cut grass reached our senses it was a green light. We knew when the school bell rang we could at last break away from the tarmac of the playground and finally run free on the lush school playing fields. Break-times at school became a terrific festering itch of grass fights. We made dens of cuttings and hedgerow camps, prickly with hawthorn. Girls sat in soft cooing circles making daisy chains. They flipped into handstands against the classroom walls, a line of pretty pink knickers, all with the days of the week in *Strawberry Shortcake* or *Snoopy* cartoons. Girls counted in cartwheels and chalked up squares of hopscotch on the tarmac. The lines of the netball pitch marked out territories for the tag-team games of catch and British Bulldog, that brilliant boisterous game which involved tackling each other rugby style. Coats became goalposts and cardigans were spread out on the ground for beds in the make-believe rooms of houses, hospitals or castles. With the springtime bird chorus and the first cuckoo came the sing-song of skipping-ropes and the stamping rhythm of rhyming hand-clapping games. We caught furred caterpillars and they'd tickle us as they crawled over our cupped hands. As girls we were particularly gentle with caterpillars, we tried to feed them leaves, amazed, in awe at their nature of becoming butterflies one day.

Meanwhile, boys were maniacs, they ran wildly with their coats on back to front, with the hoods up covering their faces, blindly colliding into each other and roaring like bears. They tortured daddy-long-legs, and kicked the bins until wasps flew out angrily. And oranges seemed bigger then, huge and tight. Sometimes it took almost all morning-break to meticulously peel away all the white pith to reveal the perfect orange segment.

The longer light, the heat and the dandelion seeds in the air were a call for robust games of kiss chase and war. Charging across the plains and fields, I was a lion and the boys were antelope stampeding. I played rough, flew, bundled and tackled boys to the ground. I stuffed grass in their mouths and down the backs of their shirts. As females we gathered and called other girls to unite, marching around the playground screaming *We want the girls! We want the girls!* until we made a string of ten or twenty girls, holding hands in a chain. Then we charged across the playground, up the bank and onto the playing fields, into an equal number of boys lying in wait like soldiers in grass trenches, their back-up troops at the top hill behind them. With an exhilarating roar our two armies ran at each other. We grappled and fell, the wounded crying out.

I've been shot! So you can't shoot me anymore, I'm already dead.

I can too, I can make you double-dead.

That's not fair!

Well, I just threw a hand grenade, that means you're deader than me!

We rolled on our backs like puppies, with the smell of fresh cut grass stinging our nostrils. Spring was like too much sugar, a drug that made us laugh so much and so hard we almost wet ourselves. We chased and grabbed and squeezed at each other's parts, boys slobbered kisses on the cheeks of girls who squirmed and squealed in a mixture of delight and disgust. We formed packs and hunted boys. Intentionally taking the weaker ones for our own purpose. We made them slaves. We held them down, pulled down their trousers and laughed at their Y-front pants. We took them prisoner in epic hedgerow camp games that took weeks of break-times to conclude. We ordered our boy-servants to fetch and carry for us in our houses in the undergrowth while we squashed berries with sticks on dock leaf plates.

There were compelling games in the long grass, the first blooms of *show me yours, show you mine.* In a fuzz of golden hay there were delightful flashes of truth-or-dare kisses. Suddenly, we had a good reason to really like school. Winter was a grey memory, abandoned like a shed snakeskin. Everyone suddenly looked different, there was a spate of new haircuts and growth spurts and gappy smiles as we were all losing our milk teeth.

Springfield Road

My appearance changed dramatically too, I'd had my ears pierced for my seventh birthday and I wore gold stud earrings. This was to compensate for two loathsome facts: firstly, to my disgust, I now had to wear blue NHS glasses in class for reading and writing. I thought they made me look ugly. Secondly, my mother, now working and not having the time to help me in the mornings, had cut my long, beautiful but unmanageable curly hair off. I now had a short boyish haircut, which she insisted was called a lion-cut, but which grew out fast and erupted into unruly microphone-head afro-frizz within weeks.

That spring we all grew more confident, as we became aware we were not the youngest babies in the school anymore. We had a new uniform of green skid marks staining our elbows and knees. We felt lighter coming to school in just short gingham summer dresses and the boys in those short grey shorts.

***

In our last golden term in the infants, the new boy arrived in our class. He had eyes like the sea, dark green with blue flecks. He was tanned, with auburn brown hair, brown freckles and very pink lips. He could run fast and had been to Disneyland. He had moved into the new house on Braybrooke Road opposite the sweet shop. Our teacher Miss Barclay chose me to show him around for his first break-times. That's how I got to meet him first and how we became friends. That first day, he lifted up his shirt and said,

Punch me!

When I punched his stomach he said,

Harder! Look! See, it don't hurt! Look look, see… Do it again! as he punched his muscular torso with his own fist. He was a seven-year-old with a six-pack and I loved him. With the arrival of the new boy that week, suddenly in class I was distracted. I wriggled in my seat, staring at him when Miss Barclay read us our afternoon story. Miss Barclay wore dresses with low necklines. She was pretty, with bleached hair, and when she leaned over we could see she was wearing a black bra. We giggled and nudged each other, fascinated by the otherworldly black lace cupping her bronzed bosoms. A fly banged against the classroom window lazily. We were milky and soporific with afternoon daydreams. My hair was frizzy, knotted with grass. I undid a button on my summer dress and slipped it off my shoulder to rub my bare cheek against it whilst looking at the new boy. My naked shoulder was shockingly smooth, my cheek was hot against it. Watching him hurt my stomach. I had butterflies with teeth. I stared at the beautiful new boy twiddling with my curls. Miss Barclay's voice was lulling and soft. I stroked the cool skin in the hollow at the backs of my knees. I drew a scratched love heart on the back of my hand with my fingernail only to quickly lick it off, jumping with the sudden sound of the end of school bell.

The new boy's name, I will call him Mark MacGowan. He spoke fast and excitedly, his eyes wide and sparkling. I seem to remember he wore a silver boxing glove charm on a silver chain around his neck. He showed me a grey piece of lead, like a charcoal-silver freckle, under the skin by his temple and said it was where an electric pencil sharpener backfired and could have blinded him.

Could've killed me if it had gone into my brain...

I sighed like I was being shown a hero's war wound. After school I walked him home the long way around. Mark's house was huge and sprawling compared to our bungalow. I became shy and polite when I met his mother, a pretty lady with short red hair. In his bedroom upstairs there were *Star Wars* models and pictures of him snorkelling in America. He told me what it was like to fly on aeroplanes. Best of all he had a new shiny purple Chopper, the coolest bicycle I had ever seen, and he let me have a go riding it. He gave me backies too; we rode dangerously fast downhill.

One day after school Mark MacGowan and I were out walking together after school. We were by the humpback bridge and the bricked-up train tunnel at the back of the school fields when the sky became dark with storm clouds and it started to spit with slow, fat drops of rain. We were talking about James Bond and that's when Mark looked at me mischievously and said that we should stay out in the rain and get drenched on purpose. He persuaded me that if we got wet in the rain his mum would make us take a bath together like James Bond. He told me that we should tell his mother that we got lost down the lanes and that we got caught in the storm accidentally. Mark MacGowan had a wicked glint in his eye when he said this and so instead of turning back to go home, like a dare, we stood there watching the rumbling black sky unfold above us. Thunder rolled and the lightning cracked. We looked at each other and simultaneously began to run, we sprinted fast and hid beneath a tree, jumping with each flash of lightning and calling out with each roar of thunder. Then the fast summer rain bucketed down, it poured and poured and soaked us through. We tipped back our heads and caught the drops from the branches above in our opened mouths, I span with outstretched arms and leapt about.

In my remembering, that moment will always smell like summer rain on cowslips and hawthorn. With the chestnut tree blossoming above us, this memory shines like the raindrops in his eyelashes, his eyes all glittering and laughing. We splashed and kicked in puddles at each other, wetting each others legs on purpose as we raced each other along the lane through the downpour until we were out of breath, soaked through and back at his house. As soon as we got in the door his mother made a fantastic fuss. Just as he had hoped and predicted, she said we'd catch our death and she ran a bath for us. However while I soaked in the bath, Mark sat on the floor in the stairwell and talked to me through the locked bathroom door.

What are you doing now?
Washing my knee.
I can see you.
Then what am I doing now?
Washing your arms.
Am not.
Washing your tummy?
Nope.

Mark's mother and my mother became great friends. They'd laugh about how we were dumped in the bath together after the rain, but it wasn't true, for the record, we didn't have a bath together. I did not *take a bath with my first puppy love* as my mother teased me for the rest of my life.

In the days after the thunderstorm, I lay awake in my bed and played out daydreams where I impressed Mark with my super-fast running and cartwheels. We were like Batman and Catwoman, or James Bond and one of the beautiful spies. In my dreams we waded through wheat fields of yellow and got caught in thunderstorms and I saw the rain on his long eyelashes, our clothes were soaked see-through as we held hands and ran like the bionic man and woman.

***

It was not until later that week that Mark dared me to kiss him. We were in the building site by the side of his house and we had crawled into some unused concrete pipes. Inside the pipes it was secret, shadowy. We closed our eyes tight, held our breath, scrunched up our faces, puckered and pecked lips. That first kiss was quick and ticklish. I covered my face and cracked up laughing and he waited for me to stop and then leaned towards me and we did it a again and then a few more times. Each time lingering a little longer, sitting side by side.

Then Mark dared us to kiss with open eyes. At first I kept giggling and it was an embarrassed mess of slobbering and a clashing of teeth, but I remember the heat of another mouth being so close to mine, and the feel of it on my cheek when he exhaled through his nose. Then he dared us to kiss in the open air. I took some convincing. I was afraid of being seen as we stood on top of the pipes and kissed under the naked sky, in full view of all the birds and the trees. We kissed with the teatime sun burning above us. God could have looked down and seen us and Jesus and anyone else who was watching to see if we had been good or bad. My cheeks flushed, the hairs on my arms and neck stood on end and my heart pounded in my chest.

In the cool of that summer evening we locked ourselves in his dad's shed with the lawn mower, plant pots and the spades, to play James Bond. The game was to act out the part when James Bond kisses Miss Moneypenny. Mark asked me to take off my cardigan so I could be more like Miss Moneypenny. We both agreed that she would take off her cardigan to be kissed by James Bond. Then he lay down and asked me to lie beside him on the floor of the shed. We kissed as we had seen adults do in films, with our lips glued and our heads turning slowly at different angles. We were in a movie of our own and he was the hero, the handsome James Bond, and I was the helpless, beautiful girl wrapped in his strong arms. We put my cardigan over our heads and in that hot pitch blackness, we sank into our own school cardigan world of soft first kisses.

Springfield Road

I ran home then, when I thought I might explode and when I could take no more kissing. I ran faster than I ever could, all the way up the hill and home. The steep climb didn't even hurt my legs as they pumped on the adrenalin of kissing and the fire of the secrecy surging through me. The neighbourhood kids, my classmates, were playing and racing on their bikes out on my street, it was still early and light, but I ran past them. I burned and I couldn't bring myself to speak to them in case they saw it in my eyes. I was afraid that I had been doing something wrong and that it was there for all to read in my face. I wanted to be alone to replay every moment, to make sure I remembered the kissing, every sensation from beginning to end. While it was still light outside, I got into bed and lay there, listening to the birds' evening songs. I had a book open in front of my face but the words were not going in. When I closed my eyes I could imagine I was kissing him again and again. I was fizzing like a bee in a jar.

At school the next week, my next-door neighbour Kathy was Mark's girlfriend and declared she was the first to kiss him. I was outraged and broke my silence to announce that actually I had kissed him first. Oddly enough nobody believed me, and Mark flatly denied ever kissing me. So every day I suffered my first bitter sting of jealousy watching them holding hands together at break-times. They were much more public than Mark and I had ever been. I felt betrayed and as distracted by seeing them together as I had been by keeping the secret the week before. I decided there and then that boys and all that kissing was much more trouble than it was worth. Boys were more useful for fighting, to make into slaves or to beat at running races.

Throughout school life Mark MacGowan would still come up to me and rave about *Rocky*, whilst skipping about on the spot with his fists in front of his face. He'd pull his shirt up and ask me to punch his stomach. I'd punch him and he'd pretend it hurt him to make me laugh. Then he'd make a miraculous recovery, say *gotcha* and we'd chase and race each other on the school track. He told everyone I was *the fastest girl runner for our age in the school* and it was rarely disputed. Though I wanted to be the fastest for our entire year, faster than even the boys too. My brother took Mark under his wing and walked to boxing club with him. They went training every week. Once in a blue moon, I have dreamt about fields of yellow and I still have that silver boxing glove, somewhere.

17 / mrs tiggy-winkle

Mr and Mrs Sharkey were a friendly elderly couple that lived a few doors down from us on The Ridings. All of the kids in the neighbourhood would visit there. When we were roller skating, hurtling up and down the pavement clinging to hedges and fences, Mrs Sharkey would pop out and she always had time for a little chat at her garden gate. There she'd stand in her pinny, her cheeks a powdery peach and pink, her hair silver-white and pinned in a bun. If Mrs Sharkey had time she'd even let us in to sit at her kitchen table for a while. I liked to watch her doing her dishes or baking, sometimes she'd let me help peg the sheets and tablecloths on the line. Then she would grin at me and pause and say,

Cakey?

It was our little joke. I would pretend to think about it for a while and take my time to say, *yes please*. Then she'd chuckle and go to the cupboard in the corner where she kept the tin filled with her home-made cakes.

I can taste them now, delicious buttery currant buns in little white paper cases with pink rose patterns. They were golden, moist with sweet plump currants and sometimes even glacé cherries. Heavenly. If Mrs Sharkey was in a rush and only had a minute to spare, she'd give us a bun each to take away with us. I'd eat mine slowly, walking down the road at a lovely idle pace. I'd pick out the cherries and fruit, nibble the cake from under my fingernails, scrape the bun remains off the empty paper with my bottom teeth until it was clean, then chew the paper wrapper until it was soggy and disintegrating and swallow it.

Mrs Sharkey's husband was a chirpy Irishman. When we played out in the street after school we would see him down at the bottom of his drive with the doors to his garage wide open, busying himself there with his lathe and all his dangerous looking oily-black power tools. That summer he made me an excellent skipping rope with wooden handles and a long orange rope. I played with it in the street, cantering like a pony along the pavement. Then he made one for everyone in the street. He measured the ropes lengths to our different heights and then he carved our initials into the wooden handles so we wouldn't mix them up.

I remember Mr Sharkey often called out to me across the street because I walked looking down at the pavement. I would be peering for lost things in the gutter and scuffing up my ugly, sensible shoes against the kerb. Mr Sharkey would catch me and wolf whistle over, *Hey! Salena, Head up! Always walk proud with your head held high, that's it, chin up, that's a girl!*

Mr and Mrs Sharkey watched out for me. They must have seen me wandering around lost in daydreams, running my finger along railings and walking my fingers along the tops of fences and they'd always have a friendly word and a cake for me. During those hours waiting for mother's factory shift to end, I can remember being closer to the ground. I jumped cracks in the pavement and I poked in-between those holes with sticks and put stones down drains to hear them plop into the water. I'd sit on the kerb making obstacles for ants. I looked up at sunlight through the membrane and veins of leaves; I counted out pockets of polished conkers in a line along a wall; I filled jam jars with rose petals to make perfume; I looked down into the fuchsia jaws of snap dragons. I'd shake blossom trees to make it snow, hanging upside down off the branches, twanging and shaking the petals. I remember I liked to pretend I was blind. I'd dare myself to walk down the road with my eyes shut tight and my hands outstretched, it was a surprise to lose the ground beneath my feet and fall off the kerb or feel the thud and shock of walking into lamp posts. I'd always say sorry, but it was just a telegraph pole and I'd look about me hoping nobody saw me. And I'd go on the swings in the nearby park and swing with my head thrown back so the houses were up and the clouds were down.

When Mrs Sharkey was busy, she'd say,

It's lovely to see you but you'll have to come visit another day, dearie.

I didn't want to ever exhaust that kindness, I'd shrug and run off up her driveway, saying

Oh it was windy, I just thought you might like help with putting your washing out that's all!

I'd never admit that I was cold, lonely or running out of friends to call for.

17 / mrs tiggy-winkle

When my mother was late and it was getting dark, I'd sit and wait on the back door step and tell myself fantastic sad stories. I would make-believe that my mother had been in a fatal accident and I'd make myself cry. I'd go through every moment of the accident, her last breath, her death, right up to the police coming to find me to put me in a children's home. I would picture the children's home and an *Oliver Twist* life and I'd plan how I would run away and where I would go. I would roll with the tragic story, until I was so miserable and convinced it was all true, the sound of her footsteps and her appearance at the garden gate would quite surprise me and I would be so relieved to see her, my eyes would sting. I'd want to throw my arms around her as if she'd returned from a war, but instead I'd snap at her,

Where've you been Mum? You're late! I've been worried sick…

18 / princess leslie

Every Saturday morning I'd go to gymnastics alone. I remember walking beneath a flat white sky, plain as a chipped china plate. And dawdling down the hill, past our school all dark, empty and silent and along the lane, trudging to get to the other side of town. As a creature of habit, I always took the same route, along the high street and I saw the Indian restaurant had wooden chipboards over its front window again and the words *Pakie Go Home*. Stupid racists, they cannot even spell. There was also graffiti on the wall of the bus shelter, it had an A in a circle and read in black letters THE WHO. Anna Parris's mum said it should have a question mark. Every time I looked at those tall spray painted letters I'd think *THE WHO, they should have put a question mark, THE WHO?* Then I repeated versions of this to myself: *Are you twit twoo or THE WHO? Are you the Doctor and are you THE WHO? If I am Doctor Who? Then who are THE WHO?* I knew that the graffiti had nothing to do with Doctor Who or Doctor Seuss. I was pretty sure it had a lot to do with the glue-sniffers and the skinheads who wore parka jackets and Dr Marten boots. I also reckoned it was because of the film *Quadrophenia* that Gus was raving about.

During those solitary morning walks my head would be soft as cotton wool, re-living my dreams from the night before. As a child I had re-occurring dreams of being a superhero-athlete and winning gold medals. In these vivid dreams I could do a row of one-handed back flips and hands-free somersaults, sailing through the air and landing in the splits. In these wonderful and egocentric dreams, I wore a royal blue leotard, like they wore in the Olympics. I dreamt that I could fly above my house, my school and go to the seaside. Sometimes I would hover above my sleeping self, or sit up in a tree overlooking our back garden and watch the bunk beds through my bedroom window. I was a superhero with special powers. I had a cupboard in my stomach where I kept favourite and necessary things like bananas and ray-guns for fighting the baddies. My boyfriend was a combination of Elvis and Jesus, he lived in a shed in the clouds and had heaven-blue eyes. I would continue playing out these epic stories from my dreams as I walked to pass the time, indulging in images of breaking world records in athletics. I prepared speeches for when I met the queen as I precariously balanced along walls, as though they were a gymnast's beam.

I had really wanted to go to ballet classes, like most little girls I wanted the pretty ballet shoes with pink ribbons. However there were no ballet classes in our village and it would have meant travelling alone by bus to the nearest town of Kettering every week which was too far for me to travel alone. I also always wished I had a better leotard, mine was a size too small, a washed out green, with a gay girly trim of skirt attached and short-sleeves. I remember a girl every week that would screw her face up at me in the changing rooms. Then with a flick of her high sleek ponytail she always said,

Urgh! That's a ballet leotard, why are you wearing a ballet leotard to gym? It can't be a ballet leotard because it isn't pink!

I'd say in a pale defence but I suspected she was right because she was so perfect.

I was often wounded and sorely troubled by spoilt and more privileged girls, finding them clever and bossy. However their bribes of shiny and sweet things were too alluring for me to pass up. These girls always bothered me with the best sweets and sugary promises. These girls had ponies and took gym, ballet and tap classes, but they could never climb fences to get their own ball back.

On Saturday mornings after gym, I would go from door to door until I found a playmate and often I called for a girl called Leslie. She was a podgy girl with plaits who was two years below me at school. She had flushed cheeks that got redder when she was in a temper and Leslie threw quite spectacular tantrums. Leslie's mother was glamorous, she was blonde with bronze skin, like she had just come back from holiday even when she hadn't. She wore black eyeliner like Catwoman. Leslie didn't have siblings or a dad. We made up plays from story books. Her mum encouraged us and applauded, clapping with her gold jewellery jangling, she said I could do a really good Coco from *Fame* and we'd always end up jumping about to *Hi Fidelity Hi! High High High…*

Springfield Road

I didn't know what it was about Leslie. I think I felt sorry for her. I never played with her at school. She was an only lonely child and her father had died at sea. On the living room mantelpiece there was a photograph of a handsome, important-looking gentleman in a naval suit by a ship with the letters *QE2* on the side of it, like the *QE2* my dad was on. I never voiced this but I entertained the thought that our fathers might have met, or might even have been friends somehow.

Leslie had the latest Barbie mansion and stable. She had the new Plasticine Barber Shops, where you had to turn the handle and plasticine comes out like hair and worms from holes in the doll's head. She had a beautiful Victorian doll's house that she never played with and an almost life-size beautiful rocking horse. In the garden she had a swing, a paddling pool and she always had bubbles all year around.

The thing about Leslie, though, was that she sometimes made me kiss her. I had no idea why I had to kiss her, but usually when her mum was out of earshot or down the other end of the garden she'd lisp, *I know, let's play Sleeping Beauty. You be the prince and…*

I knew what came next.

… kiss me.

She lay back on her bed with out stretched arms, her hair feathered on the pillow. She looked up at me then closed her eyes and, in a faraway voice, whispered,

Kiss me. I have been asleep for one hundred years. I pricked my finger on the spindle and now you have to come and kiss me…

I stood with my hands in my corduroy pockets awkwardly by the bed, looking around her room, cluttered with glittery pink things. Under the button-eyed stare of the rainbow-coloured fluffy teddy bears and dolls crammed along the shelves, as she told me again to kiss her. She lay there on her pink Walt Disney bed cover, which matched the curtains. I looked away at her sparkly angel wings and ballet things; a china unicorn with a silvery horn; there was a musical jewellery box which you could wind up and it played a tune whilst the ballerina inside turned around. Falling out of their Weeble tree house, she had a vast collection of Weeble wobbles, *Weebles wobble but they don't fall down*; hanging above my head was a mobile of fairies. Leslie opened her eyes and looked up at me directly.

If you kiss me I will ask my mum for you to stay for tea and you can watch Jaws *with us.*

It was a fair trade, but it was strange kissing Leslie. She made me lie on top of her and say,

I am the handsome prince and you are the princess… while she wriggled beneath me. She liked it very much. Her skin flushed and she was overly warm and clammy, she smelled of milk and something sweet. Once the deed was done and she felt I had kissed her sufficiently Leslie ran and asked if I could stay for tea. Her mother smiled,

Of course, but be sure to ask your mum if it's OK for you to watch you-know-what! And she sang the *der der der der* theme tune to *Jaws*.

At Leslie's house we ate in the living room on the coffee table, and we were given sandwiches with crisps on the plate and cocktail sausages, fizzy soda streams in orange or cola. We'd have chocolate wagon wheels and bowls of ice cream and a squirty syrup called Ice Magic that went hard once it hit the ice cream. Best of all was the privilege of watching television. There, laying on a pile of cushions on the floor, I watched all the good Saturday stuff: *Wurzel Gummidge, The Bionic Man, Wonder Woman* or *Charlie's Angels*, followed that night by *Jaws*. I'll always remember that the opening scene of *Jaws* was rude, with a boy and a girl kissing on a beach, and there was a nervousness in the room. This was only heightened then as the music started we giggled clutching pillows and held hands squealing, Leslie's mum screamed too. We covered our faces in a pillow at the first sound of the *der der der der der der* and the first sight of the shark's fin cutting through the dark surface of the ocean, all three of us wearing cut-out cardboard 3-D glasses that had been given away for free in cereal packets but that didn't really work.

***

Another Saturday afternoon, Leslie was in a particularly demanding mood. It was raining and we had to stay inside. She kept complaining even when I let her win at card games. We had wandered into the conservatory when she decided to go through her mother's gardening tools. Picking up some garden pliers, she passed them to me then lay on her belly and asked me to sit on top of her. She then told me to pull out hairs from her head with the pliers. She put her head on her arms while I sat on the small of her back and sighed as though I was giving her a relaxing massage. She encouraged me and spoke in that whispering lisp, the *kiss me* voice.

Could you just pull out my hair with the pliers…

I took some hairs in the pliers and pulled very gently as she hissed cattily,

Are you even doing it? I can't feel anything.

Yes, I'm doing it.

Harder then, pull harder, pull my hair out one by one. I gave another tentative tug.

Then she leaned up on her elbows and, looking at us straight ahead in the reflection of the glass conservatory wall, said in this affected toffee-nosed voice

Come on! Just do it! Just get on with it! Pull my hair out of my head!

She haughtily exhaled through her nose as though to say, is it too much to ask? I didn't like her horsey tone of voice at all so I took a good few strands and pulled sharply. As though I had flipped a switch Leslie screamed, one long pure note. Her mother ran in to find me sitting on top of Leslie with pliers full of her daughter's hair. How could I explain what I was doing, straddling her daughter with pliers full of hair? Leslie put on a magnificent show. She roared with tears, and even started saying '*Mummy Mummy*', which I knew was for maximum effect – as kids we said 'mum' and only said 'mummy' if it was very serious and we wanted to get full cream attention. Leslie's mum looked at me with astonishment and said maybe I should come back to play another day, but it was best that I went home now. As I closed the front door behind me I could hear Leslie howling and coughing. She was being exactly like the *Just William* Bonnie Langford character from TV, I knew she would *squeem and squeem and squeem* until she was sick. I turned out of their drive and walked miserably to the street corner. I stood and looked down at my shoes. I felt dreadfully ashamed and the worst part was I think that I had made her head bleed a tiny bit.

19 / spaghetti legs and curly top

Standing on the street corner I heard my name

Oi curly top!

I looked up and saw the gaping, toothy grin of Tara Collins on the corner. Tara Collins had a long face – in fact she was a very long girl. She was the tallest girl in our school, and taller than all the boys too, apart from Darren White. She towered over us in netball, effortlessly slam-dunking goals. She had a big toothy smile and bandy spaghetti legs like a baby giraffe. This afternoon, she was wearing striped knee-high socks, plimsolls and roller skates. She had spit stuck a rose thorn in-between her eyebrows and she had strawberry lip-gloss on. I was kicking stones down a drain with the toe of my shoe when Tara asked,

What you doing?

Nothing much.

Where are you going?

Nowhere.

Where have you been?

Ermmm… dunno really, round there.

I pointed to Leslie's house and shuddered guiltily.

Wanna come skating? she asked.

I noticed her brother and a few boys with skateboards outside her house, which was set back off the road at the bottom of a steep sloping drive. The uneven plastic wheels of her roller skates scratched across the surface of the bumpy concrete pavement, first one foot, then the next. I said, *There's some lovely new smooth tarmac on my road, they've just done it this week.*

Brill! I'll come with you to get your skates then…weeeeeeeahhhh!

Tara scooted towards me. Us kids were always looking for new smooth bits of pavement to skate on. The council was slowly doing all the roads around our way, the potholed old streets becoming sheer, sleek and black with gleaming yellow lines, as smooth as ice to skate on. We were all hoping for those new yellow and blue roller boots with stoppers for our birthdays and Christmas, but for the time being most of us made do with skates that fastened to our shoes. They had laces and a buckle and hard uneven wheels; if you undid a nut at the bottom you could slide them to fit your growing shoe size. They were handed down from sibling to sibling and they lasted forever.

Come on, I'll come with you to yours. Let's get your skates and then we'll come back round here to mine and smash our heads into the garage door. We've been going down the drive so fast. Look! Watch! We've been taking it in turns on Dad's crash helmet... Do you want a go?

She pointed to her brother. Marcus Collins was wearing his father's shiny black motorbike helmet, which nearly swallowed his shoulders. He was sitting on his skateboard with his knees drawn up to his chin. He put the visor up and gave us a thumbs-up, then he put it back down again and gripped his skateboard, ready to launch. Tara burst into applause as we screamed a countdown: *Ten, nine, eight...!* He had already gone, zooming down his drive. Almost immediately there was a thunderous crash as he hurtled head first into the garage door and fell off the skateboard. The boys fell about laughing.

Brilliant!
Quick! I want a go on the crash helmet!
Do you?
I do!
Ace!

Seeing Tara laughing with her strawberry pink lips, clinging to the lamp post, all spindly arms and legs, I felt that all was well with the world after all, the guilt and shame about Leslie began to fade. I heard the tinny music of an ice cream van in the far off distance. It was an ordinary Saturday afternoon in Desborough in the late seventies. Above us a mild and ordinary sky we neither noticed nor cared about. It was the neither season – neither winter nor summer. I knew that at home, my stepfather would be watching the football on television, my mother would be in the kitchen, sorting out the washing or cooking. There were glow-in-the-dark stickers of The Hulk on the bib of my skates, I sat on the kerb lacing them up and Tara held out her hand to help me stand up. Later that same afternoon, we'd go and have a turn on the motorbike helmet; and we would scream a countdown and speed down her drive, bashing head first into her garage door making a racket with an almighty crash.

But first we are here – we are holding hands, our wheels vibrating on the rough road until we hit the new oily black tarmac and glide smooth and as elegant as figure skaters. With outstretched arms we hold each other by the wrist and spin dizzily in a circle, the lovely sound of innocent laughter and skating wheels rolling across new tarmac.

20 / once in a lifetime

I was wearing my favourite summer dress. It was pale turquoise cotton, with a pattern of tiny yellow primroses and blue forget-me-nots scattered all over it. It had powder green ribbon at the front and pearl-blue buttons up to the neckline with dainty puff short-sleeves trimmed with ribbon. It came all the way from America, a hand-me-down from my cousin in New York, I thought it was beautiful and that summer I'd finally grown into it. It was a Saturday, a sunny day, my stepfather was out at the tennis club and Mum was sitting at her Singer sewing machine. St Giles church fete was that day and I was looking forward to singing in the choir. There would be a coconut shy, bric-a-brac stalls, home-made jams and cakes, and a myriad of other fun things. I could hardly eat my cornflakes I was so excited. I chattered incessantly, pestering my mother to do my hair for me. I wanted everything to be perfect and this included my hair. I often wanted my hair to be twisted into braided hoops like *Princess Leia* and I couldn't do that on my own.

It was just the three of us having breakfast and a pot of tea together, sitting around the dining table. Half of it was cluttered with Mum's mending and cottons – she made me dresses sometimes, recycled out of the material of her old clothes. Gus and my mum began reminiscing about our father. It had been a while since we had mentioned him.

I remember when he taught me to pour my first pint, Gus said and laughed.

Oh yes, he took you around the other side of the bar and lifted you up. That was funny, you must have been only two or three. That was in Ramsgate…

And when we went go-karting… Gus continued, and I wished I had a memory of my father of my own. I had nothing but a shape of how our life was before and these inherited stories. I laughed, copying them, my eyes glazed and glassy as though I was remembering these times too. It always felt good when we talked about my real father like that, the three of us together.

By the time Gus and I got to the church it was a warm lunchtime. The gardens were strewn with flags and balloons, the trees and hedgerows were decorated with streams of colourful bunting. There were doily-covered stalls of cakes and books and tables of jumbled clothes. There were games, competitions and raffles with fantastic prizes. There was a one pound note for the person with a hand steady enough to follow an electric wire with the hook of a bent coat-hanger without it buzzing. I met classmates and fellow Brownies, all with hair tied prettily with silk ribbons in bunches and swishing ponytails. We had a run-through in the cool of the church then marched with a clatter of Sunday best buckled shoes in twos, down the side lane and into the centre of the gardens. The music started and we performed songs that had choruses of *Laugh Kookaburra Laugh* and *Solider Soldier, Won't You Marry Me?* My cheeks ached from grinning. In the audience I could see Sunday school teachers, Brownie leaders, the vicar and all the mums and dads cheering and applauding. My mum wasn't there, but Gus was.

With the sky perfectly blue above us, we tore around the church grounds. We hid in the graveyard, behind the tombs and raced across the back fields, playing hide and seek with countless new places to make camps and ambushes. We were given chocolate cornflake cakes, we had cherryade moustaches and water pistols. New white socks crumpled and wrinkled below grass-stained knees. Chubby boys sweated, tying their best shirts around their waists. I sat up a tree with a girl called Rebecca. We had disappeared together, claiming the tree as a safe place, *home*, where we couldn't get tagged. Rebecca was a pretty blonde girl who chased boys all the time and who the boys chased back. Jealous girls called her a flirt but I liked that about her. On this day, though, she was upset, and we lowered our voices as we spoke and patted each other's hands, as we had seen our mothers do. We were sitting opposite each other on a branch, in the hollow heart of the tree, as deeply engrossed as teary aunties on the gin in the kitchen at Christmas, confessional and whispering. Our faces were hot and sticky, our legs were scratched from the tree bark and whipped with running through the rough wild grass of the back fields. Up there, in the soft green rustling leaves, Rebecca started to cry.

My mum and dad are getting divorced, but nobody knows, but I do…

I touched her hand as Rebecca continued.

My daddy's not going to live with us no more now. I don't know when I'll see him…

Springfield Road

She was crying quietly, holding in any noise. She looked down at her fingers, fumbling, tearing at a twig, ripping the bark off it with her dirty pink nails. Her big hazel eyes reddened and her blonde hair had fallen out of its French plait into gentle, silky curls around her oval face. I told her,

My mum and dad are divorced. My mum says it's for the best sometimes. We have to live with her new husband, my stepdad, but we do have a real dad and he's a musician. My real dad plays on the QE2 *and that's the Queen of England's own ship, Queen Elizabeth. And he's cruising the world playing in the band and Mum says that is why we never get to see him.*

I gulped, the words stuck in my throat, she sniffed and replied,

My dad works in Market Harborough.

Well at least you can see yours, that's not very far away is it? Dry your eyes Rebecca, don't cry. Come on now, silly, it will be all right, don't cry.

We sat in that tree, muttering details of our parents' divorces. I bragged about my father. I told her he was funny, like when he taught Gus to pour a pint of beer, reiterating the morning conversations with my mother and brother from breakfast. I made Rebecca chuckle through her tears until she snorted and blew a snot bubble, which made us both laugh. She wiped her nose on her cardigan sleeve and dried her red face.

Suddenly Anna Parris shouted up,

Salena, your dad's here.

What dad?

Gus said to come and fetch you, your dad's come for you.

The idea of my stepfather being here at the church fete surprised me, but I thought he might be with Mum. Maybe they had come to see me sing after all? They were late but I could show Mum the makeshift stage where we had performed. As I climbed down the tree I saw my brother running towards me. His eyes were lit up and urgent and he held out his hand to take mine. I knew then it must be something important – my brother and I had long past the age of holding hands.

Dad's here! Come on…

Dad?

Yes, Paul, our dad! Come on, Salena, hurry up. Come on!

His voice was excited, wavering with soft and strange love. There was a kindness in his face, like he had a wonderful surprise for me, something beautiful to show me. I scrambled out of the branches, trembling in my limbs.

I looked at Rebecca and Anna.

Paul?

Who?

Paul, My real dad, Paul, you know, the one I just said about, he's only flippin' here…

My brother took my hand in his and led me up through the church garden to meet this man I had never known, the man who was my real father, for the first time. We hurried. I skipped to keep up with Gus's longer stride until all of a sudden I could see him. He was striking, tanned and wearing mirrored shades, a black shirt and dark blue jeans. He stood nervous as a groom at the front entrance to the church. In my memory of that day, he looks like a rock star and my first impression was a swooning feeling. This was followed by a compulsion to make a good first impression. I hoped my hair wasn't too wild so I patted it, feeling wayward frizz at the top. I pulled up my white socks and smoothed the front of my dress.

In those first few seconds I was on full alert to remember the smallest details. My world went into slow motion as though these minutes meant life or death, and it did, it meant everything to me. As I walked towards him I studied him, how he looked in the churchyard I knew so well, how he stood as we approached, how his shape grew bigger as we got closer. I listened to hear his voice for the first time. I was the most awake I could possibly be but I felt like I was sleeping, as though I was in a dream. I could not believe he was really there, that it was really him.

There was a surreal quality to those first minutes. Time poured as slow as golden syrup, in the amber light of a perfect afternoon. The balloons softly bumped against each other in a slight breeze, the mottled shadows of the old tree on the paving were littered with soft, trodden cherry blossom and old confetti. The sounds of the fete and other kids playing and the music slipped away. The only three people on the planet were my brother and me and this man of mythology. I could feel my brother buzzing too, as his hand left mine and the skin on our arms touched briefly. We were both feeding off this first moment, two chicks in the nest both wanting the worm at once. I searched my father's face, looking for clues. I yearned for him but I also wanted to know the truth.

Where have you been? Who are you? Who am I to you? Do you think I am like you? What do you know about me? Are you proud of me? Will you come and visit us again? Why have you not been to see us ever before?

There was a sense of relief, and also an urgency; a need to be reassured, to be liked, more than that, to be loved. I was aware of my great neediness. A need so big and so hungry, I realised I had been starving for that moment all of my life.

I want you to see me in you, to see we are the same. I want to say that word, your name: Dad. I want to call out the name Father and for it to be ours and for it to be true. My real dad. I want to be held in your arms and for you to tell me stories. I want you to talk to me and to tell me that all of this has been a test and we passed it. That this is like that story, where a king comes to find his long-lost children to take them to his palace to live together. Then I want you to say you are sorry, I want to hear how you are very sorry you took so long to come to see us. Promise you will never disappear and go away again. How we waited for you, we blew out birthday candles and wished for you. We called for you in our sleep and in our dreams hoping this day would come. That you would come one day, one perfect summer's day, exactly like this. Finally here you are. I want you to say that now you have seen us and what you have been missing that you want us in your life, say you want to make up for lost time and cannot believe you haven't been to see us before. Say something about how we have grown and that you'll look out for us now. Say you missed us. Say that you love us. I need to hear that you love us. Whatever the reasons and excuses for not coming before, I don't care, because you are here now and that is all that matters. You are my real dad and you are here and I love you. I'll say it first if you like, for you Dad, now you have to say it, say you love me.

We were awkward as strangers, nervous and self-conscious. We walked side by side into the church. We stood at the altar and admired the golden eagle bible plinth. The sun shone through the stained glass windows and made rainbows on the floor, puddles of gold, red and indigo. I tried not to stare at you Dad, but I couldn't help it. Then we showed you the church gardens and the stage; I told you that you missed me singing. You said you were impressed by that, you said you would have liked to have heard me singing. You asked me if I had been nervous and I said I had butterflies and you smiled at me like there was nothing wrong with getting nervous. You told me you got butterflies when you went on stage too sometimes. I remember thinking – we both like music Dad, see, we have so much in common.

I felt so proud when you took my hand. We looked at the stalls and the cakes, and you offered to buy me something but I didn't see anything I wanted. I didn't want anything because you were holding my hand and that was all I ever wanted. I had everything I wanted walking beside me in the church gardens. I pointed out classmates and teachers. I kept thinking, look I am holding hands with my very own real dad. Your hand felt soft and warm. Mum had told me you had piano-playing fingers and now they were holding my hand.

We got to the electric wire and coat hanger game and you asked me if I would like a go. I had been eyeing the one pound note prize all afternoon. There was a series of loops, bends and 's' shapes to weave in and out of with a hook without touching the wire. I tried for you Dad, I tried so hard. I could feel my cheeks burn as you watched me. I could feel you watching me and I wondered what you could see. I was trying so hard and thinking how I must do this well so you would think I was clever and good. What steady hands you would say. I didn't want to disappoint you Dad, I wanted to make you proud. I made it only half way and then the wire beeped. I was crushed, I trembled, but then I looked up and you smiled beautifully with a genuine warmth and you said,

Don't worry, Salena, it's just a game.

When you said my name and you said it softly and I felt a jolt of familiarity. When you said my name it echoed over and over down a long tunnel of memory. The way you said *Salena* it sounded like something more than my name, like a lovely song I once knew. Then you had a go, I watched your hands, they were shaking, much more than mine, and the machine beeped.

Looks like we're both not very good at this… you said and patted me.

Every time you touched me my heart pounded. Both of us are the same, I thought, both of us are not very good at this game. I was giddy with you, to be with you, you made me laugh. I said something cheeky and I managed to make you laugh too.

Springfield Road

The three of us left the church and you asked us if we'd like to go to the park. On the way to the park you bought us both orange ice lollies. Gus and I didn't really play on swings together any more and we certainly didn't usually get taken to the park by an adult, but we understood that this was one of those making-friends exercises that grown-ups do with children. We went on the slide, my brother and I, and from the top of the slide we looked down at you. You looked small, thoughtful and quiet. You were smoking and wearing your sunglasses. Gus and I looked each other in the eye, unspoken questions that neither of us had the vocabulary for, and Gus shrugged and said,

Go on, go down then, Salena.

I went down the slide on my stomach and head first. You watched, sitting on the park bench in your dark sunglasses. You seemed so distant over there and almost sad. I wanted to know what you were thinking and what you saw. What did we look like to you, my brother and I, playing nicely together, going down the slide on our bellies, backwards and upside down to show off for you? Did we look like the kind of son and daughter you'd like to have? Gus and I exchanged looks, but we kept acting like kids, dumb cute kids who can play nicely together at the park.

After the park, we went back home and I ran in to tell Mum I had you with me. She already knew you were here, of course, and she had told you where we were. She had seen you earlier, she said, you came to call for us and she told you we were at the church. Now, I think she knew you were coming. It was meant to be a surprise. You had a cup of tea, Dad, and I sat on your lap. We were all in the living room and there I was sitting on my very own real dad's knee. Mum told you about our schools, she told you that I was in the Brownies and that Gus was in St John Ambulance. We were happy and the sunshine seeped through the venetian blinds in stripes of orange coppery light on the white walls. It was all so easy and I felt so happy to be so close to you, Dad. I looked at you intently, the tiny hairs on your knuckles. I noticed the way Mum was smiling too and being different somehow, she was sitting up straight, attentive, her eyes were shining.

Then as you sipped the last of your tea I sensed you preparing to leave. That part wasn't ever going to be easy. As you stood up I saw you and

Mum exchange a look and I told you I wanted to come with you. I needed to hear you swear you'd be back again and very soon. You asked me,

Hey, have you met Henry?

I could see through this trick to take my mind off you leaving, Dad, and I started to cry. I wanted to go with you and I asked when we'd see you again, you said soon. Then Mum joined in with a great big stupid smile on her face, which irritated me as she repeated,

Who's Henry, Salena?

I clearly remember thinking, *I don't care who Henry is, I just don't want you to go, I need you and I need more.* I started to cry and Dad, you said,

Ah well if you don't want to meet Henry then I'd better tell him to go!

Then you gave me a winning smile, so I played along and said,

Who's Henry then?

Please! Mum said.

OK, please! Who is Henry, please?

Oh! No, no, no, you didn't want to know before, I won't tell you now!

You teased me, you did, my dad, my lovely real dad teased me and I giggled through hot tears.

Please can I meet Henry, Dad! Please!

Oh you want to meet him now do you, Salena?

Yes please Dad! Please!

Come with me.

You winked at my mum and took me to your car and gave me a huge stuffed dog, a teddy bear that was a dog, not a bear. It was half my height, with a big floppy red tongue and ears. I hugged him.

I love him! Thank you.

I squeezed Henry and Gus looked on, and I could see through the blur of my tears that he wanted something too. I could sense my brother watching me hug this huge Henry and I wondered if you had something for him too. Then you gave him your sunglasses. Gus loved flying, he loved books about Biggles. The sunglasses were the kind pilots wear, aviators, he was thrilled.

Now that you had taken off your sunglasses I could see my reflection in you, when you crouched down to say goodbye, I recognised those eyes. For a second as you held me I recognised something in the feel of you, the shape and the smell of you, your hair, your neck, your skin. Something I thought I had lost was now close to me and so familiar.

I don't remember what promises you made as you stood up, I don't remember your exact words of comfort as you said your goodbyes. I started crying again and you told us to be good. Gus cried too and you hugged him and you probably promised you'd be back another day, wait and see and soon. We cried as we heard you turn the key in the ignition and back up out of the drive. We cried and watched you drive slowly away.

I searched everywhere in the universe and in everything you touched in my world for your scent, for flakes of your skin, for the strands of hair, of each minute of that one afternoon. Every tiny triviality, like water retaining memory, seeping through each crevice of those few hours we spent together. That afternoon became a shrine, a cave. I stroked the walls of those few hours with all five senses, second by second. I took a stick and scratched our names there and every minute detail I daubed and highlighted with paints. I felt the coolness and the heat of those walls against my cheeks. I can still smell that day; when I think of it I inhale some form of dust, it sticks in the back of my throat. I can still summon the sensation of waiting for you Dad, of having you and losing you. Those few hours are an animal carcass. I devoured all its tender flesh. I boiled the bones to make a glue soup to keep us together and I slept in the hide of the beast to dream of you.

All we had was that one day when you appeared from nowhere and then you went again. For those moments I looked into your eyes, I saw something I now understand was regret or guilt. I also believe I saw love and that was all we ever had, Dad.

PART TWO – AUTUMN

my mother

21 / the other woman / London 2009

excerpt taken from my diary

The manuscript finally arrived but as I turned the pages my heart sank, it had been almost five months since I submitted the last draft, what takes these people so long? And now this version was way too far the other way, it had been stripped of love and humour, warmth and kindness, this miserable edit was hard as a black snowball, I did not intend to throw a black snowball into the world.

I switched off the phones and unplugged the internet to be alone to re-read the new harsh edit. I wept all weekend, it was as though I was going backwards all over again, covering the same old hurt and frustrations. I knew I was giving myself a very hard time, I was crippled by fear of failure and fear of the dark.

Outside my window, as I write this, I can hear the rustle of dry leaves, the death rattle of autumn at the end of such a high summer. I am crashing, coming back down to earth with a hard bump. I always did hate the end of the party, the end of the summer light. Now here is the early dusk and dirt in the corners of my rooms, the kitchen floor needs mopping, everything feels grimy. The rent is late and God only knows how I am going to find it this month. The fridge is empty, humming away with nothing to fill its cold belly. I feel utterly empty. And this book is a big, mean, black dog digging me up, digging up the past and gnawing on my bones. There is nothing I can do now though, but get over it, dry my eyes, roll my sleeves up and go through this book from the beginning all over again. There's no going back, there is no unwriting this, there is no unremembering, it's started now.

On Monday I had no choice. I had to get away from this black dog and the past, put on the lipstick and heels and go to do the gig – The Book Club Boutique at Dick's Bar, Romilly Street. This week's theme was 'Smash The System' an anarchic gig with the boys from *The Idler*, it was a lively show with Tom Hodgkinson and Penny Rimbaud. When I arrived at first the world seemed very sharp, jagged and loud. I felt small and introverted. However there is nothing like the adrenaline of a gig to pull me back into the present. And a decent martini. Besides we had a packed house and there were lots of friendly faces.

During the interval I was on my second espresso martini, smoking outside Romilly Street when she walked towards me. She looked out of place among the usual BCB crowd, she was trembling and shaky. A woman, in her sixties and well-heeled, with sleek, bobbed hair. She approached me and said *Are you Salena Godden? I knew your dad, Salena...*

Here we go, the past smacked me around the back of my head with a cricket bat. Just when I was back in the present, here I was being dragged back into this book. Who was she, but an old lover of my dad's. Is this normal? I mean, do all old lovers of fathers come out of the woodwork to seek out the children thirty years later? She told me she had found me on the internet. She apologised for shocking me and showing up out of the blue. I could see she was quite surprised herself to be standing there too. The book isn't even published, but I was now meeting the woman who possibly contributed to the end of my parents' marriage.

She seemed kind, I mean harmless enough, she was oval faced with a freshly bobbed head of blondish hair. Shorter than me, homely and plump, soft features and very curious, round shiny button eyes, like a rabbit. So then what could I do but offer her a drink? I asked her if she drank wine, and then lead her to the upstairs bar where it was quieter. She was with a friend, presumably for back-up. (Where was my back-up?) I could see she had done her nails and put her best blouse on. I could tell she was very nervous to meet me. But I still didn't fully understand what her intention was. I was wondering if there was something important she needed to tell me? She clearly felt compelled to make contact with me. She made a joke, she wasn't a mad stalker, she smiled, she was happily married. But she told me she had sneaked away and her husband would kill her if he knew she'd come to see me. It was then it dawned on me that she didn't know about Dad perhaps when she asked,

When? Was it was alcohol-related? and I heard myself reply unintentionally icily,

Springfield Road

Well you don't do something like that when you are stone cold sober, right?

As she probed for the sensational details, she produced out of her handbag yellowing photos of my father and herself from the early to mid-seventies. She placed these images along the bar like playing cards; the barman served our drinks and wiped glasses looking on casually. Dad was wearing *that* sheepskin jerkin I have seen him wear in photos of him holding my brother, with my mother, at home, in Hastings. If this was a game of poker she had a full house. There was one photograph of my father taken sitting on a bed on the *QE2*. She even said something like … *this one is your dad on the* QE2…

I now know that when my mother told us our father was at sea, he really was at sea, but now I can picture him at sea with this woman. So this is where my father was, who he was with, when my mother was struggling to feed us. This was the missing image of my father during those lost years.

Then she produced poetry and letters he'd written to her. Hard evidence, with the dates 1975, 1976 on the top, I recognised the green ink and the handwriting. My knees felt weak and I was grinding my back teeth. I would have been two or three years old, my mother a newly single parent on benefits, she was working part-time stacking shelves in a Co-op supermarket. How much stinky truth can I take? Should I take?

You should have this… she continued and handed me a book that she said she had always meant to give to Dad. A collection of poems by Frances Thompson, with ragged yellow pages, musty and perhaps a first edition. Wasn't Dad's dog called Frances when he was a boy? The dog grave in Grandpa's garden?

As I write this, I look at the photocopied letters and poetry she gave me. These are not like the sweet letters I've read, the ones to Edith, from a young man coming of age and about to be wed. These words are written from a depressive and darker version of my father. They have tones of self-loathing, self-sabotage and regret. Maybe there is the possibility of another sibling? Or am I reading too much between the lines?

She sang from the same song sheet – she told me my dad would be so proud of me, she told me I was just like him, I reminded her of him. Her eyes misted over as she announced he was the love of her life.

And all these things I have heard before from my own mother's lips.

She said she could never forget him, she couldn't stop thinking about him and that she was compelled to come and see me. But why now, and after thirty years? What could I offer her? Maybe she just simply wanted to visit her old flame?

As she spoke, I decided I wouldn't run and ring my mother to tell her she had come to see me. At least, not for a while, at least not until I had figured some of this out all for myself. My poor Mum has been trying to protect me from exactly this. I told the woman she was brave and bold. I shook her hand and I meant it, because we all mean to have certain conversations, but often never have the balls to do it. We tell ourselves to let sleeping dogs lie, we tell ourselves, let sleeping dogs lie after lie, but we all have apologies and peace to make with somebody – we are all someone's last thought before they go to sleep.

And as I shook her hand she looked at me, searchingly, she looked into my father's eyes and before I knew it, I gave her what I believed she had come for; I hugged her. I held her close and felt she was small and a little afraid.

So I was to be the strong adult. And it was as though she could somehow touch my father through me. For a split second, I felt I was passing on my father's love and that he would have wanted me to hug her. This soft thought was swiftly followed by a cold and horrible sense of duplicity – I was holding the enemy in my arms. On the phone in the morning would I really say: *Good morning, Mum, I cuddled Dad's old mistress last night?*

We separated, I drank, swallowed fat gulps as she twittered to me nervously, talking me through the photographs. There was one of a pub landlord and his wife. I forget their names, but she asked me if my mother ever mentioned them. Then she told me what a good baby I was, and how they'd put me to sleep in a room above the pub. This was painful, the way she remembered my father putting me to bed *what a good girl she is…* she said he said. So where was my mother? Working? Dancing? Picking potatoes in a field for 50p? While this woman was there, in the background of the pink cottage, the shadow in our rose-tinted time. I now have an image of my father and this woman looking over me as I gurgle in a cot and as he dandled me on his knee, she is there too.

Springfield Road

This morning, I received emails and more photos of them and of then. I did give her my email address. I thought I could handle it, but today in a harsh and sober daylight I am not so convinced I want to or need to know any more – not for the book, and not for research, and not for me.

In these pixelated shots, Dad is wearing the same neckerchief and smile I've seen in photos of him when we were a young and happy family. Am I clinging onto fiction? I am certain there was a once upon a time, in a kingdom faraway, when my mother and father were very in love, but now it's all scrambled and confused. Reading her email, I feel a creeping familiar sense of betrayal and I am dealing with the same old abandonment issues again. I might not have taken all of this so much to heart if I hadn't been re-writing the book, again, if I wasn't back in the jigsaw puzzle colouring in the missing pieces again. But then again, she might not have found me, if I hadn't been writing it in the first place and sending ghost smoke signals. What is this? Coincidence or fate or the threads that connect us all? Did I somehow summon her and her version of my past? I now picture the launch for this book and a very funny queue of women of a certain age all clutching poetry and old photos of my dad. I asked for this, I poked the skeletons in the back of the closet and now I have to watch the maggots squirm and wriggle.

I will always be in love with him, she said, *he was the love of my life*.

The love of my life.

22 / bonfire treacle

Home and school life continued much as it had before. That one visit, that summery day with Dad, was stored into our memory; we'd got carried away with hopes, and high expectations were like stubborn stains from blackberries as the summer drew to its close and we heard nothing more from our dad. During those longer dark evenings of the coming winter months my brother and I were like cellmates in our small, shared bedroom. Sometimes we'd do homework or read and sometimes we'd play cards or board games. When we were extra-bored we'd string a net across the room and tap out games of table tennis without a table – with just ping-pong bats and a ball. We'd also quietly play records on an old mobile record player that was stored as a box, when it opened the lid became the speakers. We would sing to our limited record collection, which included a seven inch of 'My Boomerang Won't Come Back' by Charlie Drake; The Beatles' *White Album* and an epic album titled *A Farewell To Kings* by the seventies Canadian prog-rock band Rush.

Every year around Halloween my brother and I made our own bonfire toffee – a slab of brick-hard black treacle and syrup, which was so indestructible we'd need a hammer and chisel to smash it up to share. It was sucked until it was as thin as glass and as sharp on the roof of your mouth. We polished and skewered conkers and had conker fights in our bedroom. Gus showed me how to take aim and get a good lick as the conkers smashed together. Champion conkers were named after how many wins they achieved. I always flinched, afraid Gus was aiming for my knuckles, on purpose, again, and more often than not his hundred and twenty-fiver obliterated my fiver.

I recall how we stood in the dark bedroom to watch distant fireworks though the window. We observed the leaves turning saffron, red and the flocks of migrating birds. These memories of autumn evenings glow with a fiery orange in my remembering; I was at that age when I was as toothless as the gappy grin we carved into jack-o'-lantern pumpkins.

Springfield Road

On Sunday evenings it was bath night. Our bedroom was silent but for the quietest fizz of Gus's radio playing the Top 40 below me, I'd lay on my belly on the top bunk and sort through my pencil case and new felt tip pens. With all their tops on, my pens were like soldiers in helmets in a row along my pillow. When a felt tip was fading I'd lick the nib to make ink come out; it tasted like plastic but was not altogether unpleasant, even sweet. If I were to lick a felt tip now, that inky flavour would be a corridor leading me to then, the first of the dark school evenings and that feeling I still always get at that time of year. Although autumn felt like a beginning, as it was the start of the new term, it was the end of the idyllic summer and the freedoms of long, light evenings and playing in the streets were no more.

***

My mother called me from the kitchen, the windows in there were steamed up and she was scribbling on a note pad as she asked,

Darling, will you do me a favour? Will you go to the shops for me?

She was leaning over the kitchen counter, trying to remember something. Her writing was curly, joined-up with loops, and it read: *SALAD CREAME, WHITE CABBIGE, CARROTTS*

How do you spell cucumber? she asked and I began to say, 'C…U…' as mother wrote, *QUE, MARROW FAT PEAS, POND MINCE, CIGGYS…*

My mother is dyslexic. It's November 1980 and this was a word we didn't understand or know how to spell. Now though, leaning over the kitchen counter, she nibbled the pen as I watched her write. She sighed and said again, *Hang on, hang on, lemme think…*

She was in no mood for a spelling lesson but to help and correct her, I couldn't help myself blurting, *Mum it's cabbage with an A not an I, see, you wrote cabbige.*

She shot me a look, annoyance twinned with embarrassment, and then she scribbled out the A so it now read *CIBBIGE.*

Oh what am I doing? Stupid woman…

She corrected herself this time and re-wrote it to now read

CLABBIGE then she exhaled and scratched that out and wrote the whole thing out again in slow loops and said in a small voice wearily, *I get so muddled up sometimes.* Her face crumbled, her features trembled as though she might cry.

I know, I know, it's OK Mummy, I know what you mean anyway, don't I?

I did know what she meant. And I knew too how, as a girl, her father bullied her over her lessons, he was so domineering he put her off learning to write and spell altogether. She told me how he'd ripped poetry books out of her hands so the pages scattered around the room like birds set free from a cage. She told me how, when she was eight, he made her struggle with Shakespeare when she longed to read *Alice in Wonderland.*

Where other children had Pooh Bear, Noddy or the Famous Five I had to read Shelley, Keats, Wordsworth and The Lady of Shalott. *I did love* The Lady of Shalott *though, I would lie in a field, in the long grass and read. Sometimes I'd just hold the beautifully bound book and watch the clouds. That's why I want to make sure you kids have what I didn't – I want you to enjoy being children.*

When my mother got in from school, her father would make her do her homework in front of him every night. He would lean over her, scrutinising her every letter and number, contradicting what the teachers had taught her. By the time she got to school the next day she'd be so confused and tired that her school lessons went badly. One day, she just shut down, that's how she put it: *I just shut that learning part of my brain down.*

Once, my mum sent my brother to school with a sick note saying he had to take his *tables* twice a day instead of his *tablets.* We laughed about it, me and Gus, as we imagined him either doing his twelve times tables or condemned to eat classroom furniture, twice a day.

Funny Mummy.

Spelling may have baffled her, but my mother was a brilliant athlete at school. By the age of thirteen she broke the school sports records by jumping her own height of five foot one, then she went on to come second in the All England Championship. In her mid to late teens she was going to try-out for the Olympics – which she reminded me was a massive achievement for a black woman in the early sixties – but she told me her parents wouldn't let her go to the try-outs, because they were in another part of the country or because of money or because it just simply wasn't meant to be. When I remembered things like this I could only try to hug her around her bump. She was round with pregnancy with pale lavender shadows smudged beneath her eyes. She cried easily, even at simple things like if you told her you loved her, this made her well up behind her round glasses. We had to be gentle with Mum, she had miscarried and lost a baby before. I made sure to cuddle her often but carefully. Also I had seen pictures of women in labour and films where women sweated and screamed in childbirth; on programmes like *The Waltons* or *Little House on the Prairie* it looked violent, bloody and traumatic. No matter how many times my mother assured me that the pain was worth it once you had the bundle in your arms, I didn't believe her and I still don't. I was afraid for her and of this vulnerable state of being pregnant.

My mother gave me the shopping list and she looked at me through those round spectacle frames and said,

Now, listen, when you go to the butcher's be sure to tell him you want a pound of mince and not a pound in weight but a pound in money's worth. Be sure its minced beef, OK?

But it feels horrible and there's drippy blood.

Then ask him to put it inside two doubled-up plastic bags so you can't feel through it, all right? That's a good girl... And don't forget to get some soapy water and wash that make-up off before you go.

Aw, but Mum!

She looked at me over her spectacle rims and held a finger up in warning so I said, *I know.*

As I laced up my shoes I heard the car and announced, *Paddy's home.*

My mother did not turn around; she was partially deaf and didn't always wear her hearing aid. She told me this was her father's fault too, he had pushed her through glass French windows once when she was a girl. I hated being reminded of these stories about my grandad's temper.

Paddy's home Mum! I repeated, tying my shoelaces. Mum looked down and heard me the second time and a resolve flashed across her face, something that could only mean *I have a bone to pick with him*. She looked down at me and arched an eyebrow. She stiffened when Paddy appeared at the door. Funny thing was, he was in a very good mood, with a dirty lopsided grin.

'Ello.

He kissed Mum on the cheek. Mum said nothing. She pulled on her yellow rubber gloves and turned on the tap. He was leaning into her neck and looking at her face close up and grinning. Mum refused to look at him; she watched the running tap and the washing-up liquid bubble up, there was an awkward pause.

What? Paddy finally said, with a sideways smile, looking amused, looking at the dishes in the soapy water and then down at me. I looked up at him behind her back and shrugged ever so slightly, as if to say *don't ask me what she's upset about this time.* I didn't mean it. I hated that I shrugged, I felt duplicitous and Paddy began to make fun and laugh at Mum.

See ya...

Where you going? Where's she going?

Shop! I said to Paddy opening the kitchen door,

Money! Wait! The list... Mum shouted, dragging off her wet rubber gloves and looking for her purse in the front pocket of her apron. Paddy picked up the list and started laughing.

Pond mince?

Oh, shushhhh up.

Pond mince? Pond mince ha ha ha...

Oh, stop, Mum said, snatching the list off him and giving it to me. *And don't you forget we've got a family meeting tonight*, she snapped at him, brushing past to get her handbag from the other room.

During my mother's pregnancy we all had to endure these excruciating 'family meetings'. They were meant to occur about once a month, to clear the air and share time. The four of us would sit awkwardly in the living room together as a 'family' for an hour after dinner with the television switched off. We didn't know what to talk about at first. Paddy would make glib, snide jokes and try to pull serious faces as Mum recited catch phrases that sounded forced and like they came from a *Woman's Own* magazine – she would keep saying *Isn't this nice, this is family time* – then we'd talk uncomfortably about our day and finally various chores were dished out. I had to clean the bathroom every weekend and polish Paddy's tennis trophies. I had to sweep the leaves in the driveway in autumn and help shovel the snow in the winter. We also had to wash Paddy's car, do the dishes, polish our shoes and tidy our room. The notion of pocket money always came up and was scoffed down. Paddy would get dead serious and launch into the budget and pontificate how come we got through so much food. He'd complain that we all had to pull up our socks and tighten our belts. During one such meeting, Paddy made a rule that we would shop only once a month from the new massive supermarket out of town. He had an unpleasant military approach to shopping, bulk buying tins of cheap baked beans and marrowfat peas, massive boxes of own-brand cornflakes, huge tubs of greasy margarine and cheap frozen fish fingers and thin beefburgers. At the end of the month Mum had to be inventive, if we ran out of anything, we went without. This always came up at the family meetings, before negotiations inevitably broke down into serious arguments with Gus about his looming mock exams and school reports. Then, after homework schedules and chore rotas were drawn up and the meeting was concluded, and once the laughter or anger had subsided, Gus and I would be sent back to our bedroom while Mum went into the kitchen and Paddy lit a fag and sank back in front of the sport on TV.

Leaving Paddy and my mother in the kitchen having an argument about the cost of the grocery bills, I walked to the shops that evening to buy *pond mince*. Crisp, November skies and northerly winds meant it was time to wear winter coats and tights again. I felt the cold against my cheeks and my knees, but I felt important walking to the shops with a folded crisp five pound note inside the palm of my glove, my hands driven into the bottom of my coat pockets.

I saw something glinting there under the leaves. I stopped and I bent down to examine it and found it was an untouched bar of chocolate. I got under a streetlight to look at it. The paper was damp but the foil quite new and unopened. I knew there would be trouble if my mother thought I had bought it and if she knew I found it in the gutter she'd make me throw it away. Either way it had to be my secret chocolate bar. I put it in my coat pocket and planned that when I got home to hide it under the blanket in the doll's cot at the end of my bed. I kept quite a larder, there under the doll's bedding were jam-smeared Jacobs crackers wrapped in tissue; a piece of old Easter egg; some chipped Hastings rock; a pinch of desiccated coconut to re-flavour old bubblegum and now there was this damp chocolate bar. I kept this secret stash for when I was sent to bed without any tea – I was a true Brownie guide, I was always prepared.

Hiding the chocolate bar deep in my pocket, the dusk light was a dusty mauve, the bruised plum and damson colours you only get at the end of the year and when the nights draw in. Breathing in the smell of bonfires and wading through dry leaves I heard the odd whistle and bang of fireworks. And my duffel coat felt familiar, but tighter since last winter.

23 / donut and lolly

One of my happiest memories of Guy Fawkes night was when we went to stay with Aunt Doreen and Uncle Laurie for the whole bonfire weekend. They were best friends of Mum and Paddy from the tennis club, not really blood-related but favourites of Gus's and mine. They took us to a bonfire, to see the Catherine wheels and rockets, coloured showers of stars exploding and falling into the night sky. They gave us our own packet of sparklers, not just one, but a whole packet. Afterwards we went to a fairground, which was always more exciting at night-time with the flashes and buzzes, the smells of popcorn and hot dogs, the thrill of all the noise and laughter. I was allowed both candy floss and a toffee apple – but most of all I remember how we went on a steam engine carousel, up and down and around I went, dizzily laughing and holding on tight to the reins, the chintzy organ music and colours were all swirling before me and through the smoky air.

When we stayed with them we never wanted to come home. I remember calling them Auntie Donut and Uncle Lolly and laughing and watching *Jason and The Argonauts* as I played with Uncle Laurie's hair, for hours, I sat up on his shoulders and he kept saying to Doreen

She finished yet? She done yet?

But I was never finished playing with Laurie's hair, it was silky but more so it was nice to be allowed, he was one of those adults that let you play with them. He tickled my feet and Gus and I wrestled and climbed all over him. We had a play fight with the cushions and then we fell in a pile on the rug in front of the fire laughing.

That particular visit, we went out to get some air, leaving the Sunday roast cooking slowly in the oven. There was a dense thick fog as we took a walk that afternoon across a rugby pitch, we could have lost each other; we couldn't see our own hands in front of our faces. Gus and Uncle Laurie walked slightly ahead, slipping in and out of sight, obscured by the veil of mist. I heard their voices and I held Auntie Donut's hand. She told me all about 'Broomy' the secret magic flying broomstick she kept in the shed that could do spells.

Someone once said – we might not remember what people did or what people said, but we do remember how people made us feel – I understand what that means, remembering these times we stayed with Doreen and Laurie.

Not long after that, Uncle Laurie had a heart attack and died in his sleep. I think it was around the same time that Elvis died – I know as a child I put them together in my head. My brother cried for hours, lying face down on his bunk and sobbing into his pillow. I swallowed all my tears up, but he let his all out and once you let one lot of crying out, there's always more to follow. I didn't know how to react, I teased him to try to make him stop, which made Gus worse. I remember there was a part of me that was convinced Laurie would be back somehow, I still hadn't quite grasped the finality of death. We all loved Uncle Laurie so very much, he was the most loving and gentle man we'd ever known.

As the years passed, I would still stay the night with Aunt Doreen but usually visit on my own because Gus grew out of sleepovers. I liked to watch Aunt Doreen as she pinned her hair into a croissant shape, at the top of the back of her head, in a sweep of soft spun silver like a Hollywood film star. She had great style and glamorous ball-gowns. She once made me a tennis outfit, an ensemble out of one of her fifties dresses; a mini-tennis dress with a jacket to match and a longer skirt of the same material to wear on top for evening wear. It didn't make me a better tennis player, but I thought I looked the business.

In the evenings Aunt Doreen would teach me to play poker, chess or draughts. She made cocktails in proper martini glasses, hers of course the real deal, but mine made with ginger ale and topped with a glacé cherry. We'd pretend to get tipsy, like *Dumbo*, I would hiccup and tell her I could see pink elephants. I remember us both cackling with laughter; she always had such a wickedly contagious and ticklish laugh.

Aunt Doreen kept me on my toes constantly by testing my spelling, stretching my vocabulary and general knowledge. We had terrific debates – she told me that the moon landing was a hoax because there was no breeze on the moon and the American flag was flying as though there was wind – and this baffled me for years.

Most of all, she encouraged in me a playful sense of humour and mischief. She once told me that the best part of the Second World War was that women got do men's work and that her sister was lucky enough to drive a red double-decker bus. I was fast and I seized this kind of opportunity by retorting

The Second World War? Why Auntie Doreen, I know you are making things up this time, you couldn't have been born then... you look like you must only be twenty-one years old.

That's it kid, you're learning! That's my girl... keep them coming, flattery'll get you everywhere kiddo!

Then she'd chuckle, we'd clink glasses and she'd reward me with a shiny fifty pence piece.

24 / black ice

I was late for Sunday school that morning. Usually we'd all get there early and kid around outside, kicking balls about on the gravel until it was time to go in. Then when we got indoors we'd mess about in the toilets with the taps while the teacher put out chairs and tables and handed out pens and Bible story quiz sheets. There was something weird that morning though. We were told to be quiet, please, to sit in our seats and pay attention. I was sitting next to Anna Parris, I poked her and she leant over and whispered in her most serious voice,

Have you heard?

What?

Tara Collins was in a car crash last night.

What?

Anna repeated herself, hissing in my ear but I could not hear her. I was so busy poking her, and mouthing *what?* trying to get Anna to repeat herself that I also missed the very beginning of what the teacher said. Anna hit my thigh, frowned and mouthed *shush* at me. I crossed my arms and thought *bossy boots* as she pointed at the teacher to make me listen. I caught words like *tragedy* and *accident* and the tail end of a sentence that ended … *sadly boys and girls, Tara Collins's mother died.*

There were gasps as the sentence took a while to sink in. I looked down at my fingernails, coloured in with felt-tip, and listened intently. I was unsure what facial expression was appropriate and looked down the row of seats and saw the other kids' faces in shock, they looked like fishes mouths. We had all imagined our mums dying. It was the one thing that you could not bear to imagine though. It was the one thing that would make the world utterly black. It was also the one thing you could think of to make yourself cry on purpose, if you had to in an emergency.

When the teacher finished speaking we turned to each other. Different versions of events were passed along the rows in hushed whispers. Sunday school that day was sombre and strange. Those of us who knew Tara formed a silent alliance; some who didn't know her acted like they did. We were closer somehow and we flocked like twittering little parrots repeating the sympathetic statements of our elders,

I just wish there was something we could do... Poor Tara.

We were well behaved, and we didn't laugh at the teacher when she dropped her book. We didn't point and giggle at the deaf old lady in the pew in front of us when we went into the church for the family service. And when the priest said *let us pray*, we prayed properly and hard, eyes squeezed tight shut and no peeking. Some girls were crying when the priest said Tara's name. Anna Parris's mum gave me a lift home and all our seat belts were put on, even though it was just up the road. I said goodbye and then I ran as fast as I could. I ran around the corner, past the sweet shop and down The Ridings and I flew around the house and into the back kitchen door. She was there. My mum. She was there and she was at the sink, the windows were steamed up, and I could smell Sunday dinner, roast chicken, and hear vegetables bubbling in the pots. She was my mum and she was wearing her blue and white apron that looked like Wedgewood china. She was finishing a ciggy, her head tilted back and her fingers still wet, as if she'd put it out in a bit, after this last drag. I felt a rush of gladness and relief and threw my arms around her round waist and began to sob.

What's all this? she said, holding her hands up. She extinguished the cigarette in an ashtray and with this movement I held on tighter. Gus came in behind me and whispered something above my head and she touched the crown of my head and listened. I loved the way she was touching my hair and listening. As though any minute she'd say *oh don't worry we have a bandage for that* or *all you do is soak it over night in a little warm salt water and it'll wash out in a jiffy*. Gus gave a blow-by-blow account, his own cold, action-packed version.

They hit black ice and apparently they swerved and... wrapped around a tree and...

I cried the way children cry, I bawled, confused and shocked by death and its final meaning. When we grow up we are surprised when we catch ourselves crying like that, finding there is so much howling inside, there is so much in there stored up and needing to get out. Sometimes, once you let some tears out, more tears flow, once you let go there is a reservoir of tears and reasons to cry, then you feel lighter afterwards and wonder why you carried all those tears for so long – it is just like letting go and laughing, sometimes crying is like when you cannot stop laughing.

Gus was still giving his comic book sensational account, speaking fast, without taking breath,

Apparently, they were only going about fifty or sixty, Mum, but the fog was so bad last night remember Mum? It was a deadly and fatal combination of black ice and thick fog. It took ages for the ambulances and the firemen to come, Mum, apparently, right, they had to cut them out with chainsaws and use winches and everything! The worst accident on that road in history! We all reckoned, yeah, they must have been going sideways for about a quarter of a mile 'cos there's glass and skid marks all the way down the road and then they must have started rolling, faster and faster, and once they started rolling, well you imagine that, hey, Mum, hey guess where it is? It's about halfway down the hill just before the… you know, where the farm is, yeah, you know? On the steeper bit of the slope on the road to Rothwell, you know, where we went strawberry-picking once, yeah? There, it's just before the strawberry farm. You should see it Mum, we all biked up the hill to have a look and the car, you should see it, Mum, it's hanging in the tree, practically in half. Lucky there were any survivors at all, they must have crashed through the fence, gone over the ditch, through the hedge and then hit the tree. Totally wrapped around it, Mum, and the car, the car is almost split down the middle where they must have sawed them out and then…

I loved… strawberry-picking… there!

I spluttered and stammered and cried even harder into my mother's apron, I could feel Mum nod, motioning to Gus to shush and he left us and went into the bedroom.

Blow your nose, I cannot hear a word you say when you cry like that, love.

But I wouldn't let go of her, I spluttered, I wiped my nose on the back of my sleeve.

Mum, listen, Tara's mum is dead… really dead… and they don't know if her dad is going to be OK. Her mum died… Imagine poor Tara… imagine? Poor Tara's mum… We have to do something Mum, Mum, you and me, we should go around there…

With tears rolling down my cheeks, I began to try to persuade my mother that we should go to Tara's house. I believed we should boil pots of water, make up beds and peel extra potatoes. I was also convinced that they could stay with us and maybe we could even adopt Tara. My mother listened as I talked and it was comforting. I felt like we were hatching a plot and conspiring. I loved it when my mum listened to me like that. I waited for her to reply, which she did, carefully, with big pauses between each word. She had a plan, I knew it, and I was ready to cling to every word. I knew she would come up with something really brilliant. She wiped my tears and asked me if I was listening and she said *blow* and I blew my nose.

Now listen carefully, are you listening? Tara and her brother will be very, very sad right now and they need to be close to their family because when people pass on it's a quiet time. If you really want to do something…

Enraptured, I nodded my head, clenching my teary snot-drenched tissue in my hand.

If you really want to do something what you should do is…

I couldn't wait to hear, my heart raced at the thought that there was one thing, one brilliant thing I could do to make it better.

Salena, what you should do is you should make her a card and put it through her door so…

No but Mum, we should go around to their house together and take them some books and some sweets and nice yogurts…

Listen.

But I didn't ever listen, I kept interrupting and she repeated that one steady word.

Listen… Listen… LISTEN.

Mum deepened her voice and looked me right in the eye,

Look, I know you're very sorry for Tara but she will not even be there, she's probably still at the hospital or with her family. It's family time and she'll need to be quiet… Listen! What you should do is make her a card and pop it through her door so that… so that… when she does come home she'll know that you're there for her… It's QUIET time and you can't just go around there and….

But Mum…

No, Salena! How many more times do I have to tell you? It's QUIET TIME! QUIET TIME!

With my mum yelling *quiet time* in my face I know I have lost the battle. *OK, OK, what shall I write in the card?*

What shall you put in the card?

A project, a task was being set and a determination takes over that there is something I can do as Mum answers slowly

Let me think… Just put that you are sorry and…

I know.

That you are sorry and that…

OK I said I know… I cut her off and ran into my bedroom.

Late that dull Sunday afternoon I walked solemnly under an unremarkable sky. When I got there all the curtains were drawn and the house was in silence. Nobody was home. The bikes weren't out. The car wasn't there. *Of course the car wasn't there.* The drive was very steep and I thought of the crash, and of the crash of helmets against the garage door and us all laughing. I didn't want to disturb anyone, not even the neighbours. I didn't know how to look or how to explain why I was there – at the house where death just happened. I felt like a trespasser. I nervously crouched at the back door. It was glass, the swirly glass of bathroom windows, with a brown wooden frame. I pushed my lumpy envelope through the letterbox at the bottom of the door. It was hard to get it in, bulky. I had put loads of things in the envelope for Tara, things she might need: my lucky conker, a real American one dollar bill, a plastic joke ring that spurted water and a rubber eraser that smelled like Coca-Cola.

The envelope wasn't fitting, so I held the stiff flap up and poked it through with my fingers. I was just getting scared that it was stuck or that it would trap my finger when the packet shifted, I heard it thud heavily on the vinyl floor on the other side, and for a split second I froze, thinking I heard movement inside. I jumped and quickly backed away as though I was doing something wrong or interfering; a chill feeling as though I was being watched.

I walked back up the steep drive and turned left down the hill towards our school, with nowhere particularly to go and nobody in particular to play with. Dusk had fallen. The orange streetlights flickered on. I walked slowly, untangling these new emotions, melancholia, and dreadful fear. I stopped to tie up my shoelaces and sat on the kerb for a while to think, nervously biting the skin off the side of my thumb. Then I walked down the lanes and to the fields on the edge of town

Springfield Road

and climbed a gate and sat on it. I called to the matted old brown horse and offered it bitter crab apples. Its breath a warm steam into the chill evening air, after I patted it my hand smelled of horses. I imagined being Tara. I felt as though my package was a litany whispered into the wind or a message in a bottle thrown into the deep sea, but it was the best I could do and it was all I had to give her.

25 / tiny tears

It was a bitterly cold day when my mother was rushed to hospital to have the new baby, prematurely. I remember being excited to have a new baby sister or brother, but I was desperate for my mother the ten days or so she was gone. My mother had miscarried a baby before this new child and so I was very afraid to see my mother broken like that again, to find my mother in darkness, her eyes red from crying. There was a depressing darkness and a stuffy warmth in her bedroom that day and I never forgot it.

My brother and I were left to fend for ourselves. We went to and from school as usual and helped ourselves to cereals and toast. The house was empty without her, silent and loveless. The idea that this could be permanent was too horrible to contemplate. After school I shivered and waited, sitting on the back doorstep in the gloomy dusk, fearing the worst, waiting for my stepfather's car to light up the drive.

There were complications with the birth. We had a new sister, but she was premature and she came out fragile, tiny and blue. She was in an incubator and there was a blood transfusion. This was all I knew and a horrible dread consumed me. During those long, dark February nights I steeled myself for the possibility that my mother might die. In the books I loved to read this happened all the time, the stories of Hans Christian Anderson, Brothers Grimm and Charles Dickens were filled with stories of orphans whose mothers died in childbirth.

I was waiting, always waiting, for news, for my mother to come home safe or for Paddy to come to let me in after school and to pass time I started walking, blowing on my cupped hands to keep them warm. It had started getting dark and was spitting with rain when I knocked on Mrs Sharkey's door. I wanted to be less pitiful, but the sight of her kind face and the gush of warmth at the open door made my eyes hot with tears. She was wiping her hands on a tea towel and I could see she was about to say she was busy and about to send me away. I was hungry and cold and as my eyes filled I looked away and down at my shoes.

Springfield Road

What's wrong? she asked and I looked at her and then down again into my upturned coat collar when I felt my lip quivering. Through a blur of hot tears I saw her face change and she asked me inside. I was grateful but awkward because this time it wasn't a game, this time I felt I needed her. Once inside I began to cry, regurgitating the things I had been told but didn't fully understand. I told her that my new sister was smaller than a doll and that she came out blue and had to have a blood transfusion.

She's in an incubator and my mum's really ill and… and what if…?

Mrs Sharkey put her arm across my shoulders and listened and assured me that my mum would be all right. She made me dry my eyes with a handkerchief, then took out a pot and heated milk to make her special milky coffee. She made me a ham sandwich – the most delicious sandwich I had ever eaten, neatly cut into four quarters, on moist white bread with creamy butter and soft pink ham that was ever so slightly salty. I found it difficult to eat carefully and with all of my manners. I was self-consciously hungry and I ate too fast and the sandwich stuck in my throat. I tried to sip hot coffee to dislodge it. Mrs Sharkey watched me. She told me to take my time and that I could stay for a while and get warmed up. Then she walked to the corner cupboard in the kitchen and her grin made me chuckle as she said her lovely catchphrase, *Cakey?*

Mrs Sharkey asked if I would like to warm up by the fire and led me into the living room. I thought I must be a very trustworthy person to be allowed to sit in the proper front room and eat my cake and drink my sweet and creamy coffee. I felt shy and awkward, I hadn't sat in there before, our chats were always at the kitchen table or by the back doorstep. Mrs Sharkey told me to take my shoes off to warm my toes and this embarrassed me, making me feel like I was really welcome to stay for a while longer. I was grateful and in no rush to sit on the cold doorstep at our house anymore. I fumbled nervously with my laces, acting as though I had somewhere else to go in a bit, acting as though I thought she was the one who might want some company – because asking for comfort when you really need it is the hardest thing.

The blue glow of the electric fire was warm and inviting. Mrs Sharkey switched all the bars on high, until they glowed orange and ginger beneath the coals. I took my shoes off and, suddenly aware of my odd grey boy's socks, I tucked my cold feet under me. She put a tartan blanket on me, she had bought it on a caravan holiday she'd had in the highlands of Scotland, she said. The room had two armchairs but we sat side by side on the big green sofa. There were lace curtains and doilies on the glass coffee table, my coffee cup sat neatly on a *Cork, Ireland* coaster. She told me about Ireland and about her family pictured in gold and silver oval frames above the mantel piece, she told me the names and ages of all of her nephews and nieces that lived in the long ago and the faraway.

As Mrs Sharkey explained her family tree I pretended to go to sleep for a joke and I snored loudly. Mrs Sharkey played a lovely game with me, she pretended to be offended. She said

Oh how rude to fall asleep when I'm in the middle of telling a story...

I pretended to sleep and snored on and she held me, I was enveloped in her warm bosom, and pillowed in her arms. Then she pretended to fall asleep too, and snored even louder. With our eyes clenched shut, we peeked at each other out of one eye and then belly laughed, as we whistled, snorted and made pig snuffling noises together.

Well, well, what a big snore for such a little girl, she said, blowing a raspberry on my neck to wake me up making me laugh and wriggle.

With Mrs Sharkey holding me by the fire, we became still and gentle. Eventually I let myself go and drifted off for a little while. I was so comfortable in the glow of the fire, the soft heat of her arms, I fell into a lovely warm haze. Just so she'd hold me safe, for just a little bit longer.

***

When they came home, my mother and sister were fine after all. My mother once told me that she had had nightmares in the hospital and got up to sleepwalk the halls in the night, dragging her drip along with her. We sat on the bed and whispered, watching my newborn sister sleep. Jo-Ann was very small, a living, breathing doll, with black silky floppy curls. I measured her against my Tiny Tears doll and Jo-Ann was smaller. Her skin was the colour of my palest inner wrist and she had a penny plastered over her belly button.

When Paddy was home I was discouraged from picking Jo-Ann up to cradle her. When he wasn't home, though, I could help out and kiss her all I liked. Paddy started coming home from work with chocolate bars for my sister. She was barely off breast milk. I watched her slobbering, her miniature fist clenching carefully cut up chunks of melting chocolate and caramel. I would salivate and pretend to help her, wiping her face with a napkin while I stole pieces of chocolate.

Sometimes in the evenings when Paddy and Mum were watching television I risked sneaking into their bedroom to her cot-side. I wound up her lullaby toys and soothed her when she cried. I liked the way she grabbed my finger with her tiny hand. I sang to her, *Goodnight Mister Moon, come again and see us soon…* Jo-Ann cried a lot, but when I was with her she'd go quiet and it made me feel as though I was her special one. I had to be ready to dive out of there pretty sharpish though in case Paddy caught me. If he found me with her, he'd accuse me of waking her. Even when I told him I was trying to make her go back to sleep but he'd tell me off: *No you weren't, you are keeping her awake now get to your bedroom and don't you ever let me catch you in here again.*

26 / stepbrother

I remember a family day out much later that same year, 1981. We were visiting my stepbrother and walking along the seafront in Grimsby. The seascape was cheerless; the tide was out, the sea a murky slurp of grey in the distance. We walked along the out-of-season beach, past shuttered ice cream shops and rides. There were fading signs, arrows shaped like orange carrots, which read Donkey Rides, but it looked like it was going to rain, again.

We only saw Tina and Graham, Paddy's two real children from his first marriage, perhaps three times a year: Easter, Christmas or occasional birthdays. Paddy sometimes went to Grimsby on his own some weekends to visit them.

My mother pushed the tan-coloured corduroy pram with baby Jo inside. I held the pram handle, while Gus lolloped separately along and ahead a bit. He had grown very quiet and his legs moved in long gaping strides. We were there in Grimsby visiting my ginger-haired stepbrother for his birthday. He kicked a stone along the edge of the pavement and kerb, with his hands shoved in his pockets. We hadn't seen Graham for a while. He had a gruff, hoarse voice that was breaking, and his northern accent lilted up and down musically at the end of every sullen sentence. If you could get a whole sentence out of him that was. He was very pale, almost bluish, with a splatter of fat marmalade freckles. When he laughed he hid his mouth with his hand. Gus and I liked him most of the time, but he was very shy until he got used to being around us again. It was awkward though, with the adults making strained efforts to make it 'a good visit', everybody all together playing happy families.

Gus and Graham got on best, they were closer in age and they'd play boys' games like football. My stepbrother had all the latest electronic computer games too. One summer the boys made a tent and camped together in our back garden. Gus told me they stayed up making shadows with torch light, burning moths on candle flames and pulling the legs off daddy-long-legs. I was the youngest and Graham was sometimes a bit rough with me. He'd laugh and swing my dolls by the arms and catapult them across the room. After we watched *Star Wars* at the cinema, Gus and Graham made me cry when they took an ankle each and held me upside down, banging my head on the floor, playing out a scene from the film.

Graham's elder sister Tina was older than Gus. Of course, I liked it when Tina visited too, they wouldn't pick on me so much then. She was pretty with auburn freckles on her nose and reddish hair with flicks hairsprayed into her fringe. She wore black eyeliner and skintight jeans. She let me brush her hair and told me secret, grown-up things. One visit, Tina showed me a passport-size photograph of a punk-rocker, with a skinhead and she whispered *that's my boyfriend*. He looked like a glue-sniffer, his ears were pierced and his eyes were hollow, but I told her he looked very nice. I liked the way she had whispered that secret to me.

I can remember that seafront, that cold November day in Grimsby. It was a depressing sight, we were pedestrian and ordinary; awkward and all a bit bored of walking. The car was parked miles away down a side street, a free parking space to avoid paying for the car park. The sky was a flat slate grey. It was raining out at sea, but we were to make a day of it. Paddy and Mum kept saying things about the view and how *taking in the sea air and a bit of exercise won't do you no harm.*

I watched Paddy making a fuss of Graham, roughing up his hair, putting his arm around his shoulders, being affectionate. He was leaning down to Graham's ear for nice chats that only they could hear. I got jealous in waves; I wanted to be my stepfather's shiny one too, to make him notice me. I loved to see my stepfather when he was like this, when he made a point of being lovable and loving. Even if it was not a direct hit, even if it was not for my benefit, I inhaled the fumes like his second-hand cigarette smoke.

It's grim in Grimsby I thought over and over. When I said it out loud Mum and Paddy shot me a look to say *don't go spoiling the day.* I said *I was only kidding around*, thinking don't you get it? Grim in Grimsby, why is it called Grimsby? Because it is so grim and… *What shall we do then?* Nobody said this. We just thought it and walked separately along the dull seafront. A brackish stench rose from the dark brown sand and an olive-green scum and froth washed up with the tide. The railings were salt-tarnished and weatherworn, metal hinges were rusted to bolted doors and locked down shutters, the deckchairs were padlocked and the posters of the summer seasons were all torn and rain battered. There were smashed beer bottles in bus shelters that smelled of wee. Mum kept calling this *exploring* and honed in on the benefits of getting some sea air into us. She kept up her cheerful banter and gave us Polo mints she found in her coat pocket. We were being careful to act cheerful and as though we were all included for a day, included in a thing that didn't really exist. We were all involved in this united nothing, we were forcing something, faking it without knowing its name. It was tense, draining, silences were punctuated with Mum's noisy deep intakes of breath and repetitive clichés about the fresh air being good for us.

The boys kicked a pebble to each other, shouting *goal!* At first it was half-hearted and then they started running, racing each other, as the pebble rolled off the pavement and down the steps and onto the sand. Mum said we couldn't take the pram down onto the sand. I couldn't ever run fast enough to catch up or get a kick of the stone. I held back, it was not about me, I knew it was not my special day. Behind us on the distant promenade my mum sat and smoked a ciggy and rocked the pram. In the other direction, the boys and my stepfather were miles away by the edge of the tide and surf. There was no distinct horizon, just a grey fog of indeterminate mist blending sea and sky. I crouched with a rustle of my red cagoule over a puddle of crab pools and poked at sandy worm shapes. There was a dead starfish on the sand, seaweed knotted in washed-up objects, plastic and rope. I wished we were allowed to take our shoes and socks off and paddle. I wished it was summer.

We went to a sea view hotel and restaurant and were seated in the window. There were chocolate brown velvet curtains and apricot tablecloths and napkins. There were different condiments in sachets in a silver basket in the middle of the table.

What is tartare sauce? I asked.

It's like salad cream with bits in it.

We had been promised fish and chips but this place was more classy than our usual chippy. We had run into the first place that was open when the rain started pelting down. The menus were in red leatherette covered booklets. We sat up and kept our hands and elbows off the linen and cloth. It was an alien experience, being a family in a restaurant. My baby sister Jo-Ann was at the head of the table in her highchair and we all looked at her as she banged her plastic tray with a spoon. We focused on her every dribble and gurgle. I wondered if our stepbrother would love his new sister as much as I did.

See she always does that... I told him. *She likes it when you do this, blow on her hand, see she likes it.*

I was aware that they were connected in a way I could never be with Paddy. I was wary that they were also blood brother and sister and I really hoped Jo-Ann would not like her brother more than me when she got older.

Paddy asked Graham, *What do you fancy?* My stepbrother chose scampi in a basket. I didn't know what a scampi was and wondered why it came in a basket. We read the menu out loud and made shushed comments about the prices. Graham said he'd eaten lobster before and he liked it; we saw it was the most expensive thing on the menu. Gus had chicken and chips and I had sausage and chips and a fizzy orange. Outside the front window, rain slurped down the weighted canopy outside, a man poked it from the underneath with a stick to drain the water. It was bucketing down, coming in at a slant, obscuring the horizon, somewhere beyond the rain and the railings was the ocean.

My hands smelled and there was dirt and gritty sand under my nails, I asked to go to the bathroom. It was on the other side of the lobby and required a walk through the posh restaurant and down some gilt stairs. I walked slowly across the plush red carpet. I sucked the inside of my cheeks so it looked like I had cheekbones and pushed my chin up. I imagined I belonged there, I saw a piano in the corner or the lounge and bar area and I imagined that my father owned the place and that I was going to the lobby to meet him for luncheon. We'd call it luncheon, my real dad and I, and I'd say, *shall we have the lobster Papa?*

I went into the grand and marbled bathrooms and washed my hands with the pink soap and dried them on pink napkins from a dispenser that said *towelettes* in curly writing. Watercolours hung on the peach walls, a painting of two cats in deckchairs dressed like humans. Dry petals filled a glass bowl and there were plastic flowers in a vase. Old-fashioned tea-dance music was coming from somewhere. I took it all in and looked hard at my reflection and watched my pupils dilate. I leaned closer and watched for them for a while. I wasn't happy. I stood in the quiet of the toilets for a minute or two, sulking, watching my pupils growing and shrinking as though they were breathing.

When the food arrived, the slick grey-haired waiter was flirty with Mum and we all laughed over-politely. When he had gone Paddy poked fun and laughed about his bow tie. We ate fast and hungrily, filling the holes in our stomachs and the gaping pauses. There were some jokes made about the size of Paddy's cod and the huge amount of chips we had to get through each. Scampi in a basket was, I discovered, like nuggets of fish finger and I tried one. Graham squeezed ketchup and tartar sauce all over them. Jo-Ann made that face, with out of focus eyes, and we laughed, the tension coming out, our lips all grease and salt and vinegar. Jo cried out and Mum nursed her away from the table saying I think she needs changing. We held our noses and said *poo-ey!* Graham giggled with Gus and me about Jo-Ann's stinky nappy.

Throughout the meal Paddy spoke to his real son. I heard him asking him about school and sports and how his sister was getting on with her exams and I heard him ask *how do you feel about coming to us for Christmas this year, it will be special because it is Jo-Ann's first ever Christmas.*

Gus and I sat quietly in front of ketchup-smeared plates and cold leftover chips. We slurped our pop through straws. The waiter returned and cleared the table and asked us if we wanted dessert or coffee? Paddy asked Graham if he would like a Knickerbocker Glory? The waiter brought over plastic picture cards of all the desserts. This was a pivotal moment, we knew if my stepbrother said no, we'd leave now and skip pudding. I twitched and Gus nudged me under the table. I looked at the photographs of luxurious ice cream creations with names like choc-mint magic and toffee bonanza. Gus leaned in and pointed to a photo of a tall glass of gooey brown chocolate and whipped cream, he licked his lips and whispered,

Hmmm chocolate fudge sundae…
Hmmm banana split more like! I pointed and whispered back.

Springfield Road

Paddy looked at his watch and said we could always get one from an ice cream van. My heart sank, imagining us all in the boring car, sheltering from the rain, licking tired 99 ice creams, looking through rain splattered windows at the dull sea. The waiter lingered, waiting for a decision as Mum returned to the table. Jo was cradled in her arms in the sleeping position, it was a bad sign, she'd want to get going. The waiter gave us a moment and left as Paddy was asking Graham, *OK? Then shall we maybe get one from the ice cream van?*

On the journey home it was quiet in the car except for the squeak of the windscreen wipers. I watched the rain make trails down the window, my eyes following individual drops until they joined with other drips. It wasn't ever really about whether we had ice creams or not – I was nine years old and beginning to be more aware of feeling as though I were outside looking in, observing my family going through the motions and wishing things were different.

PART THREE – WINTER

pull a lucky wishbone, christmas, late seventies,
desborough

27 / *wish upon a star*

The snow came in the night, falling thick and fast. By morning, there were deep snowdrifts in the narrow country lanes and jagged icicles hung like fangs from guttering. We were astronauts walking on a crunchy moon on the first day of proper snow, preparing for our expedition to planet school. Bundled up in mittens, hats and scarves, we met each other in the middle of the road, a brave new world, the white world. We wore plastic bags on top of our socks inside our wellington boots. We had eaten sticky thick porridge for breakfast believing it would glow blue like low flames and central heating in our bellies. We puffed and stamped our feet through frozen puddles. We left our mark, dirtying the fresh clean snow of garden lawns with footprints and names. In gangs we rolled massive snowballs until they were boulders and too heavy to push. These would become the round bodies of snowmen, with pebbles for eyes, carrots for noses and sticks for arms.

What did one snowman say to the other snowman?
Don't know? What did the snowman say to the other snowman?
Can you smell carrots?

We threw snowballs all the way to school. The first one in the back of my head surprised me with that sudden thud, thump and sting. I retaliated, skidding and chasing around the shapes of cars. Then we scooped big hands full of clean soft ice cream to eat,

Eating snow is dirty…
No it isn't! It's only frozen sky! It's natural.
Urghh, you ate yellow snow!
Did not it was clean from that wall… look!
Yellow snow, yellow snow, you ate yellow snow…

Boys mercilessly rammed snow down the backs of necks and rubbed it into faces, making them red and rashy. We slipped down the hill to school, claiming the middle of the road as cars were few and far between. We sucked icicles, our free ice lollies. We goaded each other that school would be closed for the rest of the week and that there would be a blizzard and we said:

> *It is going to drop to ice age temperatures, that's below minus zero!*
> *No colder than that, minus below twenty!*
> *There is no such thing as minus below, it's below zero.*
> *You're a Joey.*
> *Deacon! It's called sub zero minus actually!*
> *Sub-zero minus whoopee! Ice age!*
> *It's going to be below sub minus zero! Hooray! Ice age means no more school!*

We told each other fantastic horror stories – that a car had been found in a ten foot snow drift with its passengers frozen solid inside. We insisted that woolly mammoths were coming back. We talked about avalanches and Antarctica and played at being great explorers searching for the North Pole, a world inhabited by polar bears and Eskimos. A rumour spread that the river was frozen over and we made plans to go ice skating, although not one of us owned ice skates, and ice skating would have been more a case of ice skidding in our wellingtons. We spread tales that the teachers were snowed-in their homes and described how they were starving grotesquely to death. On days like these, many children were kept home, especially posh kids from the farms and remote areas, so we held high hopes that the class numbers would be too low to even bother opening the school gates.

School was a ridiculous, glittery chaos that close to the Christmas holidays. Our teacher read us Christmas stories and watched over us as we industriously made Christmas cards, cardboard stars and papier mâché snowmen, the desks a mess of glitter-glue and crêpe paper.

I remember enjoying preparing for our annual school nativity plays. I always landed the roles of either shepherd or one of the three kings, which were really boys' roles. Each year my mum made my costumes from old cotton bed sheets from home. I had a brilliant time though, once I stopped being envious of the pretty angel, traditionally that part was always given to the cutest blonde girl in the school, they dressed her all in white with a halo and silvery wings.

Each year during those last weeks of term, the school dinner ladies came around each class and every single child had a turn stirring the Christmas pudding mixture, a cauldron of currants, sultanas and plum with the sickly smell of sweet rum. When you stirred it you had to make a wish. Every year I looked into that vat of goo for the sixpence and I wished with my eyes closed tight and I made the same wish I still always make.

It took ages to undress from our winter things when we re-entered the classrooms after break-times. We blathered and fussed with talk of chilblains and frostbite, blowing on our hands and rubbing our frozen feet until we could feel them again. There was a constant distraction of snow gently patting the windowpanes, like a sparkly friend tapping on the glass. We always said *God is shaking out his eiderdown* or *the angels are having a pillow fight*. We did our lessons in our socks, with damp hair, runny noses and flushed rosy cheeks. Clothes that had been caked white from rolling in the snow dripped and steamed on classroom radiators. The worst casualties of the snowball wars were sent to the school secretary to get ill-fitting, musty-smelling clothes from the lost and found. When it snowed, the girls were permitted to wear trousers instead of skirts – an amazing freedom that evened out the snowball chases and fighting odds.

So sweet was that sound of the early home-time ring of the school bell. Always a couple of hours early due to the weather and the dark. We skidded and slid deliriously into the fields, making plans to meet at the top of the steep hills at the back of St Giles church with makeshift sledges – a black bin bag stuffed with an old pillow, tied and bound with string and tape or sometimes we sped down the slope on old tea trays. The fields were white as far as the eye could see, with black matchstick trees in the distance, an undulating cotton sheet, an expanse of endless sand dunes, as deep and untouched as the craters on the surface of the moon.

***

On Christmas Eve 1981, I was with Anna Parris, her brother and her father, walking their two golden Labradors. It was late in the afternoon as we walked towards Rothwell. We crossed meadows, frozen streams and woodland. The sky was an apricot hue, laced with a fine mist. It was like a painting with the smoke-grey hills in the distance and the branches bare as bones, like charred skeletons. Our noses were red and runny, we carried sticks and called out to the dogs to *heel* and *walk on. Merry Christmas!* We called out in chorus, happy to see someone, anyone, approaching so we could yell it again *Happy Christmas! Ho ho ho to you!*

Mr Parris was a lovely dad, he had a peppery beard with ginger bits in it and golden brown eyes like Anna's. He was the headmaster of a big school in a nearby town. He seemed to always find time to help build things with his children and their friends. Once I went to play there and found them all making a real igloo out of snow. I'll never forget that, it was big enough for all of us to get in. We sat in the round centre of it and I remember finding it warm inside.

I also recall one summer Mr Parris made an obstacle course down the centre of their long garden and he and Anna taught me how to ride a bike proficiently. He built a rope ladder and a swing in their apple orchard, and we spent hours swinging on the rungs of the ladder and eating unripe apples. Anna was my most sensible and bookish friend. She taught me how to hold my breath and swim underwater, she tried to teach me to play *Cats* with her on her piano and she introduced me to the Brownies. My Brownie Guide uniform was a second-hand brown tunic that was too short for me, with a yellow tie and a brown leather toggle. I wore my Brownie bobble hat ridiculously balanced on my afro. It looked better if you had straight silken hair like Anna's. She was a tomboy too, with bobbed straw-coloured hair, those sandy brown eyes and pale freckles across her nose. I pored over my Brownie manual, and together we competed over badges, both aiming to achieve two full sleeves; to us these sewn-on trophies not only symbolised that we had passed the tests of semaphore, cooking and first aid, but that we were smart and we could solve anything, that we could survive in the wild and live in camps and tree houses.

So that Christmas Eve, we ran through the sludge with the dogs leaping excitedly and barking. Then we stopped and called the old brown horse to come to the fence to eat snowy, muddy grass from our red palms. Standing on the gate railings, we shouted *here boy*. Our fingers were cold and dirty; we cleaned them inside our mittens. The sky was sweet above us, swept with the colour of rhubarb and custard penny chews, Fruit Salads, pink and yellow.

Springfield Road

Do you get butterflies on Christmas Eve? Anna asked.

I do! her brother replied.

I have got butterflies in my tummy already Dad, I have, Anna said softly, taking Mr Parris's big, gloved hand.

Me too, I said, shoving my hands deeper into my own pockets and tucking my chin into my scarf.

The four of us fell quietly into step as I began to think about my own dad and the letters we had written to him that week. That year particularly Mum had asked us to write to our father and say what we wanted for Christmas. I didn't know what to write, we had never asked for anything or written to him much before. I'd found the letter difficult. More than anything I wanted to ask for something to give him a clue who I was and how I had grown up. Mum suggested I ask for a vanity case, I didn't know what a vanity case was. Mum told me it was a case for young ladies, with a mirror and a manicure set, it was somewhere to keep precious things and jewellery. To me it sounded like it would make him picture me as a pretty young lady.

So that Christmas, I wrote to my father asking for a vanity case and I couldn't wait to see what he'd send and what on earth a vanity case looked like, but because it would be from my real dad, I suddenly wanted one more than ever.

The icy grass crunched under our boots, there was a lavender mist across the dusky fields in the distance. The dogs padded by our side and as we came back into town pretty Christmas lights in house windows winked and blinked on and off. Chimney smoke wisped into the evening. We caught a lovely little smile playing on Mr Parris's lips underneath his bushy beard as he listened to us talking about Father Christmas. We were discussing how Santa could get to us even though our bungalow didn't have a chimney.

We felt the magic of Christmas Eve all around us, sparkling in the frost. We were content that tomorrow would be the best day of the year. And as we said goodnight to each other the North Star was twinkling above us. We kept yelling *Happy Christmas* until we were out of sight of each other and I was walking alone. A street away, I could still hear Anna Parris shouting into the peaceful Christmas Eve, the silent night, the holy night, all is calm, all is… *Merry Christmas, Salenaaaaaa…*

28 / christmas

Memories of childhood at Christmas times blur into a montage very much depending on my mood and the hunger I felt then, and also now in the remembering. The last week of December, those last evenings of the year, often remind me of the magic and warmth of home fires, of the familiarity of a sing-song of chattering voices above my head, the voices of my step-grandparents, Nanny and Grandad, or visiting friends like Auntie Doreen. Once the novelty wore off and I'd stopped jumping on knees, I would settle and curl up, lazily flip the pages of a *Beano* Christmas annual. The adult talk was tipsy, fuelled by hot toddies and mulled wine, and cackling laughter came from the kitchen where the women fussed over the grease and jelly of the boiled ham, while the men poured whiskey or rum and stood with their hands in their pockets, rolling on the balls of their feet, chewing fists of peanuts. With ceremony, they uncorked Mum's home-made rocket fuel she called damson gin and let me have a taste as they all talked loudly over each other and over Mary Poppins singing 'A Spoonful of Sugar'.

I remember well the rose-lit, tinselled living rooms of my parents' friends, with the comfortable cacophony of those competing voices. I recall straining to comprehend the shush of talk between adults. Content, I sat underneath tables or behind sofas, out of sight, with my newfound wealth of chocolate coins and colouring with new felt tip pens.

I also remember moments at Christmas when we were like a real family, the ideal family, like the adverts showed us to be, chocolate boxes and crackers, sausage rolls and Twiglets. Then there are also memories of times when I found Christmas strange, depressing, stifling. There were times when Christmas was painful, when there was preferential treatment of favourites and jokes about Scrooge were made through gritted teeth and forced smiles. There were moments when I'd mope off and hide from my alien family and lock myself in the bathroom convinced I must have been adopted.

Springfield Road

I remember one Christmas my brother Gus and I rolling our eyes at each other as we watched our stepsiblings unwrap top-of-the-range games while we opened our presents to find a chocolate bar each. What did we expect, equality? In these moments I believed that if the stepsiblings were opening these gifts then maybe, just maybe, I'd get that Barbie or writing set I had my heart set on. I'd have a head filled with playground lists posted to Santa and I wanted the same presents classmates were asking for – then that gluey knot in the belly when we looked back at the tree and all the gifts were gone. It was all empty shiny paper and going through the motions of what Christmas is and never was.

There was a year though, when we were rich and Paddy was unbelievably generous, something to do with him being made redundant or a tax refund. I felt I must have been the best stepdaughter and luckiest girl on the planet, there were so many presents under the tree. That may have been the year we played Monopoly and watched television all day. Was that the last Christmas we all got on happily? Or perhaps that was the same year when Mum found me quiet, wondering why there was no package from Springfield Road and Grandpa George. I recall how she laughed that they were forgotten and hidden in the shed. Then when she appeared with cold damp boxes, I tore into one addressed to me, and found I had been given the most beautiful play china tea set, decorated with roses and gold lacquered edges.

There were times when we had our stepbrother and stepsister to stay. A Christmas when they stayed always meant Paddy being particularly playful and loving. We'd all sit in the living room together, *The Wizard of Oz*, *James Bond* or *The Three Musketeers* on the television. We could smell dinner cooking slowly for hours, and we were allowed to eat all together at the dining table and have a glass of wine with our dinner. One year there was a box of Liebfraumilch and I distinctly remember feeling giggly and bold and loving everyone and finding my family the most hilariously entertaining people I had ever known.

It's the white Christmas I remember most clearly though. The feel of that day when we were close, everybody was happy. We had glasses of fresh orange juice for breakfast and warmed croissants with real butter. That was the year it snowed thick and fast. We took a walk on

Christmas morning whilst the turkey cooked on a low, slow heat in the oven. Bundled up in mittens and wellington boots, we walked around the country lanes towards the town of Market Harborough, and the four of us, Gus and me and Mum and Paddy, we had a snowball fight. The sky was ice blue with bright wintry sunshine reflecting off the snowy fields and hedgerows. That's my happiest Christmas memory: the snowball fight on Christmas morning and laughing like a real happy family.

***

Christmas 1981 was my baby sister's first Christmas and both my stepsiblings came to stay. I remember watching Paddy take photographs of just the three of them, just his three real children. I wanted to be in the picture. I wanted to be in the gang. That Christmas I remember Mum being really tired and baby Jo-Ann teething and crying. Most of all I remember that was the Christmas my mum had asked us to write to my real father. Perhaps it goes without saying that the gifts never arrived, no word from Dad. Mum made excuses about the Christmas post, and Gus and I were told they just might arrive in a later post after Boxing Day or in the new year – but the truth is we didn't understand why we were asked to write to our father that particular year – and it wasn't until later that we discovered the real reason why.

29 / the end

Gus and I hoped that we'd see our father again. We knew that he lived in Bristol and that he had re-married. I privately entertained the idea of running away to see him, or imagined that maybe he'd come and fetch us when we were older. We lived with the sensation of waiting, though to say any of this out loud felt to me like a betrayal of my mother and her choices. It was a loyalty I was afraid to break. It didn't even occur to me that he might not want to know or that he might have a new life. I made up romantic excuses for his abandonment. I also believed that my stepfather didn't want my mother's ex-husband coming to the house to visit and so I blamed him too.

As long as you have the perception of an achievable dream, you can keep surviving and existing. Meeting our father, getting to know him and having him in our lives one day, that seemed obtainable, we believed that one day the privilege of knowing our father would be ours.

When Mum called my brother and me to her side, she was unwell and pale, with dark circles beneath her eyes. We three were seated in the living room. It was an overcast and ordinary day in the bleak February of 1982. I sat on her left and Gus sat on her right. My mother spoke in a low and deep voice and Gus and I looked across from each other and smirked a bit. We were restless, our mother spoke in such a serious tone it made us nervous. We pulled faces copying her, on the verge of larking about and laughing at her. She was building up to something but we were not totally listening until she completed her speech with those three words: *Paul is dead.*

Pardon? my brother blurted, and we looked each other in the face and then burst into peals of laughter. It was our mother's face, it was so strange and so serious we laughed and then slowed to a snigger. I looked at Gus, he tried to take control so I tried to mimic his features, which made him chuckle and that made me giggle. I looked at my mother, she was stroking both of our backs with the palms of her hands as you might a baby. Feeling this soothing gesture and catching my brother's eye I started roaring with laughter again which set Gus off. Gus and I laughed, we laughed until it really hurt, we belly laughed. The more I laughed at Gus the more he laughed at me, out of control, away from our mother's hands, we fell off the sofa and were face down into the carpet, hysterical. Gus looked at Mum and kept catching his breath and saying, *It's her fault she keeps making me,* which sent us both into fits of laughing again. I have never laughed so hard in my life. There were tears on our cheeks then suddenly Gus, he wiped his face and croaked, *Salena, stop...*

In slow motion, I saw my brother's face change. First his dark eyes went glassy, then his mouth turned down at the corners and his brow knotted. As though a cloud had passed over the sun, a shadow crossed his face as something registered. He couldn't see the joke anymore, though I was still frozen in smiling. I thought the cloud would last a moment only and then normal service would be resumed and we'd laugh together again. But the more serious he looked, the more nervous it made me. Mum said quietly *I think she's in shock.*

Gus's eyes were out of focus and filling with tears but I didn't want the laughing to stop and I tried to laugh some more. I forced out a fake laugh. Mum held him and he was making a noise, a low wail that I had never heard him make before and which wasn't laughing. I didn't want the laughter to ever stop. Their shoulders were shaking now, they were both weeping *Paul is dead, Dad's dead, Salena...*

Then my mother made a long sonorous cry, a single note that resonated through me. It rang underneath and inside her and through me, it was a howling, it was my mother crying and my brother crying, the two of them in front of me. I couldn't take it all in and I mean I didn't want to and then I had started to cry too.

Mum told us he took his own life. That was the bit that was hard to understand. Mum told us he was very, very sad. She said he ran out of choices and the only choice he had was to end it all. We asked how and she wouldn't tell us exactly. I was nine years old and I was trying to imagine being so sad you would kill yourself.

With this I wept harder, it was the fact that he was very sad, that one day our dad was sad, unhappy enough to kill himself. I had never heard his emotions discussed before, I never knew he could be sad. I wanted to go to him, make him happy. I heard my brother and my mother crying, his head was in her lap next to mine, her hands on our heads; she stroked our hair and we cried together.

Mum told us quietly that he died before Christmas. Before Christmas? He committed suicide on December 11th 1981. He was already dead, long dead and long gone. It was February, two months after the event. There was no funeral to go to, no goodbyes to say or respects to pay. This was the end. Those letters we wrote and posted, mine about the vanity case, they were written and posted to a dead man already long cold in his grave.

30 / the silence

Silence. It was very silent all of a sudden. The rage was silent and the grief was bitter. There was a black and cold hole inside me and I fell into it. If I could have I would have given up speaking forever. I reduced my language to polite monosyllables at school. I could not find any words to say what I was feeling. I know I felt like a fake because I didn't know my real dad, not really, did I? I didn't live with him or get to visit him, did I? It was not like Tara Collins, who lived with her mother and knew her and in any case that was an accident. Her mother would still be here if she had the choice. It was Dad's choice that I was struggling to come to terms with. My father didn't die from an illness or an accident. He killed himself on purpose.

I give up and sit by the kerb and flick ants down the drain using bits of dirt.

I climb inside the wardrobe and sit on the shoes. I inch the door closed and stay there for a while. I am in the dark, you cannot find me here, you cannot see me, you cannot hear me. In fact, I am not really here at all.

I rode my bike on my own, intending never to turn back, to run away from home. Up and down steep and winding country roads I cycled for miles, wet inside my cagoule with cold and furious sweat. Eventually I stopped and sat at my favourite spot, on the yellow, rusting frame of a broken-down tractor on the very edge of town. I climbed into it and hid, I was miles away from home. I had cycled so hard I was shaking and my legs were weak. Around me, bleak brown fields, black hills and grey roads like dull spaghetti stretched into the distance. The trees had ashen branches and there was no birdsong. I hugged my knees and shivered, damp in my rustling plastic coat. I got lost staring up into the flat dull sky. With my head tipped back I opened my mouth wide, I cried, soundlessly at first.

It was dark when I returned home. My hot head was throbbing and aching and I crawled down to the end of my bed, with my feet on the pillows. In the dark and under the covers I wondered over and over

Springfield Road

what if one day I just give up like that? You did it, Dad, you did it. You're my dad who killed himself. I had learned something new, that sensible grown-up people, with cars and houses, with family and friends, adults with responsibilities kill themselves.

Without words Gus and I called a truce. There was no speech or handshake, but a concrete feeling of uniting in this shared grief. It solidified us as brother and sister and was absolute. It was a pane of glass we carried between us for the rest of our lives.

At night, in the silence, I'd replay that moment, when we realised our shared dream was smashed. I saw my reflection in my brother's eyes; they were black as teaspoons of treacle, dark and shiny. I was looking into two black pools and seeing the twin of my own pain. I remembered his face as it went from hysterical laughter to clarity, to shock and finally that long scream of loss. We mirrored each other, sharing that unforgettable second when the penny dropped, the branch snapped, and we fell through a jagged sky to the hard ground. I rewound it and felt my own heart breaking in slow motion, I saw it again and again in my mind; my brother's eyes when he first really heard the words *Paul is dead.* I watched his face, his disbelief and the excruciating sting of the meaning of those three words. I watched my brother breaking, then I felt my own heart splintering, shattering, both of us, together at that minute. It was a hard slap of cold granite, a metallic taste of fear, of terror and a thumping in the blood.

When birth and death came screaming at me, all I could do was throw my head back and scream along. Death and birth screeched and crashed into my nine-year-old head. With the birth of my new sister and the death of my father in the same era, things were changing inside me and outside I felt my shell harden.

It was the word *choose* I have always had the most difficulties with. I struggled with the fact that, you, Dad, would rather die than ever see the sun shine again. Or share love, laughter or more to the point see us, your children, ever again. More practically, you would rather die than see if you feel differently in the morning. For the first time in my life I grew silent, I read even more books and in the quiet turning of pages, I started to imagine blackness, nothingness, I started to picture what suicidal could possibly feel like and mean.

If this were a comic book, the graphics would go to black and red now. After hearing of Dad's suicide, the rainbow technicolour pages of my childish fields of gold, sky blue summers and daisy chains, became monochromatic drawings with long charcoal shadows and I withdrew. That dark February of 1982 was the longest month of my life.

I stopped dreaming I was a superhero. I did not fly above churches and forests and fields, I no longer dreamed I was kissing Elvis in Hawaii or that I had a cupboard in my belly with bananas inside. Instead in my half-dreams, I'd see my father.

I'd see you there at the end of our bunk bed, watching us sleep, standing over us, an illuminated figure in the bedroom. I'd lie in my bed as still as stone and watch you looking down at my brother. There was a bluish light around you, as you slowly turned your head to look at me, I closed my eyes so you would think I was sleeping. My heart pounded in my chest but I was not scared, not of you or of your ghost. I was expecting you to visit. I knew they wouldn't let you into heaven because you killed yourself. I knew they wouldn't let you into hell either. Did you come to say sorry? You looked at Gus as he slept and when you turned to look at me I closed my eyes and when I opened one eye I saw you had gone. I knew you would be back though. I felt you watching me. I have always felt you watching me in the dark.

It is probably no coincidence that my father killed himself around the same date as the anniversary of his mother Edith's death. As I grew up, the more I thought about it the more it made sense. My father knew how it felt to seek his beginning. He spent much of his life searching for his natural birth parents and he suffered and grieved when he lost Edith. Now with the knowledge of that pain and emptiness, that waiting and seeking, it was as if he passed all that sad weight on to his children, so now we would also know that loss and we might also always miss something we never had. So that we might also grieve a father we never got to know. This was our shared inheritance. His second wife and new family must have been devastated, beyond devastated. Mum, Gus and I did not go to the funeral. Looking back, I think as kids we would have found his funeral highly traumatic. This was a decision made by all the adults and with the best intentions, but because of it there were many unanswered questions – my brother and I never knew the man when he lived, or the whereabouts of his final resting place. We could not say hello to the living or our last goodbye to the dead.

I was convinced that if we had been allowed to be even a small part of your life we would have been one more reason for you to hold on, Dad. One more loving and happy memory to make you stronger, to make you want to live. As a child I thought we had a wonderful time that one afternoon, I felt a bond, and your one visit kept us living in hope for years. Maybe if you had known us you would have waited to see whether you felt a bit better in the morning.

Mum always said sleep is the great healer. Sleep well and goodnight, Dad.

31 / fishing

Not long after we found out our dad had gone, I can remember my mum asked Gus to take me fishing. These two events may be unrelated but it is what was left unsaid and the feeling we shared that sticks in my memory. Gus had got the fishing rod for a birthday present in March and I'd been pestering him to let me have a go. At Mum's insistence he relented, but I could see he didn't want to take me to his secret place. Nevertheless, we packed jam sandwiches and orange squash mixed in a plastic bottle, while Mum made us take cold boiled eggs. We hated cold boiled eggs.

We walked across dewy fields, through wet grass that came up to my waist, and climbed over stiles heading towards Rothwell. It was spitting lightly and I struggled to walk so fast, my corduroys damp from the reeds and long grass. He complained and ordered me to hurry up, we begrudged and bickered at each other. Eventually we walked in silence, me jogging ten steps behind, trying to keep up.

Finally we got to *the* good spot, according to Gus. I couldn't see anything more remarkable about this place than the stretch of river behind or ahead of us and I grumbled as much. Gus tutted and started work, feeding his line through the loops on his rod. I watched, feigned interest, trying hard to enjoy my first fishing trip. We sat on cold, damp grass. I looked at the dun, muddy water and waited for something to happen. Gus had maggots for bait, which revolted me. I couldn't take my eyes off the sickening sight of the guts through the wire. Gus cast his line and settled. There was only one rod and I very rarely got a turn to hold it. When I did, I invariably did something wrong – wound the line too tightly so it snapped or let it out too loose so he'd have to reel it all back in – and that annoyed Gus further. So for the most part, I sat in my red cagoule with my hood up, elasticated and tight around my face, padded out by my fat, curly hair. I absentmindedly lobbed cowslips into the river.

Don't do that, you'll scare the fish, Gus growled.

What fish?

Springfield Road

Shush, don't talk, you'll scare them away.
Scare who away?
The fish! Now like I said, shut up.
But Gus?
Just shut up will ya.

I was about to launch a volley of *shut ups* right back but he gave me the look. Since I had insisted he take me in the first place, I knew my best bet was to shut up when he gave me *that* look. Gus began lecturing me that fishing was a relaxing pastime for people to get some peace and quiet and that fish can sense predators and hear noise above water – but I was ignoring him. I couldn't see any fish, the water was murky and there were no other fishermen. I reckoned fishing was a load of boring rubbish and I said so, under my breath.

Time passed so slowly but it seemed we had eaten our jam sandwiches hours ago and we were beginning to get hungry. I looked at things floating in the water, plastic bags and other rubbish. Then I busied myself picking flowers for Mum, but there were only dandelions and cowslips. Gus said they were weeds, so I cast them aside and stared gloomily into space.

When Gus and I recall this fishing trip, he thinks we probably caught a minnow. I do not remember the thrill of a single bite or a catch. We both remember that I was annoying him, though, and that we were cold. Sitting on that bank, on a mulch of damp sameness, we must have looked like two bored apes in the zoo, scratching a bit and not doing much. We were quiet, the sky was darkening and I could see a sheet of slate clouds in the distance, rain heading in our direction.

Then with nothing else to do, I studied my brother, his habit of intentionally biting the skin on the side of his nails and spitting out the chewed bits. I watched him for the first time in a long time, taking in the new fuzz of his moustache, his bony long legs, his coarse hair in need of cutting. But more than that, I saw his eyes had no twinkle. I looked upon my brother as though I were seeing him for the first time, as an outsider, the way you might look upon a stranger. He was hunched over, his mouth had none of the usual curl of smiles playing at the corners. Gus was never one to talk much, but for the first time I could see a new melancholy in his demeanour. I wanted to touch him, reach out, I wanted to talk to him but I didn't know where to start. I could see he was sad and trying to be brave. It was awkward. I tried hard to stop thinking about talking all the time so much, something I have always found difficult. We sat moodily apart and together.

I started to shiver, concentrating on staring wordlessly at the brown motion of the muddy water. After a long pause, Gus finally looked over at me and we caught each other's glance and shrugged. He said gently,

You all right, sis?
Yeah.
You sure?
Bit cold.
It's getting nippy.
Gus?
What?
Doesn't matter… Nothing.

Gus nodded at me, lifted his chin as though encouraging me to continue. Both of us knew there was something to talk about but instead I just said,

M'ungry… you?
Starvin' Marvin.

Then we remembered the eggs, we opened the tin foil they were wrapped in and the stink was foul. We were hungry but these eggs were really unappealing. Out of boredom I peeled one and saw the yolk was grey as the sky above us. We threw them in the river and watched as they floated away downstream. I watched the bobbing eggs, food for the fish, and twenty years passed until we hugged each other and finally had that conversation.

32 / golliwog!

I soon read every book in the library at my primary school. The headmaster joked that they had to order in new books just for me. When I had read all the books at the school library, I became a proud public library member and I started borrowing books by authors like Doctor Seuss, Enid Blyton and Judy Blume. I devoured big sturdy books by the Brothers Grimm and waded into hefty compendiums with titles like *A Thousand Adventures for Girls*.

On the walk to the public library I passed through the older part of town, the factories and the council estates. Some of those houses still had disused outdoor lavatories in the stone backyards. They were industrial boom houses, built from dark, sooty slate and brick when Desborough was a roaring leather and shoe-factory town. I usually avoided those streets, the windows hung with St George flags, the growling dogs, the child-lynching mobs I tended to attract. They'd tease me, telling me that their dogs were ex-police dogs that were trained to bite *blackies*, *nig-nogs* and *golliwogs* like me. They called out these names the moment they saw me. In gangs they took up chase with their dogs snarling, hounding me across the back of the new estates and muddy building sites, caterwauling, *Golliwog! Golliwog! Get back on your marmalade jar!*

Once in the safety of the library I immersed myself in books. Among the encyclopaedias and atlases there was a heavy biology book I peeked at on each visit. It had pictures of a snake dislocating its jaw to eat a whole frog and bare-naked African tribespeople. There were illustrations that showed apes morphing into cavemen, children changing into hairy adults and vivid spaghetti diagrams of the insides of women where babies came from. Most often though, I turned to the centre, a double-page spread of a bloody baby, mid-birth, with its head coming out of a hole. The caption below the picture read *The Miracle of Life* and to me it was the goriest thing in the whole library.

It was dusk, closing time and I was nearly the last person in the library. This part wasn't unusual, I would often get lost in all the books I wanted and be so indecisive, knowing I was only allowed to choose four.

Outside, I heard the dogs barking. I glanced out of the window and saw six or seven itchy, snotty-faced kids with bikes and dogs waiting for me outside. They looked bored; they chewed gum with slack jaws. I recognised at least two of them from my school, a vicious girl with a long greasy fringe that always hung in her eyes. Smithy – she was tough, one of about eleven brothers and sisters, with a rusting car in the middle of their front yard. Next to her stood a boy – I knew him, too, he had a girlish name, something like Marion. He was albino, with white fuzzy baby's hair and sharp pointed teeth due to some calcium defect. He looked like a vampire's baby. They were with bigger, older punk kids though and loitering. I knew they'd try to take my books off me and that they'd call me names and their dogs would snap at me and chase me all the way home.

They were swelling in numbers and blocking the entrance when my hero was on his way down to the boxing club and he saw the gang. He knew they had no use for books. My brother appeared at the entrance to the library and I beckoned madly and waved, Gus saw me through the glass in the doorway,

You all right, sis?

As I checked my books out, he waited for me, then we walked through the swinging doors together. Gus looked down at me, he didn't take his eye off me once, holding both my shoulders and asking gently if I was all right,

Did anyone hurt you? Which one was it?

My knees were weak. I was trembling. They jostled, bristled and called us niggers and wogs. Quite suddenly, Gus swivelled from the waist and threw a direct punch at the biggest of them, hitting him in the face with rapid precision, twice, then three or four swift jabs, bloodying his nose and knocking him clean, clear off his bike and onto the ground. It was so fast, nobody had time to blink and even the dogs barked too late.

Leave her alone! She's still only in juniors...

Gus swore at them

You're all older'n her... leave her alone unless you want more!

Springfield Road

Marion jumped on his bike. He wobbled in his hurry to speed off as fast as his thin white matchstick legs could go. From the safety of the other side of the street he yelled *Niggers!* and something about getting his big brother, but Gus brushed that threat off like a fly. The punk he had punched sat cradling his face with cupped hands, blood dripped through his fingers, from his mouth and nose and down the front of his slashed Iggy Pop t-shirt. Gus stepped over him and hoiked up a good thick greeny from the back of his throat and spat.

Don't go near my sister again.

He swore and then he took my arm and walked me across to the zebra crossing opposite the library. Gus looked down at me and told me with an assuring authority,

You're all right sis, now go straight home…

And as I started hurriedly up the hill, cuddling my stack of books to my chest he called out,

Oi! Salena!

What?

Don't tell Mum.

33 / the day the glass joke broke

War broke out the day the glass broke.

I was inside, in our bedroom on my own, and it was winter. I was reading when I heard a knock at the window. I started, but I was relieved it was only Gus. The doors were all locked and he asked if he could get in through the window. I opened the window and then closed it before he could climb in. I teased my brother as Gus ran around the outside of the house trying all the windows, which I kept opening and closing. He was getting annoyed with me, which made me do it more and I laughed as I just managed to get the dining room window closed before he could get his arm in.

Stop messing about! Let me in or else!

I started juggling fruit. Then I peeled a tangerine slowly, doing a silly dance, eating the segments with my mouth open so he could see the chewed up orange mush in my teeth and tongue. He yelled,

Hey! You're gonna get done for that…

Mum said I could have one…

Where's mine then? Come on gimme one, if you can have one then so can I…

He stamped his feet, blowing on his hands and his nose was red and running. Eventually, of course, I let him in, opening the dining room window so he could climb through as the front and back doors were all locked to keep out strangers. Gus came inside and said *you took your bloody time* but his anger abated as he ate a tangerine.

We were bold enough to wander around the whole house, to snoop about and look in our parents' wardrobe, to hang out in the living room. We turned on the big stereo in the lounge and listened to music on the radio, loudly. Elvis was on the radio, I distinctly remember that. We played cowboys through the swinging saloon doors, and when we were shot we collapsed across the lounge and threw ourselves backwards over the couch.

We started playing with things on the shelves. A miniature barrel that looked like a beer barrel but had nothing in it and a soda fountain that made a whoosh noise when you pulled the handle.

But it was me, I reached up and I picked up the glass and started pretending to drink from it and that's when it snapped at the stem. The glass that broke wasn't even glass, it was made of plastic. It was a trick, a joke glass of brandy, you tipped to your lips and nothing came out, the liquid was trapped in a double layer of plastic. It was quite realistic though, Paddy had got it in a joke shop, maybe one summer on Hastings Pier. I remember my legs went to water, my heart leapt in my throat as we stood in horror with the broken joke glass in our hands. We tried to reassemble it. The stem had snapped, we balanced it against the wall so it looked like it was OK from a distance. Paddy hadn't paid much attention to the joke glass for a long while, it was a bit dusty and we thought he wouldn't notice – at least until we could get our hands on some glue.

Sheer and horrible panic engulfed us both then at that exact moment, when we heard the car coming up the drive. So they wouldn't see us through the living room window, we dived behind the sofa and snaked across the lounge to switch the radio off and then crawled on our stomachs, opening the door a crack to slither through the hall and back into our bedroom. We didn't have time to make sure the sofa was smooth and the pile of the carpet was swept straight. I was shaking and my brother lay on the bottom bunk pretending to read. We waited silently, listening for the inevitable, my heart thumping in my chest. Once, when we were in trouble like this for breaking something, I tried to drink a bottle of Indian ink, I only managed a sip, but I would have rather died of ink poisoning than ever face my stepfather's wrath.

The blood was trembling inside my veins, I paced the bedroom, waiting to see if we had got away with *it* or not. I couldn't stand the waiting; I went into the kitchen. My baby sister was crying, red in the face and shrieking. Mum said it was cold outside, that it might snow, more to herself than anyone. She was seeing to my sister and disappearing into their bedroom leaving me loitering by the kettle and I pretended I was there to make us all a pot of tea.

Salena?

Paddy said towering over me.

Is Gus in the bedroom? How did Gus get in?

I was cornered. I looked at the floor as I told him I let him in through the window and above my head I felt him look down at me with such furious disgust I wished the ground would swallow me up. He opened the very window in question and closed it several times, as if checking the hinges still worked. Then he leant out of the window and inspected the walls, outside and inside, the white carpet, the windowsill, the window ledge, the skirting board for any damage, for shoe prints or dirt marks, all the while yelling,

What's the matter with you kids? Are you stupid? Are you stupid or something?

Whenever he lost his temper, his face flushed reddish and his mouth twisted ugly. He opened a packet of cigarettes and went to put the cellophane in the bin and then he saw the tangerine skins. Two crimes, two huge and terrible crimes. One: Climbing in windows. Two: Taking fruit. It didn't matter how much I hung my head and protested that Mum had said I could have one.

Yes one! One! How many did you take? Can you count? Are you stupid?

Gus was called and we stood side by side in the living room. As was customary we had to put our hands outstretched in front of us and my stepfather had his stick, a piece of willow switch. Paddy was also prone to clipping us around the head, which left a horrible stinging in the senses and a sharp heat in the ear.

What have I told you about taking things without asking?

I was crying while my brother Gus bit his lips and looked at his shoes.

Look at me when I am speaking to you…

My mother stood beside her husband. We were told that we should appreciate the fact that we had a beautiful home, a roof over our heads and food on the table. We were told that Paddy worked very hard to provide for us and my mother told us she was tired of all these fights. She said that we should all try harder and stop making it all so difficult; that we needed to have more respect and gratitude. We were given a couple of whacks across the knuckles with the stick for taking a tangerine and climbing in and out of windows, and were just about to be sent to our rooms without any dinner… when Paddy saw the broken joke glass.

I froze.

Paddy inspected the lounge for other misdemeanours, checking and feeling the back of the television to see if it was hot. Then he felt the back

Springfield Road

of the stereo and found it warm where we'd been listening to the radio. He noticed everything, that the sofa was ever so slightly off-centre and that a tennis trophy had been moved. He questioned us about a kink in the blinds, a scuff in the white carpet and a mark on the paintwork. Lengthy and terrible tirades inevitably followed: *Are you stupid? What were you doing in the living room? Why weren't you in your own bedroom? Why did Gus come inside in the first place? Why did you let him in the window? Are you stupid? Where had you been Gus? Why did you touch my glass? Are you stupid? How dare you play the stereo! Do you know not to touch my things? Are you stupid? Well, are you?*

With stinging palms and ringing ears, my brother and I were in disgrace and sent to our bedroom without any dinner. The row continued burning in the lounge between my mother and Paddy that night. My mother has since told me that they had the biggest fight when she told him he was being petty, that after all it was just only two tangerines and a plastic joke glass that was just collecting dust. They fought. Then, when my mother told him he was going over the top she slapped him, he gave her a good slap back, and all hell broke loose. All we heard was screaming, yelling and then the most awful, deafening, miserable silence.

Lying on his bunk with his back to me, my brother told me it was all my fault. I knew he was right and I was so sorry. Gus hadn't told Paddy it was me that reached up and got the glass down off the shelf, Gus shared the blame. I was weighted, the pockets inside my head rattling with the loose change of guilt. Nobody spoke. There was nothing but the wretched stink of silence interrupted by the distant television cheers of Saturday football. I knew Paddy would be slouched in front of the television, whilst Mum slammed pots and pans in the kitchen, both silent and furious. Gus lay still, facing the wall, also silent. I stood in darkness behind the closed bedroom curtains, pressing my nose against the cold windowpane, watching for night and snow fall. My stash of chocolate bars and crackers in the doll's cot at the end of my bed was already depleted. I was hungry, but I knew we wouldn't be allowed any dinner, so I filled my hunger with regret. Besides, I felt I deserved to be empty because I was bad. A bleak darkness fell and the bare tree branches made the intimidating shapes and faces of monsters against the inky sky, while black ice coated the roads.

34 / swings and slides

At the age of nine, I rehearsed a new sentence: my father committed suicide.

When the other children finally found out and asked me how he died, my honest answer slapped the air. I could feel each of them rehearsing that sentence in their minds, fingering the material of those two unfamiliar words: *Committed. Suicide.* A phrase so heavy with purpose, its final meaning, a piece of information that kills conversation, words that meant something difficult and final was committed and done with intention – it was a sentence you couldn't take back or change.

I heard the other children whisper *Salena's dad killed himself* and I wished they wouldn't. It was the topic of lunch-break and we were sitting in a huddle. Sheila Sparks touched my arm and I looked into her round freckled face, at the hollow blue shadows that lived under her eyes. I shook my head. I knew I shouldn't have said a word to anyone – for weeks this was a private conversation I had been keeping with ghosts, with shadows, nightmares and clouds. I was regretting it now. It was as though my classmates were poking about in the private shrine in my head, moving the flowers and knocking over the candles.

It was windy and Sheila's blue eyes became glassy, I focused on her single fat teardrop like a sliding window and through it I could see her brown freckles. Then I patted her patting hand back, sniffed hard and stood up too. What had been a silent sadness was thickening and becoming some new emotion I had no words for. As they discussed my father's suicide, I believe I began to grow angry. News like this was like fresh bait, it reminded me of seagulls swooping down on bins and tearing old chip packets open. A brassy girl called Joanne Brown looked like her mother down the factory, all she was missing was a fag drooping from her lips, I distinctly recall how she folded her arms as she said,

You'll be all right, girl. Know what? Us lot, we never even ever knew our dad, know what my mum calls him? She calls him a bas-stud! He is one too! He did a

Springfield Road

runner as soon as my mum got herself pregnant with my youngest sister. My nana says, men are all bas-studs... she says it's so!

I flinched at the way Joanne said bastard, the up-north way, as though it was made of two words: bass / stud. I was also very impressed at the way that word came out of her mouth with such vitriolic ease. We all repeated that magic word and it sounded good in our young mouths and to our soft ears. And the first hard scabs formed inside me and over my raw wound.

As the bell rang for the end of lunch break, Kate, another girl in our class announced spikily,

What about my dad... Good riddance to him, he may as well be dead... bas-stud.
As we walked across the playground Sheila confided,

We never hear a word from our pa, Mum says our pa was a right bas-stud too...
My dad was just really unhappy... I began to say.

For a while my classmates tiptoed around me. They let me win at things, they pretended it was my turn when it wasn't. They shared their crisps, fed me segments of oranges and Kit Kat fingers. I was rarely left alone at break-times, I was interrupted when they caught me staring skywards and making out shapes and faces in the clouds.

The truth is, we all seemed to have parents who were in some way or other absent and we all had parents who fought. We all lived in a mess of stepfathers, stepmothers and split up families. Now, looking back, perhaps Anna Parris was my only close friend who had what I considered a sensible and normal family. She had her two real parents that were solid and together, and to me that was the most enviable thing in the world.

***

Sheila's mother was a silver-haired firecracker; a tiny woman with a wheezing laugh that ended in a machine-gun cough. She was a fine example of how much fun it can be to have a single parent and she was older than all our mothers. She seemed to have a very different way of doing things from other mums, an old fashioned way. She washed Sheila's hair in the kitchen sink and let her stay up until past midnight. Mrs Sparks was a chain-smoker who regularly gave the pair of us money to go to the smoky working men's club to get her fags. We'd love it in there, nestling up to the boozy bar to buy fags. They sold sweets and pop, we would loiter there as long as we could without getting noticed, sucking cola bottles, inhaling the stale boozy aroma, blue smoke, foul language, taking in the sight of toothless old men coughing and swigging ales.

Then with our loot of sweets we would retreat to her bedroom to make radio plays. I remember having to press the record and play button at the same time as we recorded our harrowing horror stories. The plot usually required an orphan receiving a beating and so we'd create these sound effects by whipping a belt on the bed or slapping our hands together before the microphone. Once finished, we'd hear ourselves on tape and laugh because Sheila did the same voice for all characters, but for the male parts she'd pull a different face, which obviously could not be translated onto audiotape.

I can picture us now, down the park, standing upright on the swings, bending our knees and swinging in unison. And how on warm days we'd spin upside down on the roundabout, sucking on two pence Mr Freeze ice pops as long as our arms, the raspberry flavour dying our tongues blue. We'd play *dare, truth, kiss or promise*, taking it in turns to knock on doors and run away or go under a jacket with one of the boys. We kissed boys in the dark orange, furry underworld of their parkas. And we'd kiss them up the top of the slide but only to the count of ten – any longer than that count to ten meant you loved them and you'd have to get married.

35 / coffee and sherbert

It was the half-term school holidays and I was passing Tara's house, hurtling down the hill on my bike. When I got to her driveway I felt odd as I remembered I hadn't been there since *that* grey Sunday. The early morning sunlight glinted on the wet black tarmac as I screeched to a halt outside her house. It looked normal, the curtains were open. *Well since I was here and was passing I thought I'd call for you.* I practised it again, *I was passing on my bike and just thought I'd see if you wanted to come out to play or something,* and then I planned to yawn like it was no big deal if she was busy or if she had plans and I'd leave again. I remember waiting until it was OK and wondering when she'd come back to school, so I went and called for her.

Nervously, I knocked on the low letterbox of the glass door. It took a while for anyone to answer, then Mr Collins surprised me by coming to the other door, the kitchen door. He looked different; he had longer hair and sleepy eyes. He was in a hurry, grabbing a slurp of coffee, late for somewhere, work? He looked surprised, almost happy to see me. He invited me in and asked how I was and would I like a coffee? *Coffee?* Then Mr Collins called Tara who came in smiling and in her Mickey Mouse nightie. I was suddenly aware of the time. It was way too early for visitors – perhaps both too early after her mother's funeral and too early in the morning – my brother and I often went out first thing in the mornings during the school holidays, as if we had school to go to. Most kids didn't come out to play until after *Why Don't You...* and the mid-morning cartoons had finished. I felt like I was intruding and I wished I had gone for a nice long bike ride first and killed an hour or two.

Thought you might wanna visitor today or something... I said trying to sound casual.

Tara smiled and offered me coffee telling me, *I like mine black with six sugars.*

She said this as though she was sixteen and all I could say was, *Me too.*

Her dad hollered from the lounge that he couldn't find his car keys and Tara shouted,

They're under the newspapers, by the cushion...

Tara shook her head and rolled her eyes and walked towards the doorway to the lounge,

I'll keep an eye on the kettle in case it boils, I offered.

You don't have to watch it, it's electric...

I looked at her blankly and she explained, *It switches itself off.*

She seemed so grown up. She wandered out to help her father find his keys and I could hear them in the other room.

There.

Where?

Oh for crying out loud, Dad... here!

Oh yeah... Thanks Tara! What would I do without you, Princess!

Mr Collins said he'd left some money on the side for her lunch. They talked about dinner, Tara said she wanted spaghetti and then he laughed and went out the door saying something like, *Again? You'll turn into spaghetti one day, no wonder your legs are so long! Spaghetti legs!*

They kissed and said *I love you* and then he got into his car, beeped the car horn and was gone. Tara's brother was still asleep in his bedroom.

Take your jacket off then. Come on, let's take our coffees in the lounge.

I sat in the lounge and looked at the photos and felt conscious of the silence. Tara reappeared, changed into a stripy t-shirt and purple jeans. She sat with her feet tucked under her bottom and held her mug in a cupped way, as though she was warming her hands. I mimicked her. There was a slight awkwardness as I remembered the last time I was in this house her mum was alive. There was a photo of her mother on the sideboard. The room was messier than before too, with some clothes on the floor and newspapers, but it was really homely and comfortable. Then Tara asked me if I wanted a bit of jam on toast. We watched telly, a black and white *Laurel and Hardy*; they were dressed as cotton-picking slaves with shoe polish on their faces. We talked about school and the netball team we were both in. Well, me as a reserve, Tara actually really on the team. Sitting in her lounge, I remembered how, when she first returned to school she'd quietly thanked me for the card I made her and how I playfully punched her arm and told her it was a real American dollar bill. Now, though, we did not mention the death thing, my death thing or hers. Suddenly, it dawned on me we didn't have to. Instead we deliberated over how to spend the day; it had started to rain again and the school holidays yawned ahead. I suggested we do some colouring and she looked at me and screwed her face up, *Colouring? You are joking?*

Yeah. I just thought…

Colouring?

Tara started laughing, and then coughing and I laughed too, nervously. I felt like an idiot for saying colouring. My mum had told me if I went to see Tara that she might want to be gentle, she might want someone to sit with her, to do some colouring or a collage. Clearly, Tara thought colouring books were for babies. She made more black coffee, spooning in heaped teaspoons of instant powdered granules. Then she washed up the breakfast things, sighing and telling me how she needed her coffee to get her up in the morning. It did taste nice the way she made coffee with six sugars. It was as though the house was her own, and we were both much older and I suddenly blurted, *We should play that we are really old and both sixteen and this is our own house…*

Yes, I know, let's say we are seventeen even… and we share a house, yeah, ace… and let's pretend we have to get ready to go to a disco.

Tara flapped her wet hands excitedly, suds went everywhere and she pulled off her rubber gloves, *Oh I know, I know! Listen to this then!*

Tara turned the TV off and beckoned me down the hallway and into her bedroom. She had a tape of Adam and the Ants' 'Stand and Deliver'. On came the rolling drum beats and we danced. We rewound it and played it again, high as kites on coffee and sugar. We put on eye shadow and lip gloss, we tied our hair up in colourful elastic bands. We bounced madly on her bed and at the top of our voices sang, every word of 'Stand and Deliver'.

We were doing the hand gestures and the dance that particular song required – a stomping pose with the crossing of the arms in front of the face.

After that first caffeine-fuelled day of dancing and lip gloss, that particular half-term holiday I went around to Tara's almost every day. We sang and danced to Sheena Easton, Eurythmics, Grease, Kate Bush and our favourite, Adam and the Ants. We drank lots of sweet coffee and played that we had jobs as secretaries. We sat opposite each other typing on imaginary typewriters. We somehow converted half of her bedroom into an office and the other half into the disco where we'd pretend to go after work to meet our two boyfriends and dance. We chewed gum with our mouths open noisily and pretended to talk on the phone to each other, taking it in turns to be each other's boss or boyfriend.

Yours are really growing now… Tara said to me one day,

No they're not, not like yours, I replied dolefully.

Yours are! Look, so are mine, look at mine…

Tara closed her curtains and lifted her t-shirt to show me her nipples. They were swollen to different sizes, like two sweet plums pointing out in different directions, brown and mauve coloured. I thought hers were amazing and I told her,

Mine hurt sometimes. Do you really think they're growing?

Mine hurt sometimes too but that means they're growing, look at them, yours have grown loads, especially lately. Look at them now, show me them and I'll show you what I mean…

I lifted up my t-shirt to show her and we both stared at my bumpy nipples in the mirror.

My mum calls them bee stings, I complained, and then realised I said 'mum' but Tara grinned and told me, *My gran's got whoppers and she thinks mine are going to be big as hers!*

We stood side by side with our tops up under our chins to compare in the mirror.

See mine were like that, like yours at first, but yours are coming along nicely now…

Tara sounded like she knew what she was talking about. The golden news that mine were growing normally too gave me a rising bubble of excitement inside.

Tara taught me how to smoke sherbert. We'd buy Refreshers, the oblong yellow fruit chew sweets with sherbert in the middle and she'd break them open and roll the sherbet in the sweet wrapper to make cigarettes. Then when they were rolled up, she'd gently blow the sherbert out the other end so it looked like real smoke. Tara also showed me how to take two rolled-up socks and twist them into your vest to make a bra. She taught me that if you tuck the extra vest material up the middle, pull it through and down to make a knot, your vest becomes a kind of sexy bra top with the socks sitting in place like real boobs. After the disco dancing, we would lie on the bed and take it in turns to be the boy and the girl and pretend to kiss, with our mouths closed and our heads smooching mechanically from side to side. We took our socks out of our tops and put them down the front of our trousers so we'd know which of us was being the boy and which was the girl: Sandy or Steve, Candy or Chris. We'd get it wrong and make Chris and Steve kiss.

Oh Chris, I mean Steve…

No, I'm Sandy now…

No hang on, my socks aren't in right then.

I have such vivid memories of Tara and of that particular school holiday. We'd both lost a parent, but she seemed to be getting on with living and I followed her shining example. I remember her once showing me photos of her mother and sharing memories with me, but only once, whilst we waited for the kettle to boil and switch itself off.

We were almost ten years old, but we escaped into caffeine and sugary bubblegum play days, each day inspecting our growing pains. It was all glittery silver disco and lip gloss, it was all pretending we were not where we were, and for that school holiday we were really old and grown-up and all of seventeen.

36 / game, set and match

It was June and although my tenth birthday was coming up that month, June really only meant one thing in our household: Wimbledon. In our street everyone got Wimbledon fever, that particular year everyone was tennis crazy. John McEnroe was making televised tennis dramatic with his outbursts, his infamous tantrums, coining the catchphrase *'You cannot be serious!'* which we in turn mimicked and cried out whilst lobbing tennis balls across the road at each other. After school and under long rose-perfumed, midsummer evenings we hurled grassy-green balls against walls and we sent them crashing against garage doors. Tennis balls got everywhere, on rooftops and in guttering. We bounced them so high they hurtled over the telephone wires.

Sometimes I went with my mother and stepfather to the tennis club. Whilst my parents competed in tournaments, I'd push my sister in her pram and talk with Aunt Doreen. Having a tennis coach as a stepfather ignited an ambition to play tennis to please him. I tried to play tennis, but I was heavy-handed and lacked any of the natural skill or subtlety required. My stepfather even looked a bit like John McEnroe, he had similar curly hair and wore a headband. I saw sharing his enthusiasm for the game as a way to maybe creep into his affections and for that season I even harboured aspirations to be a ball girl at Wimbledon one day. It was the only time I really ever talked about him to my friends. I cringe to admit this, but at school I'd boast, *My stepfather is a tennis coach, he actually goes to Wimbledon every year for the special dinner and for strawberries and champagne and everything.*

On the morning of my tenth birthday I opened a present from my mother of new running shoes. They were two shades of pink and I loved them. I was excited that morning at breakfast, skipping about in the kitchen in my new trainers and pyjamas.

It's my birthday today! I told my stepfather.
Is it? How old are you now then?

I thought he was joking so waited for him to smile. When he didn't, I replied,

I'm ten and, and that means I am now in double figures.

I waited for him to smile like he was only joking, to say he knew how old I was really and *happy birthday*. I held up my leg to show him my new trainers. He nodded but clear and sharp as glass I remember feeling ignored. Mum had made a fuss, telling me it was an important and monumental birthday because I was nearly a teenager. Paddy flicked back at the newspaper, crunching on his toast.

***

At his tennis club there was an older girl who befriended me. Lucy was at least seventeen or eighteen, she wore her blonde hair in a sporty bouncy ponytail and had smooth brown legs. She was being coached by my stepfather and would often ask me to walk with her. We'd take our rackets and balls and walk, bouncing them off the grit on the nearby athletic track. Walking around the circles of white chalk lines, she'd grill me about my stepfather. Lucy asked me about my mother and how long they had been married. She talked a lot, in fact Lucy talked too much – she told me that my stepfather was a brilliant coach, an inspiration, that he was so smart and handsome and on and on she would blather… I played the dumb kid and took all the coke floats and bubblegum screwdrivers Lucy wanted to buy me. It irritated me how much she idolised Paddy and I was jealous of her version of him.

A few weeks later, I remember overhearing Mum on the phone complaining that Paddy was always out at the tennis club and coming in late. Then I heard Paddy and my mother rowing about some girl who had a crush on him. Later my mother quizzed me about these weekly walks, she asked what Lucy talked to me about. I told my mother everything, I told my mum the truth, that Lucy thought Paddy was the bee's knees.

37 / the nightmare

The Montys were Paddy's parents – my step-grandparents. They were Irish Catholics and lived in Surrey. Ma Monty was a scatty, curly redhead who wore her hair in a bouffant bird's nest balanced on her head. Pa Monty was a stern, bruiser of a naval man. Pa Monty was an ex-boxer too and he liked to clench his fist and shake it at us. He'd stand above us like a boxer and growl,

I'll give you a zonker.

He was tough-talking, hard and weathered. They were both a bit scary and mean from a child's-eye view, but they meant well. Ma Monty was partially deaf but never wore her hearing aid and so misheard everything. She and my mother were almost as bad as each other. I can picture them now in the kitchen boiling vegetables or making gravy out of the grease of roasted meats, both with their glasses steamed up over the stove, hovering over a huge broiled ham, and Mum would start,

I'm just going to see if the potatoes are done.
What?
The potatoes.
What tomatoes?
Doesn't matter…
Hang on Lorna, let me see to the potatoes first then tell me…
That's what I said…
What?
What?

Then they'd collide at the stove, both holding a fork to test to spuds.

Meanwhile, in the lounge, Pa Monty gave me swimming lessons. He taught me how to swim front crawl through the air. Lying on my belly across the dining chair, I learned how to straighten up, keep my body in line and scoop the water away with my hands and how to turn my head to breathe.

On the walls of their home were framed black and white pictures, now faded to yellow, of my stepfather as a school boy in an old-fashioned blazer and cap. Next to them stood pictures of a younger, more dapper Ma and Pa. In one picture, a ship dominated the background, while Pa Monty stood upright and smart in his naval uniform and Ma Monty turned to the side and posed holding his arm. Even in black and white she looked vivid. A blazing redhead in scarlet lipstick and fur coat and stockings with black lines running up the backs of her long legs. Now in his dotage, Pa still stood to attention, the skin of his face was lined with purplish threads from sea, salt winds and weather. Ma Monty still wore pillar-box red lipstick and a fur coat and she jangled with gold and pearls just to go to the corner shop everyday.

***

That June then, after my tenth birthday, it was Wimbledon. We were to stay in with Ma and Pa Monty while Paddy and Mum went out for the night to the Wimbledon gala dinner. My stepfather was in a tux and bow tie. My mother looked stunning in her new cocktail dress. It was royal peacock blue chiffon and it floated around her. I thought it was the kind of dress Princess Diana would wear.

It was a small house, Gus and my stepbrother would share the box room and I was sharing a room with my parents and Jo-Ann. I was lying on the makeshift bed on the floor and that is when I heard something I wish I hadn't, words too brutal for a child aged only ten. I stayed quiet and as still as possible, facing the wall, eavesdropping and letting them think I was asleep. Mum was seeing to my baby sister Jo, and she and Ma Monty were talking in hushed whispers. I heard,

What Lorna? Hung himself...?

I could hear the hiss of loud whispers, their jaws clicking, the wetness of mouthed words, and caught only parts of sentences.

...the staircase...

I had the covers over my face as I listened to snatches of what was being said.

It snapped.

Snapped?

...fell... cracked... radiator at the bottom of the stairs...

What?
It broke… split clean…
Ooh no!
…bottom of the stairs, imagine?…
That's terrible, Lorna…!

Jo was being given her milk and I heard her gurgling, soothed by the bottle. The deaf women whispered loudly for a few moments more, then I heard my mother say *shush* and there was a very long pause and then they left the bedroom. I lay in bed and thought about that for a new sentence: *my father hung himself.*

Whenever I had asked my mother how my father died she had avoided telling me any exact details, she just used the word *suicide*. Now I could imagine a noose, the knot and the thread unravelling, the sound as the rope snapped, the crack of the broken bannister and Dad falling, falling and falling. I saw him landing with a thud, his head split open on the sharp edge of the radiator and the brain and blood oozing down the sharp edges of the world below, the carpet, the walls, all thick black blood and the insides of raw sausages. I tormented myself with horrible details, brain tissue and bone, muscle and matter. I pictured a staircase, a balcony and a hallway in a house I had never seen. My father jolting and his feet kicking then swinging lifeless. *He's hanging and I am scared to look up past his feet to look at his face. I just watch his swinging feet and then I hear a snap… he is falling… thud… radiator… crack… dark blood.*

Now I had a whole film to play – I tortured myself picturing my father wobbling on the top of some stairs as though he was jumping from a burning ship, it is careering into an iceberg and either way, fire or ice, it's clearly the end. He couldn't stay and burn, he wouldn't survive if he tried to swim in ice either. He jumps with intention, to certain death.

I imagined the texture of gnarled, thick brown rope against the skin and then I imagined him trying to use his tie or a belt. I had difficulty imagining him knowing something as practical as how to tie a noose, but boys often know things like that. Maybe he didn't tie it well enough and that's why it snapped… *of course… that's why it snapped.* I imagined him waiting for an opportune moment. Self-murder would take purpose, intention and planning. I put myself in his shoes and wondered how he spent his last few hours.

Did he go out walking that dark December afternoon? Let's say he did. It would have been nearly Christmas; the streets would have been garish with a shrill chorus of carol singers, that grating, incessant 'Jingle Bells' pouring from all the shops. I imagined him going to buy cigarettes and then finding himself walking by the water and stopping to buy rope at a chandlers by the docks. I tried to imagine the misery and violence he must have felt towards himself. Perhaps though, he felt eerily calmer knowing he'd made a choice, perhaps it was soothing to know that it would all soon be over. During those last hours he must have been desperate, waiting for the end of waiting; waiting for the raging pain to go away, waiting for a reason not to live, waiting for a reason not to die.

I imagine Dad on the top of the stairs; he swigs neat brandy straight out of the bottle. I imagine him weeping and finding there are yet more tears under there. I imagine every bitter swig taking some of the waiting away, dowsing the fear and the misery in hard liquor. I imagine him convincing himself everyone would be better off without him, that it was for all our good and that none of us would even care. Then I see him suddenly calm, silent and still. With conviction and surety, he sniffs hard and wipes his wet face and grinds his cigarette out. He stands, makes a knot, fastens it rough and tight around his throat. That was it. He made a decision and let go… fade to black.

38 / 69 pink pass

It was a crisp and bright Tuesday on the 11th December 2007. The sky was cloudless, truly blue as we drove through Bristol. The winter sun cast long, cartoon-like shadows. We had seen a sky dog, a beautiful flash of rainbow in the distance, and we drove towards it, taking it to be a good omen. December 11th was the anniversary of my father's death and also my boyfriend Sam's birthday. As Sam drove, his helium-filled birthday balloon bumped lazily against the rear window. I had always imagined I would do this journey on my own. I was grateful for his company.

We travelled in silence, gliding through the traffic. I felt I was following a path, being lead by fate and destiny. I took nothing for granted: my eyes were open, my senses were alert. I found myself admiring the beauty in pedestrian things, sunlight on the river, faces in the rocks by the suspension bridge. We nosed our way through the city towards Shirehampton, counting magpies, finding significance in one for sorrow and two for joy. Uncanny road names gave us old clues that we were close. The hairs stood up on my neck as we passed Hung Road, and then a Springfield Avenue.

My brother Gus stood at the iron gates, alone and smoking a roll-up. He looked lost and cold, tight around his features. He was relieved we had arrived, he said, he had been there since nine that morning. We'd arranged to meet at the graveyard gates at midday but he'd got there keen and early. He'd found it, he said and nodded: this was it. It wasn't a wild goose chase; this really was the final resting place of our father. I felt a quick, sharp wave of envy that Gus had been there first, without me, that he'd had time alone with the grave. Gus showed us to the local shops and I went into a flower shop and bought pink freesias and a small pink rose bush. The roses, I decided, were from Mum.

My father's plot address is 69 Pink Pass. Even in death his grave number is loaded with innuendo. When I telephoned and told my mother, she said, *That's your dad for you, he was always the one with both the wife and the bit on the side. He just couldn't make-up his mind what he wanted.*

When we entered the cemetery gates, magpies flew in pairs above us. This is it then, this is where he is, I remember thinking, I am going to see my father once and for all. I had telephoned ahead and the cemetery caretaker was there to show us to the plot. Although Gus knew the way, we followed him, walking in single file. I walked last, I walked slowly, I wasn't sure how I would feel to see it. I was afraid I would feel nothing. I was afraid I would feel everything. For all my life I had imagined this moment in film noir images. In my mind I always imagined I would be doing this alone under a thundery black sky, collapsing melodramatically to my knees, dragging at clumps of wet grass, sodden earth under my nails, trying to climb in or dig him up, drunk and inconsolable with rage, with fury and grief. But there was no stormy weather, no melodrama. The wintry light was primrose yellowish, the cemetery serene, peaceful and calm. On a modest, arched headstone of grey shiny granite I found the words,

PAUL GODDEN
POET & MUSICIAN
1941 – 1981

So, there you are. I thought it was nice that they included Poet and Musician. I am sure he'd have liked that. For a moment I felt as though I was seeing my past and my future, my own grave. I stared at the name on the stone and did the maths – he was only forty years old. *How long do I have left?* I looked at my brother, who looked down at the grave. We stared in silence at the headstone and the grass for a very long time. It was tidy, the gravestone was tasteful. I imagined his funeral, more than twenty-five years ago, and I wondered who had been there. I started to feel faintly embarrassed and awkward, as though I were gate crashing. I had made all these plans of how I would like to react and they all suddenly seemed far-fetched. My father was long gone; he wasn't here at all, not really. I wasn't sure what to say, so instead I crouched down and kept quiet and thought about the person my mother loved to describe, the bones and the heart of the man six feet under the ground, under the grass roots. In my head I said *there you are, there you are, I found you finally, nice to meet you again…*

I knelt on the wet cold grass and touched the letters. Although they were engraved into the granite, some of the white paint had faded. No religious waffle or even a *greatly missed father and son*, just his name, his poetry and his music. There were no other flowers there, no evidence of recent visits. I was jumpy and half-hopeful that we'd be caught here, that someone might catch us trespassing in the past, others he'd loved, others he left behind. Gus said he thought he had seen a young lady earlier who may have been someone, but she went to a different grave. We both dared to hope that by finding the dead we might find the living.

And suddenly, I felt ridiculous. I felt self-piteous, pathetic and I hated myself for making such a fuss. *Is that all there is then? Is this all there is then, Dad?* I felt cheated.

Directly above our heads the sky was a chilled December blue. Two planes crossed paths, white lines making an X to mark the spot, or maybe it was a kiss. I sat with my legs crossed on the cold muddy grass, running my thumb over the letters on the headstone. I brushed it clean, the ledge where the flowers go. I heard Gus saying that the stone was protected by the hedge beside it. He said Dad's was the only grave without morning frost. I placed the pink freesia and the roses beside my brother's pink carnations. I took a swig of brandy and then poured some on the earth at the head end. *There you go, cheers, Dad.* Sam asked if we'd like it if he planted the roses, he said they'd last longer. I stood back and watched as Sam knelt down and dug into the earth with a stick, getting mud on his hands. As he jabbed the stick into the earth, I pushed away horrible thoughts of being underground and seeing the stick from the underside, the view of the tip of the stick from inside my father's coffin. In horrified flashes I pictured my father's skeleton.

Sam poured water on the freshly planted rose bush and I told him indignantly he had just watered down Dad's brandy. I realised that was when I felt an awful aching in my chest and throat. I squirmed inside, hurting. I asked Sam to put the roses in straight, they were slightly askew and too far to the right. This was me trying to get things perfect, lost in a compulsion that it mattered, that we had to get things in the right order.

Springfield Road

Sam dug up the roses and shifted them along to the left a bit. *Better?* Sam asked gently and touched my sleeve. I nodded, *yes, that's better*. I was still thinking about the watered-down brandy. I took another little sip and poured some more straight onto roses.

Sam wandered off to leave us alone and I felt Gus put his arm across my shoulder.

I cried when I came on my own this morning, but there were workmen and I…

Gus didn't finish his sentence. I heard him crying. Just like when we were children, his weeping moved me. It sounded like off-key laughter. I wanted it to be laughter. I was hoping he'd laugh instead. I kept my jaw clenched tight until it started aching. Hearing him crying, my eyes grew hot, but I pushed it all down. I whimpered gruffly, a short and soundless sob. Then Gus said thank you. He said in a broken voice,

Thank you, for finding him… Salena.

Then Gus said, *oh dear*, and sniffed, holding me close around the shoulders. It was Gus and me again, Gus and me and our real dad. This was what was meant that day when we went fishing all those years ago. This was the unsaid, this was the conversation and this was what we wanted to find together. I closed my eyes tight as a school bell rang on the other side of the fence. The silent cemetery was littered with the sounds of children's laughter and a cacophony of kids shouting and singing. I liked that my father could hear children at play.

Gus wandered off towards the car and it was when I was alone at my father's grave, I took out a piece of writing from this book. I read the last paragraph under my breath to the headstone and saw it for what it was: I saw that once upon a time there was one day, it was a once in a lifetime moment, and now I was here. That was all we ever had, my father and I, and now I was a thirty-five-year-old woman, standing in a cemetery staring at the letters on a headstone, trying to make sense of my need to see this, rationalising my sense of the importance of counting magpies, sky dogs, flight path kisses and street names. I started to weep but pushed it down again and coughed. I told myself *cowboys don't cry*. I don't know, I have no idea why I was trying to be a cowboy about it.

I wondered if that was all there was to a life and a death. Perhaps the most we can hope for is that twenty-five years after we die, someone may remember us, that someone will come looking for us and put roses on our grave. All in the name of what could have been, all for the promise of those *what ifs* and *buts*. Is that the most we can hope for? I felt bitter and said goodbye and walked away. I left the writing in a sealed plastic wallet by the flowers and walked toward the exit, hands in pockets and shoulders hunched, shivering. I couldn't help looking back to see my father's granite headstone, so small next to the grander graves, and so very small in the grand scale of things. I faltered and found it impossible to actually leave and for a few minutes I was that lost little nine-year-old girl, looking for her father in a crowd, looking at his grave among all the others.

I remembered all the anniversaries and the 11ths of all the Decembers before. Days when I had wandered into random churchyards to cry at the feet of strangers' headstones and lit candles in unfamiliar churches. There were times at school when I'd sit in my classes silent and withdrawn for that whole day. The times when I had walked miserably along the city streets of London alone, searching for ways to numb this feeling I got every year on this day. I was pale as the rain and thin as December, and, as usual, so skint in the weeks before the holidays. I walked down Oxford Street, with Christmas music jarring me, surrounded by normal, happy, plump holiday families with rosy cheeks and bellies warmed with mulled wine and mince pies. There were times I sat and drank by fires, burning writings to my father so he could read them in the smoke. And times as a teenager I'd cry and throw pebbles into the sea at Hastings, searching for him and a way to let go.

I bowed my head and wept into my scarf and coat collar, kicking a stone at a puddle through fat hot tears. I found I couldn't leave the graveyard. I kept looking back and then walking towards him. I couldn't let go, I couldn't just leave. *I don't want to go now I have found you, Dad.* In the back of my head I heard the reply, *you are on your own now kiddo*, and with that I cried – *Am I on my own now, is this really goodbye? Will I still be watched over? Will I be able to sleep with the lights off? Will I still wake up sometimes and feel something, someone, at the end of my bed?*

Perhaps you were never there, maybe I really am blessed and lucky and it wasn't my father's intervention that ever helped or guided me.

Springfield Road

Perhaps I was always on my own. Perhaps there are no such things as ghosts and guardian angels – *you are on your own now, kiddo* – maybe we were all always alone.

I heard children laughing and playing in the sunshine in the school next door, alerting me to the poetry and beauty in living things. I heard a squawk of a crow and my tears dried as I watched it take flight overhead. I looked up and felt a rush of relief, a certainty and reaffirmation that everything was going to be better. I said several times out loud, *it's all going to be all right now*. I felt like I had closed a door and opened another inside myself. It was as though this wouldn't hurt quite as much again. This was the beginning of healing, the start of this story and not the end. I finally had the evidence I needed. Maybe now I would no longer look for my dad in strangers' faces, or seek him across a crowded world. I had been given the chance to say hello and goodbye properly and I walked away under the canopy of tall trees this time without looking back.

We drove away in convoy towards London. Behind us and in the west, the winter sun set in a vivid and breathtaking fire of scarlet and fuchsia. The birthday balloon bumped against the car window. At the back of my mind I remembered a poem I had been writing, *Today I Found My Father*, and as we drove, I remembered the ending lines; *and the nine year old inside me, the lost little girl is found, she is released like balloons into the sky.*

I played with the mud on my fingers and under my nails. I looked over at Sam's hands, filthy on the car steering wheel, and at the muddied knees of our jeans, and felt somehow comforted, that we were both covered with earth from my father's grave, there was something real, tangible about it. I smoked a cigarette and listened to the radio but whenever I closed my eyes I saw my father's granite headstone. With the lull of the engine and the car heating I started to feel sleepy, memorising every moment and detail, the exact fading letters, the rose and pink petals against the flecked grey headstone. I put that image firmly in my mind, just as though it was a photograph of his face that I wouldn't allow to fade. Just like the eternal picture I have imprinted of the time I remember looking into my father's eyes, how he crouched to my height and looked into my face, and I swear I saw love and that was all we ever had, Dad.

PART FOUR – SPRING

the knee-high banana yellow platform heeled boots

39 / mickey

When we visited the Montys in Woking I had a friend called Mickey. I must briefly mention her here because I never forgot her. I wanted to be like her. When I think of her now, I imagine her at Glastonbury or The Burning Man Festival with a whole crew and circus, I imagine her as a wild and free sprit on a permanent rock and roll world tour.

I remember she was a tomboy from a gypsy family. She was wild with long black curly hair falling out of her ponytail. It was a great and memorable friendship because we'd just pick up where we left off each holiday and it was always as if no time had passed, as if time were rubber. Mickey whistled and walked with a boy's gait, slouching with her hands in her pockets. She was skinny and shabby and always had holes in her plimsolls. I liked that about her, I was scruffy too. She spoke like a Cockney, dropping her Hs and saying *I ain't going…* rather than *I en't going…* the Midlands slang I used.

Mickey couldn't walk past anything without investigating it. If she saw a low branch she had to swing off it, if there was a post she had to try to leapfrog it. She skidded on any surface that promised you'd get a good slide out of it, especially in supermarkets. She always had some bruises or a cut covered with a dirty plaster. She rooted around in bins, skips and gutters, stuffing things in her pockets saying to herself, *That'll be 'andy…*

Abandoned shopping trolleys were a favourite. We had many precarious, white-knuckle rides in shopping trolleys we'd found. I remember on one occasion Gus and I pushing her up a steep hill and then letting go. The trolley zoomed away and we ran down after it and found her in a crumpled pile in some bushes at the bottom of the hill. She brushed herself off and laughed crazily. She didn't show it and I am sure she was hurt, but that was Mickey.

I remember we'd go to visit Truck-Man. He was an old tattooed hippy with long hair and a grey beard and he lived in the car park behind the shops. His truck was not always parked there, but when it was, he'd let Mickey and me nose about inside. It was bigger than you'd think inside. It had a real toilet, a sink and a bed, loads of cassettes, books and his guitar. He sat on the bunk and rolled cigarettes while we poked about, and he let us sit up in the cab and talk on his CB radio. *Roger Roger… over and out.* He said he could hear the police signal on it and we tried to listen in. He would make tea in stained chipped mugs to demonstrate that the kettle worked. We thought it was cool to be allowed to look inside his truck. I remember the tapes he played too and in particular that song about *The Marrakesh Express*. We watched him playing guitar with his long yellow dirty nails with a fag drooping from his tar-stained beard.

Heading to the swings, Mickey said she'd like a truck like that one day: *Imagine if you had one of them, you'd be free to go anywhere. House on wheels, you could just pitch up and take a snooze, then have a cup of tea and drive off as free as a bird!*

As she said this, she made a little run and extended her arms like wings as if to fly and said,

You could travel the world with no cares, just you and your truck, your own kettle and stuff, you could even go to France.

You could go further than France even!

Yeah, yeah, Sal! You could go further than France even!

America.

Yeah America, imagine that! How could you drive to America though?

Dunno Mickey, under the Atlantic… I know, I know! Mine would be a submarine truck?

Ha! Then mine, mine would be a flying truck.

If mine goes underwater and yours is a flying truck, I reckon I'd like yours more if it's going to fly.

Me too, I'll tell you what lets both get one of each, yeah… Or I know… we could get trucks that fly and go underwater at the same time.

We stole matches from Pa Monty's garden shed and went down into the woods behind the swings. We feasted on sour fizzy cherry bomb sweets, salt and shake crisps downed with cans of fizzy dandelion and burdock. Mickey taught me to smoke. She sniffed knowingly and, with her dirty bitten nails and bony fingers, showed me how to straighten out and smoke a fag butt she'd found in the gutter. She lit it and took first drag, making it look easy, then passed it to me. I tried puffing on it, but it was disgusting and it made me cough. Mickey took it back, holding the ashy butt expertly between her thumb and finger and gave it a good pull, then she collapsed in fits of coughing, her eyes watering as I banged her on the back.

We were always busy with mischief and on missions, making fires with cardboard, crouching down and blowing into our cupped hands over smoking twigs and melting plastic. We stank of smoke and tree bark and our clothes were stained moss green and filthy. Leaning logs against trees, we karate-kicked them to break them up for firewood and we smashed up dank wooden crates. We spent hours in the woods by the river, amongst the broken prams, shopping trolleys and junk. Best of all we climbed inside a burnt out, rusted old car, with ivy on the bonnet and growing inside but the steering wheel and gear stick still intact.

We never talked about any of the outside world or the crazy adults, why would we? It was about escaping, running away, smoking and making fires. Instead we felt tough if we managed to smoke fag butts without coughing. We imagined driving to wild places in that mildewed, rotten and rusted-up car, which to us would be capable of being both a submarine and a plane. We had a secret camp and a burnt out car in the undergrowth, we didn't need nothing and we didn't need nobody. We acted like we could sleep out there any time we liked – but we never did.

40 / six times six

My stepfather had a special stick, a switch reserved for hitting us. I have no idea where he got it, but it appeared in our bedroom one day and was thereafter used mostly to hit our outstretched hands. I can distinctly remember Gus and I putting it precariously behind the heavy books on the top bookshelf, hoping the encyclopaedias would fall on Paddy's head and kill him the next time he reached for it. Needless to say the books never came crashing down onto our stepfather's head and he lived on and the use of the switch continued. My mother wasn't usually witness to these episodes. I suppose if she heard a commotion coming from our room, she assumed it was Paddy sorting out another sibling squabble, and that was often the case.

My stepfather liked to keep us on our toes. If he found some mud on the precious white carpet, he would come into our bedroom, inspect the soles of our shoes to identify the culprit then demand we polish them all as punishment. We didn't own many shoes, but we had to polish them perfectly to his almost military liking. On other occasions he'd come into our room, stand in front of my brother and me, and demand answers to maths problems

Six times six?

We looked at him blankly, neither of us daring to speak or move. I knew if I said the answer then I would have to watch Gus getting hit; and if Gus answered correctly then I would get it. Gus would always remain silent as Paddy would repeat.

Six times six?

Thirty-six

I was asking your brother! Are you stupid?

After my father's death I often found myself in terrible rages and sometimes I was unable to contain angry tears. It took years to try to learn how to manage these episodes once they started. One night, my brother and mother were both out, I was alone in my bedroom and looking for

Springfield Road

a worksheet I had to finish for school homework. I couldn't find it and I began ripping the bedroom apart, as I looked for it, I worked myself up in floods of furious tears. It felt as though there was a pressure valve in my head, and once I opened it a little bit, much more would follow. I screwed up and tore apart papers that were the wrong ones. I even bit them and jumped on them and slapped inanimate objects as though they were hiding my particular piece of paper on purpose. I hit the side of my own head with my fists and sobbed. Eventually, I collapsed onto my knees, hitting myself in the temple with my fist. My teeth were clenched so tightly that my jaw hurt. I was curled over, growling and bawling into the carpet.

I looked up hearing the bedroom door fly open. My stepfather stood there and saw me in this hysterical mess, amongst the ripped paper all over the floor and the books all strewn. Seeing him there made me howl even harder. He told me off, telling me to stop making a racket, to shut up and stop grizzling, he was furious that I had woken my baby sister. I cried even louder, my head was hot and throbbing. He must have seen I had worked myself into a state but he lost any patience he may have had. He picked me up by the scruff of the neck so I was standing, my legs buckling under me. He shook me and asked me again if was going to be quiet, and then he lifted and threw me down, somehow clouting me mid-air. I landed face first on the bedroom floor. He yelled at me to bloody keep it down, to clear all my crap away and behave. Then, as suddenly as he had appeared, he left. I picked myself up from the floor and felt my mouth. My bottom lip was bleeding a little. I looked in the mirror and the sight of blood stopped me dead. I was stunned. It was stinging. I looked again at my lip in the mirror and sucked it. I blew my nose and saw blood on the tissue. I examined it then threw it in the bin. I felt very calm as I tidied up the torn pieces of paper I had thrown around the room. I put everything neatly back in its proper place. I was numb – the physical shock somehow counterbalancing or quelling the fury. Once the bedroom was immaculately tidy, I made my bed and then lay on top of it and stared blankly at the ceiling, waiting for tomorrow to start.

I never spoke of that night or other times like these; I didn't tell Mum, I felt like I had made a racket and had a tantrum and I deserved it. I knew I had to learn to control this rage, the fury and the grief I was feeling. Looking back, I suppose this attention from my stepfather was better than being ignored. His temper was his feedback. To be honest, I am not sure how I would have reacted if my stepfather had ever put an arm around me or hugged me, any affection from him would have been alien. Around this time a double bed sheet was hung across the centre of our bedroom. We dismantled the bunk beds to make two separate single beds. The sheet was to give the illusion of two bedrooms in one. We were running out of ideas and out-growing the rooms of the bungalow – and of this story.

41 / the red suitcase

Under the bottom bunk, Gus's bed, was my mother's red suitcase. It was battered and covered with peeling old stickers of foreign countries. Occasionally, on rainy days, I'd remember it, drag it out and go through its secrets. There was an old photo album with *Cyprus* written on the cover in gold lettering. Inside were photographs of my mother as a skinny teenager, her cocked head looking too big for her body and her face not yet grown to fit her big smile. She was dressed like Nanny, the two of them in identical outfits, wearing lace gloves, standing side by side, squinting in the tropical sun.

My favourite photos were a sequence of pictures of a wild looking fancy dress party. I didn't recognise anyone but my mother. In one picture she stuck her tongue out at the lens. In another, a man with a comic moustache picked her up, twirled her around and he nearly dropped her. The party people were all laughing and moving, their elbows stuck out like chickens dancing the twist. My mum was dressed like a pirate, wearing a beard and an eye patch. I wished I could turn the volume up on these images, and hear all the laughter and the music. And later in the album there were the few photographs of us as babies with Dad.

A flat yellow envelope held all my mother's stunning modelling shots and contact sheets. She was so beautiful; in some she was lying on sand dunes and in others she was dressed in go-go dancer's clothes – a waistcoat, top hat and black, short wig – and looked like Liza Minnelli. And I remember there was the silk, burgundy and pink, paisley cravat that had once been my father's. The material was crumbly and worn, I sniffed at its musty perfume of roses and cinnamon.

That red suitcase was like a Russian doll with hidden pockets and bags within where I'd discover theatre programmes and old bus tickets, silver glitter stick-on stars and gold eye shadows, handkerchiefs folded around lost single earrings, bags of beads and hippy jewellery and four-leaf clovers wrapped in tissue. There was a bag of wigs, a pair of knee-high banana yellow platform heeled boots and a tiny black PVC minidress.

This was the evidence of my mother's life before I was born. Her triumphs as a young athlete in the All England championships; her Olympic dream and her Royal Ballet dream; her Gold medals and *Swan Lake* dreams; her teenage years in Hong Kong and Cyprus, and also her wild go-go dancing days. My mum used to hint that she had partied and performed with a cool sixties crowd, mentioning the likes of Englebert Humperdinck, Tom Jones, Stevie Wonder and Georgie Fame. With her best mate Leslie, Mum was the tall skinny dark one and Leslie the tall blonde and the way my mum tells it, the world was oyster-like for the pair of them. During the day, she had a civil service job before she met my dad. She told me they made her sign the official secrets act. I used to imagine my mum was a spy, that one day I'd find her fake passports and a gun in that suitcase. My mum was a spy and she used the modelling and go-go dancing as a cover – but accidentally she went native when she fell for my dad.

The truth was it always felt as though my mother could drag her suitcase out from under our beds and slip back into herself if she wanted to. I thought of these things as her superhero costume. That she could stick the glittery stars back on her face, put on the yellow platform boots and use a bus ticket from before to get back to then and who she really was.

***

My mother was often on the phone for hours talking *grown-up stuff* and chain-smoking. I'd play peek-a-boo with my sister, holding her on my knee whilst eavesdropping on these long conversations, often with Aunt Doreen. Mother suspected that Paddy was having an affair with a woman from his work. I heard her saying his car was spotted, parked up on one of the country lanes with the windows steamed up. It was sleazy and it was almost the last straw.

Then one day I came home from school to find my mother dressed beautifully in her red suitcase clothes. It was four in the afternoon and she was in full make-up. She was stunning, immaculate in a long flowing gypsy skirt, patterned with huge purple, lilac and orange flowers. She wore a belt of bells and a bobbed black Cleopatra wig. We went out together, strolling down Braybrooke Road, the High Street and through the village. Everybody looked, cars slowed down and the people inside turned and stared. I pushed Jo-Ann in the pram as my mother walked by my side with a confident stride and her head held high. My mother looked sensational and she kept repeating to me,

This is how I looked when he fell in love with me… I think you-know-who needs reminding.

Every time she said it she seemed stronger, more convinced as she said,

You know what I think? I think a certain someone has forgotten exactly whom he married…

We walked past Mark MacGowan's place and his mum was out front in pink rubber gloves, watering the flowers and rinsing the car with a hose in her hand.

Wow! Lorna!

They talked above my head for a very, very long time. I played with Jo. My mother was saying things like, *This is who I was before, this is what I looked like before he married me I think someone needs reminding…*

Mrs MacGowan grinned and patted my mum's arm. She said things like,

You show him Lorna, that's right…

When Paddy came home and saw her he chuckled,

Ha ha ha! What's the big occasion then? What's with the get up? Did I miss something? Are we going to a fancy dress party or something, what's with all this then, hey?

Before they started to argue, I was told to go outside and play with my sister in the front garden. Much later, I saw my mother had been crying and was back in her dowdy jeans and jumper. Hugging her, I felt as though we were in some unspoken alliance, perhaps we were silently unified by the finality of Dad's death, but the worm turned and my mother wasn't taking any more nonsense. She had borne my stepfather a child but this didn't strengthen their bond, they were not closer for their new daughter, if anything quite the opposite. I sensed there were some great changes in the air.

42 / big lessons

There were tears on the last day at Loatlands, our little village primary school. I cried and hugged my classmates whilst saying goodbye to Anna Parris and Sheila Sparks – we roared our eyes out as though we'd never see each other again – and some of them I really didn't. It is funny how even now I remember them all, the names from the school register: Teresa Fitzpatrick, Hannah Parry, Kate O'Keefe, Shelley Luxon, Joanne Green, Claire Maslen, Claire Munday, Janet Reay, Tammy James, Nicola Hughes, Jason East, Darren White, Christopher Perkins and Anthony O'Donnell.

We were not all going to the same secondary schools, we were spreading out and beyond the comfort of the village. No more walking up and down the hill, chubby-faced, sleepy-eyed, scabby-kneed with our hands full of blackberries. No more sitting on the gate and feeding crab apples and grass to the old horse. No more lolling about making daisy chains or charging with war cries into the long grass of the backfields. No more soft, easy teacher reading us milky afternoon stories.

Now we had to wear stiff white shirt collars, ties and blazers and we'd have real homework. We had new tin pencil cases with protractors and compasses to learn how to use. We had to take the school bus up the hill to the big school where the older kids smoked and gobbed on you from the top deck. We were told the big kids stole your lunch money and flushed your head down the toilet when you were a new first year.

I remember the night before my first day, how my new school uniform hung on its hanger looking like a headless ghost of a schoolgirl in the dark. September skies were crisp and blue and russet leaves gathered in the gutters. We were scared, like stiff frozen penguins, in the queue at the bus stop in our new uniforms and sensible shoes. We stared up in awe at the older kids smoking and swearing, pushing and shoving past us to get to the front.

Montsaye Secondary School was a castle compared to our tiny village school. I joined the swimming club and skipped lunch just so I could swim

Springfield Road

every lunch break. My blazer was huge on me, my tie was worn with pride. I was very keen. We rushed to find friendships to replace those we missed from primary school. These alliances ended in tears. Eleven-year-old girls fell out and made up every week. We were two-faced and fickle, giggling over special sign languages and sending notes to each other using secret words and code names. I took after-school classes in athletics, drama and music. I tried to learn the euphonium and then the cornet. I played jazz instruments and ran in cross-country competitions – with my lips pressed against the cold brass and my feet never fitting into my mothers old spikes – I felt I was literally following in my parents' footsteps.

Every morning my mother made me take cod liver oil. It was bitter, foul stuff. One wintry morning I refused to take it. My mother angrily asked me why and I said,

Because it makes me sick! All the way to school! Every morning!

Really? Why didn't you say? Maybe I'll see if I can get the tablets instead.

She told me if I had spoken up I would not have had to take it and I took note of this.

43 / runaway

I will never forget the morning my brother went to school with a black eye. That morning the rooms had the kind of silence you find in a house where illness has been, as though something got lost and sick, there was a scrubbed wet bit of living room carpet, a scent of bleach. In my memory that particular morning had a foul, greasy air, it stuck to the skin and coated the inside of the nose.

I absorbed myself in the routine of morning class. There was the usual talk about last night's television. Somebody picked on somebody else's new pudding-bowl haircut. Whilst I replayed the events of the night before, and in my head I imagined scenes where I ran in and saved the day. I hated the passive role I played as onlooker and witness. I felt guilty for being the girl and being younger. Perhaps if I had been older, if I had been a boy then it would be me sitting with a black eye in class today.

I listened. I couldn't do anything else. I listened at the door to the living room and so I saw nothing. Gus had been summoned to the lounge by stern voices and then I heard shouting. I crept out of our bedroom and crouched down small in the hallway, between the doors leading to the two bedrooms, the bathroom and the lounge. I knelt on the white carpet, rolling balls of white carpet fluff between my fingers. If someone came I planned to dart back to the bedroom where I had a book lying open on my bed.

I heard Paddy read my brother the riot act, the list of his crimes. This was not such an unusual scene: an angry father figure reprimanding a stormy teenage boy about his CSE mock exams or lying about a party or smelling of cigarettes. Then the teenage boy digs himself in deeper by denying everything as the adult becomes more irate and impatient. We have ringside seats and we mouth the answers. We know it's a trick question. The answer is to apologise. Own up to everything, act humble and contrite, say sorry a thousand times and maybe if you are lucky, you will just get grounded and it will all blow over.

Springfield Road

This time though, my brother was defiant. He got tongue-tied, his answers became mumbled and confused, his story came out different each time. From the wings, I heard him slip into slang and I tried to nudge him the answers telepathically. To use the letter H before words like *haven't* and say *cannot,* not *ken't.* With each misuse of the Queen's English, Paddy grew more vitriolic.

Gus seemed to always be in trouble with my stepfather. This wasn't an isolated incident, but this was the worst in my memory. What was his crime this particular time? Was it that he came in late after curfew? Was it simply that he was a normal teenager dreaming of living with his friends' freedoms? Or that he was growing into a young man and becoming some kind of threat? I don't remember and, as usual, the crimes were never as memorable as the punishments.

I was frozen there, by the door, crouching down. I stared at the door hinge with the bits of white paint on it and the place where the carpet and wall meet the skirting board, my eyes misting over. All I could do was be there, listening, just feeling everything. I wished that Mum would speak so I could tell if she was there in the room. I wished that my stepfather would back down and be gentler. I wished that Gus would say sorry, accept blame and let it pass over like a black cloud. I wished that my brother and I were smarter and faster and more like the kind of kids Paddy liked, more like his real kids. Mostly though, I wished I was as small as the piece of fluff between my thumb and first finger, so I could cram myself in between the wall and skirting and disappear beneath the carpet.

Then with the first blow and the bang that followed I jumped out of my skin. I heard a heavy weight thrown against the very door my ear was pressed against, and I leaped to the other side of the hallway. I guessed that perhaps that had been my brother's back hitting the other side of the door between us. It sounded like someone fell, there was a scuffle, something got knocked over. There was a crash accompanied by the sound of a struggle. Maybe my brother threw a punch, and was fighting back, maybe he got one in. With all that boxing Gus did, it was bound to come to blows one day. My mouth was dry, my heart thudded. My mouth filled with the metallic taste of fear and I could not move, frozen by awful, conflicting feelings, until finally I heard Mum scream, *That's… ENOUGH… STOP!*

I ran into the bedroom to pretend to read a book. Gus was sent to our bedroom while Mum and Paddy continued shouting. My baby sister started crying from the other room.

After it was all over, Gus climbed into bed and we whispered in the dark.

Are you all right Gus?

No.

I forget what was said exactly, but I will always remember the dread. Mum and Paddy were having the most terrible fight once Gus had been sent to the bedroom and we passed fear and blame like a hot coal between us.

I remember lying in bed in the dark, hearing Mum and Paddy fight, and then that horrible silence. I listened to Gus's breath calm, his restlessness cease, and I sensed him falling asleep. While he was sleeping his eye grew purple and swollen.

Again, my mother has told me that she slapped my stepfather and told him he had gone too far and yet again all hell broke loose. I switched the light off and climbed into my bed and I listened. I'll never forget the next morning and how ashamed I felt when I saw that my stepfather had given my Gus a black eye.

***

My brother got into some scrapes as a youth and the police came to the door a handful of times. Once they came because Gus and some friends climbed into somebody's house. While the other boys were upstairs in the bedrooms rooting around for things to steal, for money or jewellery, my brother sat in the strange kitchen and ate all the chocolate biscuits and drank the milk. This was my brother, the kind of lad who just wanted to be able to watch telly, eat nice things and be left alone. All Gus ever wanted was a quiet easy life, without melodrama and confrontation. However, the fact remained that some jewellery and things were stolen that night and hidden. The police were called and a week or so after the event, they came knocking on our door looking for my brother. Gus was made the scapegoat – Mum always said in his defence that he was easily led.

To this day, Gus belly laughs about it. He swears he just sat in the strange dark kitchen and ate all the chocolate biscuits. I believe him, I know my brother: a packet of chocolate wagon wheels is worth all the gold in the world to him. What use was jewellery to my brother? Sharing a bedroom with his irritating little sister in a tiny bungalow, he was left no privacy for secrets and no safe hiding places. Once the police had come and gone, Paddy leathered him for it. Gus had to do youth community service on Saturdays while I believe the other boys got away scot-free, which I never thought was fair.

Mostly though, the police came because Gus started to run away from home. He ran away a good few times, and on each occasion Mum called the police and gave them another recent school photograph. I remember their efficient manners, their little black notebooks, the way they noted every tiny detail, everything Mum said they scribbled down. Mum chain-smoked fags, worried sick, her eyes red and watery. Deep down, I was so impressed each time my brother ran away again. He managed to hitch rides heading south with lorry drivers. By the time the police caught up with him, he had covered hundreds of miles, across the whole country, all the way from Northamptonshire to Hastings, to Springfield Road and Grandpa George.

Until now, I never told a soul, but I saw Gus go. One night I saw him, get dressed and silently open the bedroom window. I asked him to take me with him. In fact, I begged him, but he told me I was too young, I wouldn't be able to keep up, and that it wasn't safe for girls. He told me I had to stay to cover for him and look after Mum and Jo. He held his finger up to his lips for me to be quiet. I loved him then, so very much, in the darkness. And so I obeyed him when he asked me to close the window after him and go back to bed. I thought he was brilliant and brave. I let him go.

Afterwards, I lay in bed listening to the night and imagining his journey. He would have trouble getting through the rusty back garden gate without it creaking. Then he would have to pass down the side of the house, remembering not to tread on the wobbly grate, which I also didn't hear. The crucial point would be when he would have had to pass the living room window, on the very other side of which sat Mum and Paddy watching late-night television. I pictured it all, my brother legging it up The Ridings and turning the corner onto the high road.

There would have been miles of black open lanes, nothing but night and solitude. There would be rustling in the woods, night creatures; wolves, badgers, foxes in the shadowy ditches and hedgerows. Acres of fields with sleeping animals and the jingling of scarecrow bells and tin cans. There would be so much black ahead and surrounding him, just the occasional flash of oncoming traffic, a sprinkling of car lights. I wondered whether he would hide when a car came or if he'd stick his thumb out. I wondered if the driver might be the Moors Murderer or the Yorkshire Ripper. Restless in my bed, I imagined my brother jogging steadily to keep warm, with his hood up and his fists clenched in determination, his breath visible, his heart racing in his chest. I didn't imagine him being at all scared.

I pictured Gus running down dark, open country roads until the streetlights of Desborough were just a glint in the distance behind him. He ran and then he spat up a ball of phlegm with a snort from the back of his nose, the way he always did, flicking it off his teeth and tongue and flobbing it onto the wet tarmac. He wiped his nose on his sleeve, looked behind him and saw how far he had gone and how far he had to go. He thought of the road ahead, maybe he was driven by the thought of his destination, of Hastings. He'd look behind him to see the bungalow, the street and the whole bleak town become inconsequential and finally disappear. Until we were a blot of lights on the landscape that grew smaller than an expiring star.

44 / one knife, one fork, one cup, one plate

Gus had to finish his exams and the tension in the bungalow continued. Until one Sunday morning, my brother and I were woken by the sound of an argument and a slammed door. My stepfather had driven off leaving my mother sitting on her bed in tears nursing a bloody nose and a cut on the bridge of her nose that would later leave a small scar. She said she had knocked it on the wardrobe door. I got her some tissues and we switched the kettle on. Then I took my reluctant brother by the hand into the dining room where Mum was drinking a cup of tea and after a pause I blurted,

Mum, we don't like Paddy.
What do you mean?
Like cod liver oil Mum, he makes us sick.
What do you mean?
We don't want to stay here, Gus say something… I nudged my brother,
Why didn't you come and talk to me before now?

We had tea together around the dining table; the three of us had a very long talk. We remembered the good days in Danesholme, recalled our lives together in the pink house when Mum and our real dad were still together, when Gus and I were babies. My mother said Paddy had been a big mistake, she repeated what she always said: *the day he got that ring on my finger everything changed, he changed.*

Shortly after that Mum told Paddy there was a teachers' strike and that we had no school the next day. I don't know if she waved him off that morning, but I like to think she did. She had told us the night before to stay in bed until he was gone. This was it then, this was the last day. This was my last morning waking up in that bedroom, in that bungalow, in that street and in Desborough. We didn't say goodbye to anyone, to my new school classmates or the neighbours.

44 / one knife, one fork, one cup, one plate

As soon as Paddy had gone to work, Mum got us up and out of bed and we started packing. Mum was a ball of frenzied energy. She zipped about repeating to herself,

Leave everything!… I'll leave this marriage with everything I had when I walked into it. I will not take anything that is his, let him have it all, he can keep that for a start, urrgghh and he can keep that… leave everything that's his! I'll take my own clothes but leave him the rest, he can have everything, he can have it all, the sofa, the bed. I want nothing to do with any of it, he can have it all!

It was like a warped Christmas, it was that exciting. There was the rustle of paper everywhere, the filling of black bin liners and the sound of wrapping, boxes being filled, taped up and packed. I had to run to the shops for more boxes. I thought to myself *this is the last time I will run to the sweet shop around the corner.* I sprinted all the way. My breath steamed into the wintry air and my heart pounded in my chest. When I asked for the boxes I thought *this is the last time I go to this shop and speak to you, to the dwarf shopkeeper with no thumbs, goodbye scary sweetshop lady, goodbye dwarf shopkeeper with your stumpy digits, you'll not give me nightmares about my thumb-sucking ever again…*

This made me laugh and I ran back home clenching cardboard boxes in one fast gallop. When I came back, Mum asked me to pack up the kitchen. There was an almighty crash from the back of the house, Gus was dismantling the bunk beds with a screwdriver – end of an era, end of a war. Mum was busy caring for the plants and boxing up her cuttings. I started on the kitchen stuff I remember thinking, *I'll never forget this day, not ever, not for as long as I live.*

I opened the cutlery drawer and looked into the plastic compartments, wondering out loud what to take and what to leave. I grabbed the knives and counted: one, two, three, four and leave one for Paddy. One fork, one knife, one spoon, one teaspoon. The crockery was next. I counted one, two, three, four cereal bowls; we are four, and one bowl for Paddy. I left him one bowl, one plate, one cup, one saucer, one pot. I counted and Mum heard me and we laughed together wickedly and nervously.

One knife, one fork, one cup, one plate, now that's all he'll ever need won't he Mum?

We loaded up the truck and left, we drove away from that bungalow and never turned back. Leaving my ex-stepfather with a lonely one of everything, *now that's all he'll ever need won't he.*

45 / patriarch

For a couple of wintry months we went to stay at my grandad's house in Danesholme. Nanny was away working as a nurse in New York and only Grandad and Uncle Gerry were living there. We were back at another beginning. I walked around the estate and towards our first home, where we lived when we were three, when Mum had left dad.

The immense Danesholme of my imagination now looked small and compact as a rabbit warren. The streets were inhabited by ghosts and memories. I heard the eerie music of the ice cream van and the sound of little children counting, skipping and hiding in doorways just as I had before. My dreams so often took place in a surreal version of Danesholme, that the sensations of the memories of those dreams and actual events of my life before were merged and jumbled.

Digging around in memories and the past often leads to another, unexpected piece of your story. Once you start recalling the past, you keep remembering, and it can arrest you as though you are momentarily trapped in the then. In that moment, it is as though you are under ice, scratching at the underneath of the surface of what it is you feel or hear. Memories don't always come when they are summoned but creep up and flash you when you least expect them. And so it was, as I walked around Danesholme, I found I slipped into a trance, lost in a chain of nostalgic thought and it wasn't until the present moment interrupted me, the smell of food or feeling cold, that I realised I had stopped walking. I was standing still and staring dead into space, lost in the sensation of layers of memories. I suppose that is why the mind forgets, so we can function in the present. I expect that is why we should be glad we don't remember absolutely everything.

I found myself outside our first house, gazing into space. I blinked a few times, shook my head and carried on walking with no real destination. Ahead of me I could see the tunnel that led to the woods where the bears lived, where Mary and I followed Gus when he found the chicks that died in the airing cupboard and the hillside where Gus and I once caught crickets in a jam jar.

What are you doing here?

Mary said when she abruptly answered the door. She had grown taller than me. She wore a Catholic school uniform, a striped tie and bottle green skirt. I grinned taking that as a *hello*. From inside the house I could smell a familiar warmth. Her mum appeared behind her, wiping her hands on a tea towel.

Well, well, don't leave her standing there…

Her mother ushered me in.

Well, come on in! How's ya mam, love?

Mary showed me upstairs to her bedroom. A clutter of clothes and pop posters adorned the walls. I thought *here I am in Danesholme then, we are here again* and I thought it felt safe, as safe as nostalgia would allow.

***

Grandad mellowed as he got older and as his hair grew white around the temples he seemed to shrink, or maybe I grew, but he still scared me and made me nervous. In his prime he was a hard booze, knock-it-back kind of man, a tough guy. His voice remained deep and smoky and when he said, *honey*, it was literally honeyed, syrupy and smooth. He would quote entire passages from Shakespeare or Edgar Allen Poe and he never hid his disappointment when I couldn't name the author or the piece. Even if I did recognise parts, I would freeze, terrified, in case I got it wrong. He delivered explanations of Greek gods and mythology, how the planets work, the historical and Latin meanings of words but as soon as he reached for a pen and paper, it became heavy data, condensed dates and numbers. Just as I was with my stepfather, I always feared forgetting to listen properly and failing his lessons. It's hard to listen when you are thinking the word 'listen' over and over again.

Grandad is a big old lion, the patriarch, rumbling and restless. Maybe I am a lion too. Our dirty guttural laughs are similar, we are frightfully alike when we are loud and boisterous. I sometimes feel I inherited more of Grandad's bravado than the patience and quiet dignity of Nanny. My mother is his daughter. I will always be my mother's daughter and she protected me, installing a wariness of men, in particular my grandfather, for good reasons.

***

For two or three months of the winter of 1984, we stayed at Grandad's. The three of us, my mother, Jo and I shared a bedroom. My mother and grandad got along OK, we all managed somehow. Those weeks were highly strung and although my stepfather asked, my mother was adamant she would not go back to Paddy and Desborough. She spent long hours on the phone to him in tears. *What a mess I've made with you kids, I'm so sorry…* she said to me more than once a day.

We were planning to go to Hastings for the Easter holidays, we were daydreaming about moving there, Gus was already staying there with Grandpa George. Mum and I grew closer than ever during this time in the small confines of that shared bedroom. When Mum got dressed in front of me I saw the stretch marks of her pregnancies and motherhood. I saw the scars on her back.

Mum, when did you move to England?

You know!

Tell me again!

I was seven years old. I arrived in Dover in 1951. It was winter and the first and only thing I remember is the cold! Oh it was so cold and all I had on was a cotton dress, white socks and red shoes, how I hated to wear shoes…

As she speaks she lays on the slightest of Jamaican accents, her eyes twinkle, she pretends to go back to her book. I've heard it all before, of course I have, but I still say,

More, tell me more. Then what happened?

You know what happened, I remember how I loved to chase my chicken…

Chicken, what chicken?

Oh yes back home, I had my own chicken, and we killed it and ate it on the boat to Dover on my birthday…

I don't believe you!

It's true, I remember my mother making a birthday party for me on the boat and cooking my chicken…

Of all my mother's stories, I never believed the story about the chicken, I have heard it one million times: it was her seventh birthday on the boat from Jamaica and they had a party and it still always makes me laugh, picturing my grandmother, Nanny, slaughtering a chicken and plucking it on the deck of a boat, which took six weeks to sail from Jamaica to Dover. Was there no health and safety in those days? With my eyes watering I ask her to tell me more.

What do you want to know?

OK what was Jamaica like? What was it like there?

OK, I remember swimming and splashing in the cool river and I remember walking through the coffee groves. In the evenings my Marma told us stories as she fed us fruit, fresh mangoes… she smoked a clay pipe and wore a red bandana… When she died, my afternoon naps were taken on her grave of white marble under the mango tree and…

You slept on her grave?

Oh yes either there or in my feather bed where the hot rain beat on the tin roof and lulled you to a sweet slumber… now you go to sleep! You have school in the morning!

But tell me more, what was it like to come here, it was cold and what else, what about the first time you met Grandad?

Well he was stationed here and waiting for us. He met us off the boat and well I remember King George had died. I asked why is the flag at half-mast? Quiet child, can't you see I am talking to your mother? That is the first thing my father ever said to me.

Were you afraid of him?

Afraid… yes. I can remember overhearing my father saying to my mother, she isn't a baby, you mother her too much, you're too soft with her, this world is hard, when you gonna realise you a black in a white man's country now? You not on Colonels Ridge now you know!

Mum pulls that face and mimics Grandfather's deep baritone and frown and then looks more serious as she continues *I remember him telling me; you are no good at anything, you will never be any good at anything… and I remember him once waking me from bed to beat me because I had forgotten to brush my teeth… and then…*

The teacher?

Then yes well… Then one day my teacher noticed blood on the back of my shirt and how I flinched if anyone tried to put an arm around me or touch my back. For the first time I was encouraged to talk and my dad had to see the headmaster and she called him in and he laid off for a while.

But, what did Nanny do?

When?

Mum looked at me over her glasses

Well, after?

Nanny always bathed my cuts and bruises and sent me off to school…

But why?

My mother took off her glasses and pinched the bridge of her nose, then looked directly at me

But didn't she ever do anything?

Oh there would be tears, she said we would work it all out…

But… why?

Why what? Darling, don't upset yourself, I don't know why. I suppose she just thought that it was best. You know things were so very different back in those days, you forget your grandparents are Victorian, from another era… we just carried on, much like we do now. We stay calm and we carry on.

Then what happened?

Then I left home and I started dancing and… well that's when I met your dad… and well it's all in the past now, isn't it. Now you go to sleep, you have school in the morning. Actually I know someone who needs new winter boots, what do you say we go into town on Saturday?

Yes! Can I have pixie boots please?

They'll ruin your feet…

I could save them for best… please!

We'll see, now get some sleep, night love.

Goodnight Mum, I love you.

Love you too, sweetheart.

That night as I fell asleep I dreamed about grey leather ankle boots with a kitten heel. I wished hard, prayed for pixie boots with pointed toes. I thought they would look great with leg warmers and… I wasn't a little girl anymore and the distraction and shine of new boots wouldn't ever quieten the things we never talked about. All the pretence and the scars and all the secrets and the lies were nicely swept under the lumpy carpet. Keep the past in the past and let sleeping dogs lie, lie, lie. In my family there wasn't an elephant in the corner of the room but a whole herd. My mother confided in me, she told me all her secrets and the lessons she has learned, probably to protect me, but this left me with so many questions burning in my head; questions which sitting here today, as a grown woman I still have no answers – and all of these questions begin with the same simple single word – why?

46 / girls just wanna have fun

Every Sunday, I'd take Jo-Ann to Desborough to visit Paddy. Mum was paranoid Paddy would kidnap Jo if he had her alone. Gus was in Hastings and he said that if he ever saw Paddy again he would knock him out, so I had to go. My ex-stepfather was alarmingly nice to me, and much more relaxed and jokey than he had ever been before. I didn't mind going back to Desborough because I got to see my old school friends like Anna Parris and Sheila Sparks.

However, during these wintry months living back in Danesholme we were on a threadbare raft in a sea of transition, our clothes and belongings were all in black bin liners and boxes, we had no space or room. I started going to an ugly new local school, Kingswood, while Mum figured out what to do next. I stood out at this school and the kids could smell the shiny keenness on me. There was no uniform but for some reason I still wore my old one. Combined with my national health glasses and my huge afro, this just made me more geeky and weird-looking. This school was rough. There was no swimming pool and the possibility of continuing training or lessons in the euphonium or cornet was greeted with smirks and whispers. I remember in music class we had to sit through *Peter and the Wolf* and the teacher had us guess and discuss each instrument portraying the narration of each character. I sat at the back of the class feeling like I was in some thick kids' school.

Worst of all was during PE I was always paired off with the only other girl of colour in our year, an Indian girl called Ruby who was introverted, slow and clumsy. She ran like a girl and couldn't catch a ball to save her life. She hated sports and resented being lumped with me too, I suppose. When teams were picked for hockey, it was always Salena the *blackie* and Ruby the *paki* left till last on the icy pitch. We eyed each other hatefully, standing side by side, shivering in gym knickers and knee-high socks on the snow.

The two of us tackled the wintry wind up and down the freezing pitch, volleying the ball to each other for practise. I used to wish she could for once return a serve or run a bit faster so I could at least keep warm.

I eventually made friends with a bony girl with eyes too big for her head, Michaela. She was also into athletics and we started meeting up after school to run cross-country together. We'd jog across the woodland and back fields of Danesholme, past gypsy-traveller caravan sites, chained up dogs and burnt-out cars, towards the cereal factories and the industrial estates. I also made friends with a tough, Scottish girl called Mandy, who had acne on her chin. Mandy liked to sit on walls and kick cans, put on make-up and listen to Cyndi Lauper. I remember Mandy wore a white fake-paint-splattered denim jacket. The three of us would walk about Danesholme with our hands in our pockets and spend Saturday afternoons in the cinema watching films like *Flashdance* and *Footloose*.

Kingswood was a red brick box of a school, covered with scrubbed out racist graffiti. I was often called *blackie* or *nigger* by girls who hung about outside the school smoking fags, their hair sprayed in flicks, black kohl and stripes of neon blue and pink eye shadow across their eyelids. Many of the people in Danesholme had come down from Scotland to the Midlands in search of work in the seventies. As a result, almost everyone spoke with a thick guttural Glaswegian accent. The Scottish accent was nice when we were reading poetry in class, but terrifying when I heard it shouting *you're going to die you black nigger bitch* as I ran through woods.

I ran being pursued by about fifteen kids, five or six of them were on BMX bikes. I saw them all waiting for me at the school gates. I went out through the lower gate and ran blindly across the traffic of the main road, a car horn beeped, alerting them. I ducked under barbed wire and made a run for it into the woods. They were shouting *get her, get her, blackie, blackie*. As I was running, branches scratched my arms and legs, but I tore through and kept going.

There was someone with me, it was a chubby girl called Claire. She was my partner in home economics and she was running next to me. She said *uh oh look, they are all at the gates*. I thought she was stirring me up but then that was when I looked and saw the gang, all waiting, waiting for me, waiting to fight me. *Come on*, Claire said, *if we go this way they won't see us* and I followed her. Claire and I ran through the woods, my heart was in my throat, I was dizzy with adrenaline and fear, I had never run so fast in all my life. I was way ahead but they were leaving Claire alone, the BMX bikes were cutting in front of me. I swerved, jumped over a broken old tree trunk as the bike tyres cut into the earth and dead leaves. I was a fox and the BMX bikes were dogs with my scent on their tyres. I could hear them behind me, a braying crowd who ran behind the bikes on foot, shouting names and jeering.

I was outnumbered and out of breath. My legs were pistons, they ran without me. I could not feel them, and if I had stopped running they would have given way like watery jelly beneath me. My eyes were focused on finding any clear path but the bikes kept appearing in front of me. I switched direction, ducking and diving. I ran, I ran out of options, the way was cluttered with bracken, with brambles and the trees were in the way, thorns and thistles that twanged and snapped. Two bikes pulled in at once then another raced in behind and I was finally surrounded by trees and bikes, and circled by a crowd in the centre of the woods, miles from anywhere, miles from anyone sensible, miles from home and this had all gone far too far.

You's been getting too big for your boots! said Mandy, it sounded like *youse bin gittin too big fer yer booootz.*

Earlier that day my friend Mandy had decided she wasn't my friend anymore. At lunch-break Mandy and some other girls with hair-sprayed flicks had said to me,

Youse betta watch yer step, youse got a wee surprise after school…

A surprise? I love surprises!

I had laughed it off and then she spat,

Don't youse be getting so cocky, you've got a fight tonight…

youse got a fyeet tneet.

Woo I'm scared.

Youse betta be!

Now I was scared and I was cornered in the woods, they stood around me calling me names and discussing who was going to fight me. They said that they could smell shit, that I was covered in shit, that's what made me black. They told me I didn't come out of my mother's vagina, I came out of her arse.

Have you seen her black mum? Her mum's got shit all over her...

Listen, I don't know why we have to fight...

Youse bin getting too big for yer boots, ya need t'be brought down a wee peg or two, you black bitch... Mandy snarled at me pulling off her coat and rolling up her sleeves,

But I thought we were friends...

Well you thought wrong, you black coon. And what's that shit you have around your neck anyway, some African voodoo black magic black nigger shit is it?

Everyone laughed. I looked down and saw I was wearing one of my mother's sixties necklaces. It was a peace symbol in black, orange and yellow, a flat beaded circle on a string of orange beads. The gang sniggered. They said I should be wearing it in my bottom lip, like when I was with my tribe in the jungle. Claire was bright red in the face. She often blushed, but it was especially beetroot colourful. She said,

Why don't you all just leave her alone...

They jeered at Claire and teased her asking her which side she was on? She shouldn't spend too much time with me or she'd get shit all over herself. She'd better watch it or she'd get a fight too.

Mandy squared up to me, a boxer getting ready for a bout. She looked like she knew what she was doing. I knew that if I so much as flinched she would throw the first punch. I didn't want to be hit, I didn't want to fight and then she surprised me by saying,

Fight me then!

I didn't know what to do. I avoided her eyes and fiddled nervously with my necklace.

Come on then bitch... you scared or something? Come on fight me, blackie... blackie...

The crowd started chanting: *Fight! Fight! Fight! Blackie! Blackie! Blackie!* Improvising, desperate to do anything to avoid coming to blows, I held the necklace up like a crucifix, my hands shaking. I found my voice was steady though, and then my mouth suddenly started saying, *Curse you...*

What?

I curse you, may your crops fail...

What? Yeah right...

There was a pause, a silence and then I took a deep breath and continued,

Springfield Road

I curse you. Your crops will fail and your water, may your water be poisoned, may your children all be born deformed, may your fields be ridden with flies and your food rotten, I curse you all, may you all suffer, disease and hunger and may you...

I had no idea what was coming out of my mouth. I allowed my watery eyes to gently go out of focus as though I were in a trance and talking in tongues whilst I kept repeating things about disease, deformed babies and failed crops holding the necklace up like a crucifix. Mandy was the first to shout,

Are you doing black magic voodoo shit on me?

Kids started backing off and getting on their bikes and then riding off, swerving in the leaves and screaming,

Shit! She knows voodoo shit, run!

Shit! Wait for me!

The stragglers ran off into the woods as I was still babbling, screaming,

... may this curse follow you for all eternity, no matter where you go this curse will follow you, your crops will fail, as long as you are under the same sky you will be eternally cursed!

When everyone had run off I burst into sobs of tears that dried as soon as they came. Claire was still there, standing still, scarlet-faced and trembling. My tears turned to relief as she touched my arm and asked if I was all right and I thanked her for sticking up for me. The woods were quiet and growing dark, it was getting late. I bent down to pick my satchel up off the earthy leaves and brush the muck off it. I saw my hands and I was still shaking, then the crying suddenly was laughing as I said,

Crops? What crops?

I looked up at Claire and a rush of brilliant laughter overtook us. I was kneeling on the leaves, holding my bag, hardly capable of picking myself up for laughing, both of us were in total hysterics. We hooked arms and starting walking slowly homewards, through the thick of trees towards the flickering of urban orange streetlights, doubling over in fits of laughter every time one of us said,

Run! She knows voodoo shit!

47 / and we don't wear no shoes

It was May, the warm spring of 1984, when we finally arrived to live on Springfield Road.

I now had my own room on the second floor, but I also had a single bed in my mother's room. Jo slept in the king-size bed with Mum. I slept in the spare bed in Mum's room most nights in the beginning, I liked being close to her and I thought the house was haunted – at night the old floorboards creaked and the sash windows rattled. Grandpa George had lived there all alone since Edith's death in 1972. There were four floors of disarray and dust. It took some work, but Mum got it shipshape, homely and the kitchen in the basement was cleaned and almost hygienic to cook in.

I started a new school called The Grove that was very close to home, the lower school was situated right at the bottom of Springfield Road. It was a narrow, crooked and decrepit old school house, which they have demolished now and re-built. There was a national teachers' strike that year, so we finished classes at lunchtime every day. My afternoons were idle and often spent on the promenade and beaches. Sometimes we'd sneak into the closed-down Lido on the Marina, or go to Alexandra Park to climb trees and play on the swings. Grandpa George gave me an old grey tape recorder and often I'd go up into my father's old room in the attic where nobody went, and in contented solitude I made my own radio shows and songs.

My brother and I liked to go down to the seafront to an amusement arcade called Out Of This World. For the price of a day pass, you had unlimited plays on all the electronic games, Pac Man and Space Invaders. There was a darkened room that was an all-day music video disco. I remember watching Chaka Khan's 'I Feel For You' and realising that my big curly hair was cool thanks to her. Racism was uncool, thanks to hip hop and pioneers in rap, being in any way black or of colour gave you a certain street cred. Beatbox and rhymes were creeping into the popular consciousness too. Break-dancers wore nylon tracksuits and wet-look hair gel, strutting about Hastings town with chunks of linoleum or cardboard under their arms. They were always preparing for a burn, to impress the girls they'd spin on their heads and caterpillar across the polished floors. With legs twisting, they'd windmill, their hands and necks jolting and juddering with robotic moves. There was a constant war, a rivalry between the body-poppers, the robotics and the break-dancers. I also remember a cool older girl whose dancer name was Boogie Bush and she could break-dance as well as the boys. She also had big curly hair and I looked up to her and cheered for her to win. We loved to mimic the film *Breakdance*, I remember with great amusement, Gus scribbling a letter G, turning the title of 'Ain't No Stoppin' Us' to 'Ain't No Stoppin' Gus' on the cover of his seven-inch single. I also remember my brother playing the latest Prince album, which I'd steal to learn the lyrics off by heart. Listening to it intently when Gus was out, I felt I was privy to a whole new exciting world and I started to try to write political and sexier lyrics for my private a cappellas.

Sometimes, my brother and I would stay home and watch the big television down in the basement. A channel called MTV had just been launched and pumped out the hits of Michael Jackson, Wham! and my favourite girl singer, Madonna, twenty-four hours a day. I now prayed for crop tops and lace fingerless gloves. The basement was still almost as Edith had left it, cobwebs hung heavily from the ceiling and mice scurried in the corners. To my delight the pantry light still worked illuminating the same tins of beans and corned beef dating back to the seventies.

The very first friend I made in Hastings was a brilliant tomboy called Florence, who showed me how to soak second-hand jeans in the bath so they'd fit better. I also made friends with a red-haired girl called Caroline, we went to Christchurch every Sunday. We liked church and especially Father Jonathan, the cheery young vicar there; he had a pot belly and glasses. We all got confirmed because of him. He was enthusiastic, funny for a priest and he started a church youth club called TCs – The Christ Church Crew – The Three Cs. Every Monday evening, we'd meet and play pool and ball games. Father Jonathan's energy and generosity knew no limits, organising Shrove Tuesday pancakes; trips to the cinema, swimming and camping holidays. I went to church every week, not for Grandpa George, but because of my friends, the cute choirboys, Scott, Justin and Andrew. How I'd applaud and cheer, watching them burn and compete, attempting windmills on a piece of linoleum in the churchyard which we all thought was the ultimate in cool – spelled *kool*.

In the first year while we were living in Springfield Road, my mother discovered that my sister Jo-Ann had a rare condition called Williams Syndrome, as well as the asthma and eczema. This meant it took my sister a long time to learn to talk and to speak in proper sentences and she remained elfish and fragile. She was my living doll and I doted on her. That first year in Hastings we nearly lost Jo-Ann when she had a chronic asthma attack. Her breathing was so laboured that we had an old kettle on constantly until we could find a doctor, turning mother's bedroom into a steam room to help her breathe.

Hastings is a long drive from Desborough – but that's no excuse – Paddy visited Jo-Ann only once. I had to go with them, as Mum was still paranoid he'd kidnap her. (What on earth she thought I would do if he did try to abduct her I still have no idea.) We sat on the beach near the town and had ice cream. It was a grey, boring day. Paddy was staying at the Queens Hotel on the seafront and he disappeared in there, leaving me with Jo in the pram waiting for him for a while. Then he came back out and we sat and stared out at dull sea some more before he dropped us back home and left. Apart from divorce proceedings and lawyer's letters we never heard from him ever again. Never, ever again. Not that we expected anything, but not a birthday or Christmas card or anything for his real daughter.

Now I lived on Springfield Road, in Hastings I became one of the naked summer children and *we don't wear no shoes*. Writing this I am listening to that song by Jane's Addiction 'Summertime Rolls' and remembering us: we were barefoot all summer, we lived on the beaches and scooped rivers and irrigated moats around pebbled turrets of wet mud-castles. We jumped from rock to rock with nets, paddling in shallow crab pools. Teenage girls in jelly shoes slathered coconut and olive oil on each other's shoulders, cooking themselves in the midday sun, trying hard to get the attention of young wannabe surfers with no real waves to catch who lay on their bellies on their surf boards, basking on a flat green sea.

Springfield Road

From the beach you could always see the distant lush green of the West and East Hills, rising like two plump mounds. Walking towards Fairlight, you'd find beautiful places to think or fly a kite. We'd go meandering along the wild yellow gorse-lined paths of the Firehills in a daydream. Hastings Castle was a broken tooth above the chalky, jagged jaws of the cliff face, which in later years became the place for the sweetest flush of first love; teenage secrets, stolen cigarettes, French kisses and bottles of cider.

When the tide was out, standing out on the rocks and looking back towards land, as far as the eye could see, stretched the beaches in shades of mineral, copper and granite, swirls of slate and smooth amber-coloured stones, pieces designed especially for skimming and skipping stones across the water's surface. If you found yourself a lucky pebble with a hole in the middle, they said, you would always return to Hastings. I always thought that was a good thing.

That new beginning and the summer of May 1984, Hastings was in bloom, awash with cherry blossoms and the summer was ahead like a promise that we would surely keep. For the rest of my life I told people that this was where I came from. I never bothered to mention the life before, Springfield Road was always my home, this was where my life began, and this is where another story begins.

***

Where are you going now?
> *For a walk.*
> *Where?*
> *Just a walk.*
> *Can I come too?*
> *No, not this time, I am going to leave you here in Hastings in 1984.*
> *What do I do next?*
> *Lots…*
> *Like what?*
> *You wear wet-look hair gel and blue mascara, you obsess about Prince, you'll love Maya Angelou and you'll keep writing poetry… But listen, try to go gently and*

enjoy the journey more, smell the roses on the way. I know you think you know it all, but try to listen to Mum sometimes…

I know.

No I know, listen. When you get to fifteen take it easy with the cider and the cigarettes… in fact, don't smoke.

I don't smoke.

Yes you do.

And what about Dad?

I think he'll be at peace now.

But are you still afraid you'll die like Dad did?

Are you afraid?

Yes.

Then I am too.

Always wait and see if you feel better in the morning?

Yes, that's right, wait and see another sun rise.

Sleep is the great healer.

That's right love, oh and one last thing, please try not to be so hard on yourself so the people that love you don't have to work so hard.

What?

I know, easier said than done, goodbye then, Salena.

Goodbye… Salena.

I walk up the beach and towards the pier and leave my twelve-year-old self paddling in rolled up jeans, flat-chested in a tight striped t-shirt, short-sighted and squinting in the sun. I leave myself there in 1984, where I am content and safe with my family on the beach in St Leonard's, opposite the statue of Queen Victoria. The soft green sea sparkling in May's lemony sunlight, it is bright and warm out of the wind. Seagulls cry overhead and sit like ducks on the calm, still water. I turn back and see the tall bony silhouette of my brother Gus, staring out at the horizon and skimming stones. Jo-Ann sits in a sunbonnet on a sandy ledge, playing with a bucket and spade. Mum is head-to-toe in turquoise; she turns, shielding her face from the sun. I see her smile and I walk away. I know we are going to have a wonderful summer, we are going to get some ice cream in a bit, and we don't wear no shoes, there is sand between our toes, and at last we live on the holiday.

48 / facebook 2008

Hi Salena,

This is probably the strangest message you'll get this year but my name is Claire Godden (used to be Godden any way) and I just wondered if you were trying to find me on the genealogy website thingy???? If you are I'd really like to hear from you and if you're not I'm sorry to have sent you this weird message.

Take care
Claire x

Hello Claire,

how are you? In a word – yes! I have been looking for you, Claire Godden daughter of Paul Anthony Godden. Did you leave a message on genealogy website like back in 2001…I found the query and my name and replied last year and left a note there. Wow! hang on…Ok…I just checked and opened the site and now see your new note! I am gobsmacked and so pleased you found me here…Not sure what to write now…stunning…

Guess what, after seeing your posting, I wrote to every Claire Godden on Facebook and MySpace, to lots of dead ends…I got lots of very nice replies, one very nice letter from a 14 year-old Claire Godden whose grandfather does Godden family trees…It's been quite a road to Damascus….I am very excited to find you here. You are right though this is the strangest message I got this year. What shall we do now…? If I was standing in front of you meeting you in the pub I guess I would look at my shoes and then ask you if you want a fag or fancied a pint…or something like that…I just looked at your page, are you based in Bristol? I am in London…write back when you can…

Take care too, Salena x

Hi Salena,

I am so glad you got my message. I've always wanted to get in touch but…well I wasn't sure where to even start. My friend just happened to stumble across the genealogy thang and here we all are now! I do live in Bristol and if we were face to face in a pub (a good place to start pretty much anything) I would definitely take you up on that pint, or probably several considering the enormity of the situation! So, I know totally nothing about you – tell me some stuff. What do you do, whereabouts in London are u based, and all that kinda stuff?

I'm going to be 29 in October, living in Bristol with my hubby and two kids, always been a bit of a career girl until the deep, deep joys of motherhood and the onset of coffee mornings and nappy talk! Pleased to report I am clinging to my 'one of the girls' status with a ferocity!

I'm afraid I know hardly anything about Dad, how about you? I can't even remember him. Did you know his mum? I knew his Auntie Helen and she was an amazing woman. I visited her a few times in Bexhill and she passed away about ten years ago. I'm so glad we've found each other (how movie of the week does that sound?). I am though. I have no other siblings and I've always wondered about you, are you like me and all that, are you like Dad? I don't really know what we do next but since we have like 50% of our DNA in common I guess a rendezvous would make sense?

Looking forward to hearing from you,
Claire x

***

London. December. 2008

Dear Dad,

The most wonderful thing happened this summer – we found our sister, Claire. We met in August, one Saturday lunchtime, at Reading train station, a halfway spot between Bristol and London. The moment I saw her in the station I felt I knew her and we threw our arms around each other and held on tight and for a long time. I might have imagined it, or longed for it, but I felt something warm and familiar in that embrace. My eyes were welling up and I had to catch my breath to stop myself from crying or making a fool of myself or she would think I was soppy.

We had so much catching up to do, so we went to a quiet place on the river. We sat at a table outside a restaurant and it was a perfectly sunny day, blue sky, still green water. We ordered white wine and shared starters and chatted and when she spoke, I watched her, I couldn't help it, I knew anything she did that I did, we had both equally inherited from you Dad. I was readily observing any tiny similarities in our mannerisms and personalities and enjoying them. She makes up words like I do and loves books and writing; she's got glittery eyes and a mischievous nature; she likes a drinky and belly laughs at rude jokes… its in our genes then and I thought she's one of us all right Dad.

We were there drinking wine all day and I wanted to know everything, stupid things like her favourite colour and what were the names of her childhood pets and of course the other side of the truth, like what did her mother say about you. Where were you on those last days? I think I understand more now.

I made Claire a scrapbook, with poetry you'd written and pictures of you when you were younger on Springfield Road and she showed me pictures of you in the late seventies. You changed didn't you Dad, I mean your sideburns grew and you looked older. It was strange to see photos of you appearing a little more portly and hitting your forties. I never imagined I'd see you like that, older I mean, we've only ever seen pictures of you from way back then, in black and white.

Claire and I laughed about you Dad – we compared our mothers and figured your type out in no time, you were a legs man that's for sure, down there playing in the pit, looking up at our mums' high kicks above you.

Finally on a weekend in October all of us were united for the first time. Paul, your grandson and your namesake, was climbing all over his new uncle Gus as though he was a climbing frame. It was a very noisy and chatty weekend, there was plenty of laughter and a glass or two of champagne was raised to you, our dad, you know you should have been there.

I look forward to showing Claire around what is left of old Soho, the poets, artists and jazz musicians still here; I'll take her to Gordon's Bar down Villiers Street, maybe Ronnie Scott's and there's still a few drinking dens you'll no doubt have frequented, The Colony and Gerry's. And I'll take her up Primrose Hill or Hampstead Heath too, to listen to the wind in the branches of the William Blake tree and to look across the frosty rooftops of a wintry London from up on Parliament hill.

Dad, it's your anniversary again, but this year I don't feel the way I have before. I think that is why I'm writing you this letter, because it's not that I don't still remember you Dad, because I do, but this year I won't cry, seek your ghost and soak in your memory. This year I won't burn with poems or walk the streets of London alone at night in some private melancholic vigil. This year it's different, I know where you are and that you must surely be resting now, and for the first time, this year, it's all to do with the living.

Suddenly, I know that in a way I have always had you in the stories from my mother, in the strength of my brother and now in the laughter of my sister and the hugs from all my nephews and nieces; I am not alone and that state of waiting is done and the search is over. We all always think of you whenever we hear Gilbert O'Sullivan.

So you can sleep now and rest in peace Dad, I promise we'll look after each other. With love from me, your eldest daughter,

Sx

my grandmother, nanny

49 / eulogy

So, I tried to write this under a mango tree
remembering you, your love of mangoes,
how Marma used to slice up the fruit
and tell you all stories at bedtime.

I tried to write this passing the Blue Mountains
on the road to Melbourne and Victoria,
I knew I'd soon be on the road to take you home
to these Blue Mountains I've only dreamt of in your stories.

Then I wrote this in Darling Harbour in Sydney
and I thought of you there too, watching the boats
and the Maritime Museum, recalling history,
I remembered your passage to Dover, to England,
with my mother.

Whilst walking through the tranquil Chinese gardens
there were ornate waterfalls and fountains
reminding me of photographs of you
in Hong Kong and Singapore.

And wandering through the markets of China Town
with the aroma of rice, ginger and pak choi
I thought of you there too
how you'd wag your finger and tell me
to eat my greens.

Walking along a deserted beach at dawn
I found a coconut washed up on the white sand.

Again I thought of you and how you warned me
that coconut was bad for the cholesterol.

I was convinced that very coconut
had sailed from the West Indies,
from you to me,
to tell me it was time
to go home.

I realise now
that I will always be writing this,
no matter where I go,
you walk beside me.
I can hear you nagging me to quit cigarettes
to look when I cross the road
to take care
not to trust strangers
to work hard and to take
my time.

I can picture you now
your eyes are like tiger's eyes
and so gold.

I can sense you in the room,
a gentle mischief,
a quiet dignity,
your infectious chuckle.

The last time I saw you Nanny
I asked you to wait until I could give you a grandson
you laughed your laugh then
when I told you I plan to begin this work
when I am fifty

Springfield Road

and then you asked me to write something
to read today,

But words are not enough
and it is in the silences
I still try to write this
there are no words
my Nanny
with tiger's eyes,
just the calm in the pauses
as we all share our memories of you today,
memories that will live on.

A tribute written for Nanny, my grandmother, read at the service of thanksgiving at the Mount Carmel Church, Colonels Ridge, Clarendon, Jamaica – January 24th 2011.

50 / Kingston, Jamaica / January 2011

My Dear,

It was 4am when I was awoken by the raging storm. I pulled the curtain aside to witness this almighty cacophony of thunder and fork lightning, followed by a downpour, the like of which I have never seen before. I got up in the darkness and went outside onto the veranda. It was first light, a strange dawn with dark green clouds.

I'd picked up my telephone and cigarettes. How strange, I thought, not to have picked up my notebook and pen, as was usual, but my phone – and it was then I knew it was time to make that call to England and get confirmation of what I already knew to be true; my grandmother, Nanny, had passed away only four hours earlier.

I was so far away from home. For Christmas and New Year, we were on tour in Australia with The Book Club Boutique. My bass player, Max Doray and I were staying and playing with our Australian friends and fellow band mates Melania Jack and Patty Bom. We were travelling along the east coast; from the rain forests in Nimbin, sacred Bundjalung country, to Byron Bay, Sydney and finally down to Victoria and Melbourne. We were throwing parties, producing spoken word and music events, playing anywhere we could blag for free, beach shacks, cocktail bars and alternative theatres, whilst promoting local artists and meeting up with poets, authors and musicians in each town to jam alongside us. Admittedly, sometimes the locals were quite baffled by the arrival of four weird and wonderful looking girls in the local town hall or bar but we took it all in our stride. We made some great friends, met lots of lovely people, writers, poets and singers along the way.

However, Queensland was suffering the worst floods in history, eighty per cent of Queensland was flood affected, the tides were rising with flood warnings escalating. There were stories on the internet that a shark was sighted cruising down the water-logged Brisbane high street.

The rain: I have never seen such rain. It was like we were white water rafting down the highway in the car. I easily imagined humans as ants and that giants, Gods, were having a water fight, throwing huge bodies of water at each other above our heads. It was a constant bashing, it sounded like horses galloping across the roof. And although we were safe in Lismore and a good two to three hours from the very worst hit areas, many roads were closed, the rivers were swollen and bursting their banks. We were in limbo; we watched the weather and the news unfold via the internet, but quitting was not an option.

Following the news that my nanny had finally passed away, that night we had to do a performance in a bar in downtown Lismore. It was all right, not the best show on earth, but we made it through. I was distracted and I was hurting. But when we came home from the gig, there was a tawny frog-mouth on the veranda; a beautiful rare bird, like a fat silver owl, a reptilian kookaburra. She – we knew she must be a she – she stayed there as if she was watching over us as we drank Jamaican rum, raising a glass to my grandmother. We played music, improvised songs and poems. I recall one girl, a brilliant musician called Julz, played slide on a guitar made out of a wooden cigar box. When I went up to the kitchen to get more ice, I watched the bird for a while. Staring at its round gold eye gave me a chill, goosebumps. I said *Nanny?* And the bird ignored me. Then I said *Marma?* The bird's head span around, 360 degrees and then it winked at me and stared right at me, both gold eyes unblinking. *Marma is here*, I thought, *Marma is an owl*, Marma, I whispered and put my hand out. She flew, sailed high up into the banana tree above us. I believe she was there, watching over us, up in the branches of the banana tree throughout the whole of that night.

Phone calls to England were very strange, distant and tearful. We made plans to all meet in Jamaica on January 24th, I was determined to fulfil my grandmother's wish that I write and read her a eulogy. And there we would meet all our many relatives and take my grandmother home, back up the mountain to Colonels Ridge. Organising flights and transfers was frustrating, becoming very expensive and the time zone differences were irritating too. Was it even possible to get from Australia to Jamaica in time? Far away in another continent, I heard my mother's voice breaking on Skype and felt her heart was breaking. After more than sixty years' marriage, my grandad was in pieces. My sister Jo-Ann was in tears and my brother was quiet and shaken, and his wife Teresa was solid as a rock. I was homesick and felt guilty, I felt I should head straight home to England, but Gus wouldn't let me cancel anything and my mother also insisted that I was to complete my trip and meet them in Kingston.

Continuing the tour was quite epic, Brisbane airport was closed down. We dodged wild weather south from Lismore, to Newcastle, to Sydney and Melbourne. I recall squalls where visibility was zero and brown chocolate rivers oozed from burst banks. I remember the full moon in Sydney sent us doolally. Four girls in a hot cramped car under the full moon? It was heady and emotional. I went off on my own in Sydney, I took a hotel room in China Town alone. I did a solo show, reading poems in Bondi Beach for a friend, a musician called Jont, from London, who had established a weekly residency there. I soaked in the moonlight, took in the full moonshine, which often gets me into the worst kind of trouble. I was happy to be kidnapped; I dived in secret waters; I sat in a magic garden and drank bubbly wine, and by the time we drove those last two long days to reach the Melbourne show, we were all officially tour fried. We all needed a good bath and a few days quiet in our own beds.

The Melbourne venue, Bertha Browns, was a converted warehouse in the financial district. The crowd, though small, were warm and friendly. I look forward to returning to Melbourne one day, my twelve hours there could not do it justice. Throughout the gig my heart was heavy, knowing my suitcases were in the wings. I was in the departure lounge from this all-girl unit I had travelled and unravelled with, laughed and cried and worked hard and played so hard alongside for two months and now it was all done. I hate goodbyes – but now it was time to go home to say goodbye to my grandmother. I left Australia at 4am and flew from Melbourne to Auckland to LA to Miami and as if by magic I arrived in Kingston at 9pm on the same day and the evening before the memorial.

Springfield Road

I had never been to Jamaica before. We had not been to Jamaica before, my brother, Gus and I. And it had been dozens of years since my brother, my mother and I, had any time together, to talk, sleep and eat under the same roof. I had been re-writing this memoir for more than five years and now suddenly I'd see for myself, places we'd only ever heard about through stories from our grandparents. Here I was, walking onto the bamboo tray, the parishes of Jamaica once signified by pictures of coconuts and birds of paradise.

At Kingston immigration desk, the passport control man looked at my visa for a very long time and then he asked me if it was my first time in Jamaica.

Yes it is! I said with a huge idiot grin on my face. I was practically skipping on the spot that I had arrived, thinking, clever me, I came all the way around the world from Australia. I was so relieved I had not missed any connections.

Do you know the stories of Anancy?

Yes! Of course I do. I replied, he frowned and stared at my passport and my face in turn, slowly, his features bore great grave concern.

And what do you write about? He asked. I then wished I had written as my occupation teacher so that I wouldn't get asked these literary questions. When people know you write they say things like *everyone has a book in them* and smile knowingly as if you never heard that before or they say *you're a poet and you know it*. I felt that if I answered incorrectly he would interrogate me further so I said as casually as I could,

I write about anything, life, dreams, you know…

Do you think it is best that you write from your own perspective or somebody else's?

I think both are equally as good, I think there is no best or better. There is no wrong or right answer to that one. Do you write?

Hmmm… a little…

He looked thoughtfully at my passport and took a long time, reading all my paperwork and then choosing a page to stamp. He pointed his pen at me and said,

Whilst you are in Jamaica, you should write a story about an English person's first time in Jamaica, write about a writer who writes the stories of Anancy but with the English perspective.

He looked at me directly, eye to eye, but I shook my head *No!*
No?

No, I know what, I will write all about you, the man at the passport desk in Kingston airport who clearly loves writing and good stories. He grinned at me; beamed brilliant white teeth and bonny cheeks. He nodded then as he handed me my passport he said,

Welcome to Jamaica!

Welcome indeed; stepping out into the tropical heat, the night air embraced me and that first hug from my big brother let me know I had made it home and dry.

We were up and dressed early for the ceremony. It was already hot at 7am as we drove through downtown Kingston heading up and out to Clarendon. Kingston is a lively city, with street vendors, hustlers and bustlers. I have never been in the Caribbean before, but this place initially reminded me of East Timor. The distant blue hue of forest and mountains, fish on poles, being sold on the side of the road. Poverty in abundance, tin shacks selling fruits, cigarettes, tinned drinks and bottled water. At every street corner a bleeding heartache, at every stop sign a beggar. I was told it was best to keep your windows rolled up or you'd be harassed at every junction. I saw gullies and alleys, humble shanty towns where people lived in makeshift homes, corrugated iron rooftops, just like the ones as I once saw in Dilli, East Timor. And I saw great grandeur too, beautiful white and marbled embassies, old colonial buildings, museums, churches and universities.

Driving through Kingston, delirious with jet lag, I could easily make believe I was in the film *The Harder They Come* or any eighties Bob Marley video: I saw tiny rum shacks; a topless, toothless, bearded old Rasta with dreadlocks grown matted down past his bum; coconut trees, palm trees and birds of paradise; signs for tasty patties and jerk chicken; the two boys riding a seventies-style motorbike with a box of plantain to sell, balanced precariously on the handlebars… all that Jamaica, in real time, zooming past my car window.

The road up to Colonels Ridge grew steeper, winding and potholed. As we continued, the road grew narrower and we passed shallow muddy rivers, fields of sugar cane and bamboo. Rainforest. Up and up and up we drove until we came to a shop, a sign for a barber's, some chickens and a donkey, and we had arrived somewhere, somewhere special – we were at Colonels Ridge. The view of the mountain range was spectacular from way up there.

Mount Carmel Church was high up on the top of a mountainside. It was light and airy and the walls were painted pale primrose yellow. Inside were rows of pews and my mother pointed to our old family bench. On the back wall there were marbled plaques with the names of both sets of my great-grandparents, Robinson and Robothan, named as elders of the church, they helped build this very church. My other great-grandmother's name was Lena May Robothan. My mother tells me she had no idea, but what a strange coincidence that we are so similar, that I was christened Salena Faye. And also strange to me, below the carved dedications, dates and names were these bold words: Well Done.

The church bell rang twice and everybody came inside and sat down. We were in a congregation of cousins I had never met, some from Jamaica and others from America, people from the village and their families. We looked at the altar, the flowers and my grandmother in a box. It was suddenly overwhelming, and as the first hymn 'All Things Bright and Beautiful' began, that is when it suddenly hit me that somehow we had all made it, gathered here, to this isolated village on a mountaintop, we were finally together, I looked at my mother and we cried then.

I was the first up to read my poem, my offering, which had been written on the road, in a scuffed-up notebook. I hoped that it was close to good enough for such a crowd of strangers-yet-familiars. As I stepped up, I heard a quiet voice telling me to be myself. *Don't try for trying's sake, just do what you can do and be honest, just be yourself.* All I remember about the actual reading is that I managed not to bawl and kept a steady voice.

This was followed by another hymn and then my mother's cousin, son of my nanny's brother Sam, Patrick Robinson read his piece. He began by saying:

My father had two kinds of sisters. There were those who had the more typical Robinson woman, dominant and imperious character that brooked no foolishness from anyone, man or woman. The other set were softer and more forgiving. I loved both equally. My own father, were he a woman, would have fallen into the first category. The nieces here today and elsewhere have inherited those traits. But in the interest of my own security I will not categorise them... As he said this there was a lovely pause, full of giggles, nudging and knowing grins, for it was a certainty that we Robinson women all knew which category we might fall into, or at least we thought we did.

Patrick Robinson was no stranger – we had met him on numerous occasions visiting my grandmother. We all admire him greatly; he works as a judge, and is currently the President of the International Criminal Tribunal for the Former Yugoslavia, as well as a published author with special interest and knowledge of Jamaican Athletics. Patrick read beautifully and said: *Aunt Muriel fell squarely into the second set. She was eternally sweet and gentle but possessed of a great inner strength that was to serve her well throughout her life and in particular throughout her illness. Aunt Muriel was born and raised in Colonels Ridge. She was the fifth child in a family of ten, born to Rudolph Robinson (Papa) and his wife Theresa (Muma) née Robotham. She was the last surviving child and the one that lived the longest. Papa was an elder and lay preacher of this church when it was the Mount Carmel Presbyterian Church. Aunt Muriel would have seen her parents work hard, and although not well off, always giving of others. Many are the stories of Muma cooking and feeding the village...*

I pictured the stories my nanny told me about her mother feeding all the children after school and remembered the pictures I had in my head. With this I looked out around the elderly congregation and wondered who went to school with my grandmother and her siblings.

She told me how it fell to her to care for her grandmother until her death and she carried out this duty willingly and lovingly...

Marma – in my head I whispered her name *Marma.*

... It was in Hong Kong that Aunt Muriel started to become interested in nursing as a career. On returning to the UK they spent some time working before going to the USA where Aunt Muriel worked as a nurse in a prison. Naturally the prisoners loved her calling her their angel and respected her so much they wouldn't swear in front of her...

When Patrick finished we bowed our heads in prayer and there was a stillness and peace. I squeezed my mum's hand as the Mount Carmel choir sang old Jamaican hymns I hadn't heard before. I recall liking a particularly bluesy, soulful hymn with lyrics about the pearly gates and your place in heaven.

Then the whole church sat down to listen as Reverend David Tucker stepped up. He was a giant with a bald head, ebony dark skin and bright eyes. His voice was deep, booming and resonating as he belted the sermon. The lesson was brutal, based on 'you reap what you sow'. It was passionate and soon stopped any weeping. The Reverend clenched his fists, pounded his chest, he told the congregation to look into their hearts, he bellowed:

Do you live for just today or for today and tomorrow? When you get to heaven to meet your maker will God say well done? Will the lord look upon you and say well done? Muriel has passed. Muriel has gone. But when Muriel enters the pearly gates will the Lord say well done? And throughout this blazing speech there was a murmur of *praise be, hallelujah!* and *amen!* And thereafter I felt differently about the meaning of those two words: well done.

After the service, we walked down the dusty track to the family plot. It was ten minutes' walk from the church in the midday heat and as we walked we seem to attract more attention. More villagers joined us, people wanting to pay their respect and everyone came to their gates to watch us go by. A gaggle of school children of all ages followed, giggling and whispering. It was no longer sombre but quite sociable, with different cousins introducing themselves to us. Some folk remembered my mother as a baby, and my mother met cousins she might have played with as a very little girl too.

The family plot was beside the abandoned house that my grandmother lived in alongside her ten siblings, Papa and Muma, my spelling – Marma. We stood amongst the tombs of our great-grandparents and my great-aunts and uncles, beside a house that could not have possibly housed them all. It was derelict and I could see through a jagged window into the kitchen where my great grandmother would have cooked. There was a broken old stove there. I saw the porch where Nanny may have been sat in a tin bucket filled with roots and herbs, blinded my malaria. Now the black and white drawings my grandmother had described to me as a girl were technicoloured, those tales of Nanny as a child were suddenly in 3D, moving around me, a living, walking and talking picture. Vivid blue and violet, the world was humming in a hundred shades of life and lush green. The neglected house was swarming with hornets, I was told it was dangerous and so I couldn't risk actually going inside. I really wanted to, but I could see enough to know, we all come from very humble beginnings, from hard work and love. And looking at the congregation from the outside, I was proud to be part of this family.

My brother laid Nanny to rest; he put her box in the hole already prepared and as soon as he did so, they sealed the grave with cement and began laying the headstone. Rushing to beat the hot sun baking the cement too dry. The Reverend said some words of prayer, the choir and old ladies began to sing and everybody joined in, old Jamaican hymns from long ago, trembling voices, the rumble of blues under the yellow midday sun. I was crying quietly, looking down through my lashes, the cement slapped cold and grey, wet and final. Then one huge orange butterfly, the colour of a tiger lily settled on the grave, it stayed for a very long time, tiger lily, Nanny.

We stood at the graveside, in the shade, talking politely and waiting for the grave to be completed and the headstone to be in place. I suppose I must have stood out with my fair skin and light eyes but children started gathering around me. Children are like curious cats and they will climb all over the person that does not seem to like them. Eventually a pretty little girl with braids, by far the boldest in the school, came up to me and asked,

Excuse me… why you no got no church clothes?

Do you not think these are church clothes then?

I laughed as she looked up at me and shook her serious young head. I tried to explain that this was the only black dress I own and that I had just come from Australia. Soon her friends came over and we asked each other our names and they stared at me until my new bold friend said,

Can I have your phone number?

I managed to convince her it would be very expensive to telephone London and with that she ran off and returned with her school notebook and a pen and said,

Can I have your name, I want to see your name, please write it…

Before long I was surrounded by school children with notebooks, writing my name over and over again, they all watched and said I had nice handwriting and then someone asked,

Can you write I love you and then your name.

And so I found myself writing *I love you, Salena Godden xxx* in all the notebooks of all the village children whilst they bombarded me with questions,

Where do you come from?

England. London. You know it's the place where everyone is in a hurry and it rains all the time and the Queen lives there in a palace and she has a little dog...

Who's the Queen?

Hallelujah for Jamaican Independence!

Eventually, the headmistress appeared and shook hands with us too. My brother laughed at me and took photos because once every notebook was signed, the children all mobbed and hugged me. I haven't been cuddled by twenty-five small pairs of arms at the same time before. I wondered what my elders would think if they saw this display, and I hoped I wasn't being disrespectful. The children asked me to sing to them. I couldn't be persuaded and instead I managed to have them sing for me. They nudged and whispered, and then began an up tempo, energetic version of *riding through the snow, on a one-horse open-sleigh, over the hills we go, laughing all the way, jingle bells, jingle bells...*

I started laughing and joined in and we sang about the *snow* they had probably never seen in real life. I couldn't help wondering if perhaps these were the great-grandchildren of my grandmother's school friends, distant cousins and friends. Perhaps if we went in a time machine I would find I am somehow connected to them. For sure I felt anchored to the geography, there was a magnet and energy there. And I promised myself I would go – I will go – back up there to that school one day, back to Mount Carmel Church and back to Colonels Ridge. It really was magic and as beautiful as Nanny had always hinted it was.

***

Some days have passed and I am alone now and writing this in Kingston. I am high on the top of a hill, high enough to watch the city waking up, it is very early morning, a blue hazy smog lies above the peppery city below. Kingston hums with life, it feels fast and dangerous to me. When I wouldn't sit and be calm my grandmother told me I had pepper on my tail, I think Kingston has pepper on its tail. I am absorbing everything: This is a proud country, rich with culture, academia, sports, music, literature, food, breath-taking landscapes, history and art. It will take my whole lifetime to learn all this, to know the differences between my fictional Jamaica and the real Jamaica, but I'm an eager student.

I couldn't begin to capture it all here but my cousins have not let me rest, from historical buildings to places of great beauty; Dunn's Rivers Falls, The Jazz and Blues Festival, The Bob Marley Museum and The National Gallery. And how they have stuffed us with food: breadfruit; callaloo; salt fish; dumplings; patties; jerk chicken and festival; red snapper and bam bam.

My grandmother tried to teach me two fundamental things; to save money for a rainy day and that it was important to study and work hard. I never saved a bean but I did choose a path I enjoy and so I like to work hard at it. I remember the food my grandmother loved to eat and tried to pass on to me. I'd phone Nanny whenever I made rice and pea, just to hear her voice, I would ask her how, even though I knew the answers. I'd put the receiver in the crook of my neck and listen to her voice, as I did these meals for one, alone in my little London flat… *just fry up the onion with a little oil, then add the tomatoes, just a little seasoning, some salt and you cook it up, on a low heat…*

During my grandmother's illness the food theme continued. I knew she was ill when she stopped eating, she lost her appetite and I knew she was losing the fight against cancer. I made soup and took it to her, frozen in batches. I laboured over my recipes, as though I was making spells in a cauldron, convincing myself they would make her feel strong and well, mastering the combinations of spinach and nutmeg, broccoli and stilton, yellow lentil dhal, sourcing the best organic herbs and spices I could find. Being sure to use Jamaican root ginger and freshly ground nutmeg. The last time I saw my grandmother she was frail, papery thin and the most I could get her to eat was a plain boiled egg with a little salt. I tried so hard to conjure something of Marma, some healing power in those soups.

Springfield Road

We are descendants of the Maroons of Jamaica. And now I am in Jamaica I learn that in some company this is something to be proud of and in other company perhaps not. I have been told the Maroons were the rebels who began the fight for independence to abolish slavery. And also that some people think the Maroons were turncoats who sold out their own brothers and black slaves to the white man. In some books I have read how Maroons were brave soldiers, using early guerrilla warfare tactics to beat the British. But at other tables they are considered nothing more than black magic, Obeah-practising magicians, something like gypsies or feral bushmen.

I have discovered an interesting, ongoing debate within my family over the origin of the name Robinson. Some of my cousins are certain we are direct descendants of Colonel Robinson, a white man, a Scotsman, who was heralded for his brilliance at capturing runaway slaves and Maroons with the use of huge hunting dogs. He was rewarded a plantation and properties as payment for his work and the area was called Colonels Ridge thereafter. Another cousin goes as far as offering further explanations; that his real name was Robertson but they spelled it wrong at the Post office and it was never corrected, as poor education, reading and writing was often the cause for much confusion then. Another cousin has added that he misspelled it on purpose, so he could stay in the West Indies and hide from going back to his life back home, neglecting his first wife and abandoning his children in Scotland. Colonel Robertson, used this new misspelling of Robinson, to begin a new life, living as a king, in the blue mountains, where he went on to marry a Maroon woman.

And from this I easily begin to imagine his character, a wily fox of a Scotsman, marrying the daughter of his Maroon nemesis, who he has trapped with drooling hounds and surrendered to the Brits in order to steal the hand of the beautiful daughter, and all manner of wonderful fiction blooms and blossoms in my head. I believe this is typical of Jamaica, an island brimming with stories and folklore, superstitions, colourful contradictions and controversies, always a story inside another story, unravelling.

We cannot turn back the clocks, but I do find myself wondering how things might have been if my brother and I had come to Jamaica for our school holidays as children. How very different this memoir would be. For a start, the title might have been *Colonels Ridge* and then again I might have never written it. The fact is, it would have been even more expensive to come to Jamaica for summer holiday back in the seventies and eighties. Globally, we didn't view the world the same way, world travel now is not what it was back in the twentieth century. The world is smaller and shrinking more and more.

I can, however, wonder what it would be like if I had been in Jamaica as a child. It is for sure I would have early memories of white sands and warm turquoise oceans instead of rocky beaches and shivering in the sage green sea of Hastings. I would know that ackee actually grows on trees like red apples, but here I am, like a child looking up with wonder and anticipation waiting for them to ripen.

I would also know that when you drive towards the stadium in Kingston, there is a long wall of paintings, all in a row, of the heroes of Jamaica, and you'll see a portrait of Leila Robinson, my grandmother's sister – incidentally the netball court is also named after her. I would know that I come from a family who continue to achieve great things in sport, politics, law and medicine. If I had spent time in Jamaica as a child I imagine I would have picked up slang and patois easily; it is probably no coincidence there is a trace of dancehall rhythm and rhyme, blunt language and ska beats influencing the music and poetry I've made.

If I had come here as a little girl, I might have had more of a grasp of the geography and history of here. In English schools they didn't teach us about the Maroons. In fact, the entire history of slavery was brushed over with a brief mention of the Windrush. It was only yesterday, when I was driving out on the road to Hellshore through Spanish Town, I saw the forts and cannons, the remnants of colonialism, that I could picture the struggle for independence and abolition. And when I visited the Jamaican 2010 Biennial, the art of Barrington Watson, Alexander Cooper, Loui Davis and so many others, depicted a more accurate beauty within this island than any Ian Fleming fiction. Most of all, if we had come to Jamaica as children we would have known our ancestors as well as our many cousins, our dead and our living, and we would know them as well as the ghost of our father on Springfield Road.

Springfield Road

As one Jamaican saying goes – 'plantain ripe, can't green again' – we cannot go back in time but I do look forward to coming here again. I know now that Colonels Ridge is a big part of the salt of my earth and Kingston the pepper. And looking out across this Caribbean landscape, with the tropical palm trees, the distant blue mountains and the glittering port in the distance, I am no longer just gazing upon a bamboo tray on the wall, there is Jamaican soil beneath my feet and turquoise blue skies above and ahead, and I find myself imagining what it would be like to live here, on this holiday.

afterword / London,
January 2011

When my agent, Kevin Conroy Scott, suggested I try my hand at a childhood memoir, I really didn't want to face it, the past or myself. I started writing *Springfield Road* during the spring of 2006 but found myself in Paddington Station with an impulse to run away, with the sole intention of getting very drunk. Quite randomly, I got on the first train heading west, through Devon to Cornwall, St Ives and Penzance. As the train bumbled towards the coast, I woke up to the slow realisation that no matter where I ran to, I was there when I got there. It took six hours on the train from London to get to Penzance and staring out of the window at the lush west country, I was baffled as to how or where I would start this book, but once I caught myself figuring that out, I realised I had already started this work. And once I started to make myself remember my childhood, random memories began to flood my head, a clutter of moments I wished I had forgotten. I had just mere flashes of memories I had thought I would remember more clearly. I fell in love in Cornwall and with Cornwall and wrote some of the first draft there. I also went home and spent time in Hastings and I wrote much of this in the attic of Springfield Road.

What has it taught me? That rather than *be careful what you wish for*, we should be sure to dream harder. The journey into my past littered my present with consequences, coincidences and a sense of déjà vu. My childhood was subject matter I had always avoided writing about and I was afraid of many things, but mostly what I might find digging around in the past. You cannot go poking skeletons in the closet without making maggots wriggle.

I felt I was composing a long goodbye letter. I started work most days at four or five in the morning with little hope of light, dawn or end. It was as if these were to be the words I might say on my deathbed. I was convinced I would die on the book's completion or publication, that

Springfield Road

I would never outlive my father's forty years, though funnily enough, this macabre indulgence didn't scare me. Rather, it became a motivation; if I was going to be dead, I wouldn't hear any critical complaints, and therefore my fears and doubts of what *they* might say didn't matter any more.

Whilst clambering around in the long-forgotten but violent imaginings of my father's last hours and suicide I was forced to picture my own demise. The details of how I would actually do it – pills, knives or ropes? – However I am relieved to write that rather than a swansong, this journey was to be the beginning of a new life and a change of heart. I didn't die, I will see my fortieth birthday. Without doubt though, parts of me have died, some myths have shattered whilst others bloomed.

I also noticed that during writing this I started to dream vividly in the book, to have dreams about the past, I visited familiar childhood dreamscapes and ghosts. One night I sat up bolt upright, rudely awoken by the surreal presence of my seven-year-old self at the end of my bed, with gappy-toothed insistence, telling me to get up and get on with it.

Writers and close friends have made comments on my discipline to start writing most days at four in the morning. I would like to make it perfectly clear that it was not discipline or keenness that cruelly wrenched me from my sleep, but sheer terror that I had got something wrong followed by a rush of relief that I had another fresh whole day to try make it better, to try to get it right. I still have to eat Christmas dinner with these *characters*, they are my real living family. I'm also a Robinson, and now having been to Jamaica and watched my cousins and their heavy work schedules, the habit of rising early to seize the day is something I clearly inherited from my peppery Jamaican side.

When I started work on the early chapters about my mother and brother I fell in love with them both again, remembering us and how we once were. I love my siblings and my mother and I realise I have taken them for granted for years, as we all do with our loved ones. I feel lucky to have seen them in this warm light in my thirties, rather than later with sentimental nostalgia and when it's all too late, but now and here, whilst we are all still alive and can all still make each other laugh and cry and above all enjoy each other.

I have often been told by various family members, mainly my grandmother, that it is about time for me to *settle down* and *get a proper job*.

My mother is my champion; she has always been convinced that this writing malarky *is* a proper job. She has continually supported my choices, cheered at my success and consoled me in my failures, my many near misses and close calls. My mother encourages me to try, try and try again and I thank her here and every day. She instilled this passion and a mantra of never quitting; and this then is my understanding of her poetic heart, her artistic soul and our inherited nature of the spirit of my elders and perhaps of the Maroons.

In 2006 I started seeking my father and his final resting place. I applied to Bristol registry for his death certificate. When the letter finally arrived I burst into tears, holding his death certificate and seeing my father's name written by the word *death* for the first time. His cause of death: vasovagal inhibition due to hanging. His occupation was given as a 'sub-contract progress chaser'. How disappointing. I suppose I hoped and expected it to read: occupation – charming libertine jazz dude.

In the summer of 2007 I received an email with the address for the cemetery where Dad was buried. I will always be very grateful to the anonymous person who took the time to give me this information. I cannot tell you much more than this, that one stranger took the time to write to me. So I knew he had been buried and not cremated, and at last we could go and say a final goodbye.

Also whilst working on the earlier chapters I received an email from the boy I had my first kiss with when I was seven. He had a dream that I was singing and when he awoke he searched for me on the internet. I vividly remember kissing my James Bond, with his soft, freckled boy face, but I can barely picture the man he must be now. Once in a blue moon I dream about wheat fields of yellow and I still have the silver boxing glove, somewhere.

Whilst editing the final chapters of this book, a friend of mine took his life aged forty years old, just like my father. Tarka Cordell was stunning, a gifted and charming musician. Maybe it is the struggle, the difficulties of finding balance, faith and courage, doubt and fear, dark and light. We are all so fragile. We are all fighting the good fight, but we are way too harsh in the way we measure success and failure, the way we reward and penalise ourselves. Perhaps loathing and punishing ourselves enough to convince ourselves that we will not be sorely missed by every person's life that we touched. We may not remember what people say or do, but we do remember how they made us feel. I met Tarka when I was in my twenties, on a spoken word tour with London Cockney poet Tim Wells in New York. Tarka introduced me to the music of Charles Mingus, he made me *feel* like I was a real poet. If there is a place where we meet in the afterlife, then I like to imagine that they will all be jamming together, all the jazz dudes, with Mingus and all the rest.

One night, my mother found Grandpa George walking in his pyjamas in the rain on Springfield Road, having forgotten who he was and where he lived. He had cancer, he was slipping into dementia, and he was rapidly going blind and deaf. Shortly after, Grandpa George had to go into a care home. We discovered that he had signed over power of attorney to his solicitor and the house on Springfield Road was auctioned with my mother and sister still living in the top two floors. We had taken it for granted we would always have that old house in the family. The new landlord appeared and he flattened the front garden to make a concrete driveway. Mum came home one day and the whole garden was simply gone. He cemented the back garden, paved over the pet graves and uprooted the apple trees. Inside, he began smashing though the downstairs walls to create flats. The basement stairs were blocked, amputating the old kitchen and basement from the rest of the house. Mum said she felt a cold air, an angry chill coming up from below there. My mother went to the new wall and spoke to it: *You know me, please don't be angry with me. I am taking the dog for a walk. Will you join me or are you going to stay there?* After that every evening she called, *you coming?* and took the basement ghost and the dog for her evening walk at sunset down Springfield Road. Mum believed she was walking with Edith. My mother was the last woman standing with memories of the whole home as it used to be.

Around 1975 and after my mother left my father, in her new found solitude, she sat down and wrote out her entire life in her own words. Ever supporting and encouraging in all I do, she gave me these diaries. I spent some furious tearful weeks labouring to type them out, word for word and blow for blow, only to destroy the files, finding them too painful. So just a glimpse of my mother's story is what remains here. My mother's life story, my Jamaican roots and history should be a whole book all of its own. Perhaps I will write this when I have spent more time in Jamaica. This research seems to have started, my continued study of

Caribbean literature, history, geography, language, culture, politics, art, music and of course our brilliant successes in sport and track and field will be ongoing for the rest of my life.

During the seventies, the seasons of my childhood were distinct. There was the throng of cut grass in spring, the hot yellow of summer and the droughts; the pumpkin and chestnut of autumn and heavy white snow at wintertime. Due to climate change and global warming many of these things have started to become obsolete, just like shopkeepers that smoke whilst serving slabs of warm cheese; fish and chips served in real newspaper, one pound notes and cassette tapes. There was once a time when England only had four television channels to choose from. As children, we played outside in the streets, interacting without any health and safety, without crash helmets or internet or mobile phones, most of all, without so much fear and paranoia. I hope I have captured something of that for those too young to remember this world in Kodacolour.

Perhaps I have been seeking coincidences, making connections between my past and this present work, linking my dreams and the long lost people of before. It's that loose thread that most of us fear pulling in case we unravel the whole sweater. But I pulled and it unravelled and I sat here untangling the knots I had made.

I have learnt that remembering never meets you face to face, but sneaks up on you like a sharp corner when you least expect it. Once you take the turn you find yourself down an alleyway of memories you never knew were there. The things we want to remember are so different to the things we had forgotten. Now, for the first time in my life, I am learning to sleep with the lights off. I also try to pay more attention to dreams and all that I wish for. A fear conceals a wish, so then perhaps this fear of death was a wish for rebirth and reinvention.

The house on Springfield Road will soon be in the faraway and in the long ago, so we'll remember it here as it was, the place to find the lucky marble, a place like a pebble with the hole in the middle, and a place we once called home.

Salena Godden
London / April 2011

the heart of the home, edith godden,
springfield road

glossary

**Desborough or playground slang & popular culture references:
1972–1984**

Bazooka: bubblegum that came with a water-based tattoo

Bionic Woman: actress Lindsay Wagner played Jaime Sommers in hit TV show

Black Jack: liquorice flavoured halfpenny confectionary

***Blue Peter*:** BBC TV kids programme, informative and newsworthy

Chinese burn: a form of torture; twisting the skin on the wrist in opposite directions

Chopper: a very popular pushbike with a low, long seat and wide handlebars

***Dallas*:** TV show, a glamour-soap set in Dallas, Texas

Dead leg: repeatedly hitting the same spot on the victim's leg to create pain

***Dynasty*:** TV show, another glamour-soap, starring Joan Collins

Evel Knievel: seventies motorbike stunt hero

Fruit Salad: fruit flavoured halfpenny confectionary

Golliwog: black-faced doll; a logo for marmalade, and a popular racist taunt

***Grange Hill*:** British TV serial based on a fictional school

Joey Deacon: child with learning difficulties featured on *Blue Peter*, a cruel taunt

JR: Who shot JR? JR Ewing played by Larry Hagman in *Dallas*

Cagoule: plastic mac you pull over your head with a pull-string elastic hood

Kola Kubes:	hard-boiled cubed sweet with a flavour resembling Coca-Cola
Marmite:	brand name for yeast spread eaten on toast or in sandwiches
Opal Fruits:	confectionary of chews now re-branded *Starburst
Paul Michael Glaser:	actor from *Starsky and Hutch* – a hit US TV cop show
Plimmy:	plimsoll; a soft canvas rubber soled shoe worn in PT
PT:	physical training, PE: physical education, sports class
Refresher:	yellow tangy sweet with sherbet inside costing two pennies
Sally James:	popular children's TV presenter from *TISWAS*
Sherbet Dip:	yellow paper tube of sherbet with a liquorice dipper used like a straw
Steve Austen:	character played by Lee Majors in hit TV show *The Six Million Dollar Man*
***Swap Shop*:**	British Saturday morning kids' phone-in show
Tardis:	spaceship used in *Doctor Who*, very popular UK TV show
***TISWAS*:**	UK Saturday morning show: *Today Is Saturday, Watch And Smile*
Tucker:	heart throb character in *Grange Hill*
Top Trumps:	card game based on themes and points of strength and weakness
Wonder Woman:	TV Superhero
***Why Don't You…*:**	BBC TV programme *Why Don't You Just Switch Off Your Television Set and Go and Do Something Less Boring Instead?*

subscribers

Unbound is a new kind of publishing house. Our books are funded directly by readers. This was a very popular idea during the late eighteenth and early nineteenth centuries. Now we have revived it for the internet age. It allows authors to write the books they really want to write and readers to support the writing they would most like to see published.

The names listed below are of readers who have pledged their support and made this book happen. If you'd like to join them, visit: www.unbound.co.uk.

Amy Acre
Julie Addis
@ade
Isabel Adomakoh
 Young
Dickie Again
Patience Agbabi
Iain Aitch
Shereen Akhtar
Sarah Albery
Wyndham Albery
Kalam Ali
Wonder Allen Smith
Kirsty Allison
Titania Altius
Louise Anderson
Anonymous
Richard Anthony
Shobha Aranha
Amy Armstroing-Evans

Corinne Bacon
Daniela Badcock
Mark Badcock
Helen Bagnall
Lisa Baker
Annwen Bates
Helen Bates
Rosie Beardon
Kat Belcher
Julia Bell
Berko Berkavitch
Sam Berkson
Jo Berlowbo
Chris Beschi
Caroline Bird
John Lee Bird
Julia Bird
Billy Black
Sue Black
Hardy Blechman

Paul Blezard
Amanda Bluglass
Owen Booth
Simon Booth
Janine Bovell
Anna Boyle
Richard W H Bray
Andy Brereton
Simon Broackes
Alan Buckley
Laura Burrow
Imogen Butler-Cole
Jamie Byng
Byte The Book
Kit Caless
Claire Callender
Xander Cansell
Jamolious Carrolious
Bluebelle Wednesday
 Carroll

Roland Chambers
Vera Chok
Lana Citron
Kirsty Clark
Daniel Cockrill
Joe Coghlan
Dan Cole
Mel and Till Collinson
Joanne Conroy
Neil Conti
Will Conway
Natalie Cooper
Peter Coyte
Shanie Craig
Irene Cripps
Richard Cripps
Stuart Cripps
Matt Cummins
M Curran
Deborah Curtis
Astrid Dangoor
Glyn Davies
Kelly-Anne Davitt
Polly Dawson
Isabel de Vasconcellos
Hugo Degenhardt
Neil Denham
Miranda Dickinson
Helen Donohoe
Daniel Drage
Heather Driscoll
Matthew Duguid
Sally Dunbar
Gillian Eastwood
Simon Ellis

Elizabeth Evans
Bernardine Evaristo
Stuart Evers
Jason Evers Herbert
Em F
Michael Farrell
Jumoke Fashola
Paul Ferguson
Charles Fernyhough
William Fiennes
Ilana Fox
Kate Fox
Tina Francis
Isobel Frankish
Anna Freeman
Dominic Frisby
Vanessa Gebbie
Maggie Gee
George
Zak Ghouze
John Gill
Adrian Gillott
Tania Glyde
Lorna Godden
Paul Godden
Salena Godden
Teresa Godden-
    O'Callaghan
Claire Godden-
    Rowland
Luisa Goldsmith
Steve Gosling
Niven Govinden
Ben Graham
Colin Grant

Sola Green
Daria Grimaldi
Mark Haddon
Emylia Hall
C.A. Halpin
Katrina Hamilton-
    Kraft
David Harford
A.F. Harrold
Alice Harter
Caitlin Harvey
Como Hastings
Portia Hastings
Karen Hayley
Eizabeth Head
Graham Herbing
India Herbing
E O Higgins
Peter Hobbs
Keith Holden
Phil Holden
Derrol Holloway
Wayne Holloway-
    Smith
Roxanne Holman
Elspeth Holmes
Zoë Howe
Fran Hudson
Xenia Hudson
Rivka Isaacson
Harriet Israel
Elliott Jack
Melania Jack
Andrew James
Heidi James-Dunbar

Springfield Road

Keith Jarrett
Nick Jefferies
Henry Jeffreys
Laura Jenkinson
Emma Jones
Jessica Jones
Nathan Jones
Richard Tyrone Jones
Sarah Judd
Nicholas Judge
Peter Jukes
George Julian
kim kat'n'amy
Oliver Keen
Andrew Kelly
Mike Kennedy
Rachael Kerr
Amy Key
Debbie Kilbride
Stephen King
Katherine Kingsley
Darren Kis
Michele Knight
Jon Knox
Jo Kotas
Anna Kusner
Murray Lachlan Young
Hayley Lange
Katie Lee
Martin Lee
Xavier Leret
Beth Lewis
Paul Lewis
Kiki Linton
Amy Liptrot

Kieron Livingstone
Lindsey Lonne
Chris Lord
Hetty Los
Sharmaine Lovegrove
Jack Phillips Lowe
Justin Lowe
Jaime Rory Lucy
Cecilia Lundqvist
Alice May Lynch
Dr Penelope Lynch
Janie Mac
Ross McCleary
Anne McCloy
Roddy McDevitt
David McDonald
Rowena Macdonald
Rebekah McGill
Oonagh McGrane
Peter G Mackie
Dan Mcleod
Polly McMahon
Michelle Madsen
Anne Maguire
Sabrina Mahfouz
Paul Main
Howard Male
Gita Malhotra
Tanya Mar
Fadette Marie
Dirty Mark
Amber Marks
Irfan Master
Catherine Matthews
Hanife Melbourne

Ben Mellor
Simon Miles
Maud Milton
Bridget Minamore
John Mitchinson
Katie Moffat
Adam Moliver
Sarah Moliver
Jo-Ann Montgomery
Robert Montgomery
Steve Moran
Jonathan More
Daniel Mudford of
    Balham
Muriel
Jonathan Murphy
Mike Murphy
Tiffany Murray
Michal Nachmany
Simon Napier-Bell
Patrick Neate
Julie Niven
Keshia Nzonza-
    Delgado
Shauna O'briain
Kath O'Donnell
Mark O'Neill
Niall O'Sullivan
Renaissance One
John Osborne
Koye Oyedeji
Julz Parker
Monica Parle
The Party People
Martha Patrick

Lucy Paul
Rowan Pelling
Daveid Phillips
Bohdan Piasecki
Katja Plasse
David Polglase
Justin Pollard
Gill Powell
Alex Preston
Francis Pryor
Alexa Radcliffe-Hart
Ulla Rahbek
Amanda Railson
Svetlana Rakocevic
Keith Ramsey
Rosa Rankin-Gee
Selina Ream
Clare Reddington
Chris Redmond
Gareth Rees
Esther Reeve
Rachel Reid
Leah Hazel Jay Roberts
Patrick Robinson
Rachael Robinson
Satya Robyn
Barny c Rockford
Deanna Rodger
Rebecca Rose
Leone Ross
Mandana Ruane
Juliet Russell
Ruby Russell
Olivia Rutherford
Jason Ryall

Sarah Salway
Michele Scarr
Georgina Scott
Kevin Conroy Scott
Sara Sender
Pauline Sewards
Oliver Shepherd
Nikesh Shukla
Simon Simple
Dan Simpson
Lemn Sissay
Lara Skinner
Maria Slovakova
Alicia Sometimes
Oliver Speer
Louise Sta Ana
Vicki Stannard
Nick Stanton
Jay Starkey
Janet Steele
Deedah Steels
St.John Stephen
Neil Stevens
Tabatha Stirling
Ingrid Stone
Amy Stratton
Kay Stuart
Dan Sumption
Charlotte Tarrant
Heather Taylor
Joelle Taylor
Kate Tempest
Sonja Ter Horst
Lucy Thane
Bill Thompson

Piers Thompson
Matt Thorne
Alasdair Tod
Mama Tokus
Diccon Towns
Claire Trévien
Gavin Turk
Emma Verey
Byron Vincent
Terry Waite
Katie Waldegrave
Sally Walton
Selina Ware
Hannah Watson
Sean Whelan
Simon White
Tony White and Sarah
    Such
Kirsty Whiten
Hatti Whitman
Eleanor Whittaker
Jont Whittington
Vanessa Widdup
Heathcote Williams
Maria Williams
Merrie Williams
Michael Wilson
Kay Wise
Naomi Woddis
Peter Wolton
Steve Woodward
Andy Wright
Luke Wright

A note about the typeface

The serif Garamond typeface is named after punch-cutter Claude Garamont (1480–1561), who came from a family of French printers, and is widely acknowledged for its grace and fluidity, though Garamont himself is said to have claimed 'the art I practice is but a small thing'. Among its most definitive features are the small bowl of the a and narrow eye of the e, along with the crossed w. It is one of the most popular 'early' typefaces in the readily-available catalogue of fonts in standard word-processing programmes, and is also one of the most eco-friendly typefaces for printing in terms of ink consumption. Garamond's career began in 1540 with the commission to punch-cut the grecs du roi, a series of Greek letters which were used by Robert Estienne on behalf of the French king Francis I. In a more recent century, the iconic children's picture books of Dr. Suess were set in a version of Garamond. Garamont died in 1561 shortly after drawing up his will in which, after providing for his second wife, he instructed 'the surplus of all his goods' to be sold by a friend in order to pay for his elderly mother's care.